D0849170

Alexander Pope's
'OPUS MAGNUM'
1729–1744

ETHIC EPISTLES.

THE

FIRST BOOK,

TO

Henry St.John Lord B.

AWAKE my St. John! quit all meaner things
To puzzling Statesmen, and to blustring Kings.
Let Us, since Life can little more supply
Than just to look about us, and to dye,
†† Expatiate free o'er all the Scene of Man:
6 A mighty Maze! but not without a Plan;
7 A Wilde, where Weeds and Flow'rs promiscuous shoot,
8 Or Garden, tempting with forbidden Fruit.

An Essay on Man exordium and notes in the Harvard (Houghton) MS. version.
See transcript, pp. 21–2.

Alexander Pope's
'OPUS MAGNUM'
1729–1744

MIRIAM LERANBAUM

OXFORD
AT THE CLARENDON PRESS
1977

Oxford University Press, Walton Street, Oxford OX2 6DP

OXFORD LONDON GLASGOW NEW YORK
TORONTO MELBOURNE WELLINGTON CAPE TOWN
IBADAN NAIROBI DAR ES SALAAM LUSAKA ADDIS ABABA
KUALA LUMPUR SINGAPORE JAKARTA HONG KONG TOKYO
DELHI BOMBAY CALCUTTA MADRAS KARACHI

British Library Cataloguing – Publication Data

Leranbaum, Miriam
Alexander Pope's 'Opus magnum', 1729–1744
Index
ISBN 0–19–812051–6
1. Title
821'.5 PR3637.E8
Pope, Alexander – Religion and ethics

Printed in Great Britain
at the University Press, Oxford
by Vivian Ridler
Printer to the University

TO

THE MEMORY OF

MY FATHER

PREFACE

IN the first collected edition of the *Essay on Man* in 1734 and in all subsequent editions, Alexander Pope prefixed to the poem a 'Design' whose final paragraph reads:

> What is now published, is only to be considered as a *general Map* of MAN, marking out no more than the *greater parts*, their *extent*, their *limits*, and their *connection*, but leaving the particular to be more fully delineated in the charts which are to follow. Consequently, these Epistles in their progress (if I have health and leisure to make any progress) will be less dry, and more susceptible of poetic ornament. I am here only opening the *fountains*, and clearing the passage. To deduce the *rivers*, to follow them in their course, and to observe their effects, may be a task more agreeable.

The agreeable task that has prompted this study is an exploration of the implications of Pope's design: that is, to describe and analyse the evidence bearing upon the nature and scope of the ethic system that Pope planned to erect upon the foundation of the *Essay of Man* and which he called in a letter to Swift of 1734, 'my *Opus Magnum*'. Of the projected parts of the scheme, Pope completed only *An Essay on Man* and what we now call the *Moral Essays*, the four epistles to Cobham, to a Lady, to Bathurst, and to Burlington, and he published these together in 1735 as Books I and II of the 'Ethic Epistles'. My aim here is actually twofold: the first major object has been to gather, present, and evaluate all the available evidence pertaining to the origin and persistence of the plan from 1729 until Pope's death in 1744; the second object is to examine the eight completed epistles as inter-related parts of the larger scheme in order to suggest some possible ways in which our understanding and appreciation of them can be enriched by seeing them in this perspective. Neither part is meant to be definitive; by being comprehensive in carrying out the first objective, and very tentative and speculative in the second case, I hope to have established the groundwork for further studies along these lines. I am, that is, primarily 'opening the *fountains*, and clearing the passage'. I have been sustained in this effort by recalling

Pope's own words about the parts of his ethic scheme: 'my works will in one respect be like the works of Nature, much more to be liked and understood when consider'd in the relation they bear with each other, than when ignorantly look'd upon one by one; and often, those parts which attract most at first sight, will appear to be not the most, but the least considerable.'[1]

Despite the survival of considerable evidence attesting to the ethic scheme's existence and influence upon Pope's work from 1729 onward, in the form of records of conversations, letters, manuscript jottings, and the format and editorial annotations of published editions of Pope's works during his lifetime, there has been fairly widespread agreement among recent Pope scholars that a study of these documents would not prove rewarding. This is a judgement to which I obviously take exception, and one that seems to have arisen from several distinct premisses, each of which seems to me to be only partly valid. The first of these assumptions is that clues to the nature of the project are too fragmentary, too undefined, too obscure, to make satisfying conclusions or even useful conjectures about its influence upon Pope's poetry. Extended examinations of the *opus magnum* plan are therefore rare. I have found several sections of *The Major Satires of Alexander Pope* by Robert W. Rogers very useful, despite Mr. Rogers's tendency to smooth over many of the complexities inherent in the fluctuations of the scheme. Most readers are likely to know of the existence of the plan from the introductions to the two parts of Volume III of the Twickenham edition of Pope's poetry: in the opening section of his Introduction to *An Essay on Man*, Maynard Mack summarizes the project in two paragraphs; in the Introduction to *Epistles to Several Persons*, F. W. Bateson provides a more extensive summary of over twenty pages of packed prose, documents, and citations. Neither of these treatments seems to me to do justice to the nature, variety, and usefulness of the available evidence, and both refer the reader to corroborating documents and manuscripts that are relatively inaccessible. This study attempts to remedy this deficiency by gathering together all the available data and arranging it in chronological order, thus allowing readers to assess the reliability, weight, and place of any

[1] *Correspondence* iii. 348 (Pope to Swift, 16 February 1733).

piece of evidence in relation to all the others. Although the effect is that of a jigsaw puzzle that has many broken pieces and many pieces lacking, I am confident that sufficient evidence exists from which one can develop observations and suggestions of considerable value about this major project of Pope's mature years.

A second reason for the negative attitude towards a study of this project is a view that Maynard Mack has recently expressed in comparing Pope with Walpole, that '*l'esprit de système* was foreign to [Pope's] temperament'. Pope's outlook, Mack notes, 'involved eschewing on the whole the *thèse* and the *système*, cherishing the *ad hoc*, recognizing the flux, variety, and disorderliness of experience . . .'.[2] However, his careful qualification ('on the whole') licenses us to realize that one may be temperamentally 'disorderly' yet admire and strive to imitate those who are systematic and orderly; one may be flexible and responsive to the new and *ad hoc* and yet voluntarily undertake long-term commitments and projects; one may (however much Swift may have doubted the possibility) create, revise, and tinker with a 'system' without being ruled, reduced, and limited by the system one has formulated. All these observations appear to apply to Pope: consider, for instance, his gigantic project for translating Homer's epics, his admiration for William Warburton, and, as these chapters will indicate, his frequent resumption of the ethic project shadowed forth by his plans for the composition of the *Essay on Man*.

The mention of Warburton recalls a third reason for doubting the value of such a project as this. To all Pope's admirers, the name of Warburton is anathema. Once again this opinion by itself is amply justified, as anyone will agree who has followed Warburton's career as polemicist-at-large and editor and interpreter of Pope's (or Shakespeare's) works. However, Warburton did not begin publication of his analysis and defence of Pope's *Essay* until December 1738 and did not meet Pope until 1740, by which time Pope's project had developed its own history independent of Warburton's influence. The malignity of his influence would seem to have been greater on Pope's subsequent readers than on Pope himself, through the wide

[2] Maynard Mack, *The Garden and the City* (Toronto: University of Toronto Press, 1969), p. 204 and n. 20.

adoption of Warburton's 1751 edition of the complete works of Pope as the authoritative reading of the poems. Irritation with Warburton's claim (upheld, though possibly hypocritically, by Pope himself) that he understood Pope's poetry better than Pope himself did, has led, for instance, Professor Brower to write, 'Certainly we add nothing to our enjoyment of Pope or to his knowledge of imaginative design, by imposing schemes of the kind that Dr. Warburton provided for the "Essay on Man" and the Moral Essays.'[3] This study seconds that belief in that it rejects considerations of schemes imposed long after the composition and publication of the poems and by interpreters other than Pope himself. But I think we do add to our enjoyment and understanding of Pope's work if we clearly appreciate the nature and scope of the plans he himself projected and cherished. To keep these two perspectives—Pope's own plans and the interpretations of others, especially Warburton—distinct from one another, I have adopted an organization which follows the chronology of Pope's writing from 1729 to 1744 as rigorously as possible. I have thus tried to avoid having our knowledge of later, and frequently 'Warburtonian', interpretations overshadow a clear perception of the natural growth and development of the scheme. This kind of difficulty, it seems to me, is inherent in Mr. Bateson's analysis of the project. He first gives the detailed 'Advertisement' to the 1744 edition of the *Moral Essays*, and follows it with other earlier documents. While it is certainly true that the 'Advertisement' is the single most complete and coherent document about the scheme that we have, it is also true that the description is unlikely to be directly attributable to Pope, and, in any case, postdates by at least a decade the period when Pope was most centrally absorbed with the project.

Accordingly Chapter I presents and evaluates all the available evidence other than the poetry itself from 1729 to 1735, that is, from the first hint of the plan in Pope's correspondence until the combined publication of the eight epistles generally considered to have formed the only completed part of the greater project. Chapters

[3] Reuben Brower, 'The Groves of Eden: Design in a Satire by Pope' in *Fields of Light: An Experiment in Critical Reading* (New York: Oxford University Press, 1951), p. 138.

II to V then offer interpretations of *An Essay on Man* and the individual Moral Essays that emphasize the evolution of these poems in response to the demands of the larger project. The elements chosen for emphasis in each chapter vary in response to the problems presented by each poem and in response to the nature and availability of supporting evidence in each case. I consider matters such as dating, the evolution of manuscripts, and the revisions in printed texts not in every instance, but where I find these matters most appropriate and suggestive. I cannot emphasize enough that the interpretative chapters are far from being exhaustive in applying the results of sifting through the documentary evidence presented in Chapter I. They are intended only as a demonstration of the potential value of considering the poems as components of a larger project.

Chapters VI to VIII consider the fluctuating fortunes of the ethic plan after 1735. I have here concentrated most attention on the evidence surrounding the *Fourth Dunciad* and the manuscript plan for the epic on Brutus as parts of the over-all plan, but in the interests of being inclusive I have also given attention to documents and conjectures about the project during this period that seem to me to be less significant.

It is perhaps worth mentioning that this study confines itself very much to defining the ethic scheme and to applying that knowledge only to works Pope claimed were a part of it. I have therefore not attempted to relate the project to Pope's other works of the same period, or to his growing involvement in contemporary affairs. The decision to exclude these concurrent interests may seem to place the scheme in rather artificial isolation, but it has also provided a way to give the *opus magnum* the prominence and concentrated attention I think it deserves.

Certainly worth mentioning, and indeed emphasizing, is my immense debt to the magnificent editorial work of Professors Mack and Bateson on the *Essay on Man* and the *Moral Essays*, of Professor Sherburn on Pope's correspondence, and of Professor Osborn on Spence's *Anecdotes*. Without these exemplary modern editions this work would scarcely have been feasible, and I am anxious to record my gratitude for them here, lest my disembodied citations and occasional corrections of particular points create the false impression that I underestimate their over-all excellence.

In addition, I wish to record my gratitude to a number of institutions and persons who have helped me at various stages of this study. I am grateful to the University of California Intercampus Travel Fund for financial assistance for two trips to the Henry Huntington Library and the William Andrews Clark Memorial Library to examine early Pope editions and manuscripts, to the Canada Council for travel funds enabling me to visit the Houghton Library, the Pierpont Morgan Library, the New York Public Library, and the British Museum to complete my study of early Pope editions and manuscripts, and to the State University of New York for a summer grant that allowed me to do additional research at the British Museum. The curators of those collections showed great generosity, hospitality, and interest in my research. I wish also to thank David Foxon for his bibliographical help, Zoja Pavlovskis and William Kinsley for their helpful comments on a draft of Chapter II, and my mentors and colleagues Brendan O Hehir, Paul Alkon, Lawrence Freeman, Robert Kroetsch, Michael Conlon, and Francis Newman for their valuable and stimulating suggestions and their continuing interest, guidance, and encouragement.

CONTENTS

ABBREVIATIONS

Anecdotes	Joseph Spence, *Observations, Anecdotes, and Characters of Books and Men*, ed. James M. Osborn, 2 vols., Oxford: Clarendon Press, 1966.
Correspondence	*The Correspondence of Alexander Pope*, ed. George Sherburn, 5 vols., Oxford: Clarendon Press, 1956.
Reproductions	Alexander Pope, *An Essay on Man. Reproductions of the Manuscripts in the Pierpont Morgan Library and the Houghton Library with the Printed Text of the Original Edition*, Introduction by Maynard Mack, Oxford: Printed for Presentation to the Members of the Roxburghe Club, 1962.
Twickenham	The Twickenham Edition of Pope's *Poetical Works*, London: Methuen.
—— III: i	*An Essay on Man*, ed. Maynard Mack, 1950.
—— III: ii	*Epistles to Several Persons* (*Moral Essays*), ed. F. W. Bateson, 1951.
—— V	*The Dunciad*, ed. James Sutherland, 1943.
—— VI	*Minor Poems*, ed. Norman Ault and John Butt, 1954.

INTRODUCTION

POPE'S *Essay on Man* and the *Moral Essays* were 'originally planned as parts of a stupendous whole, the philosophical *Opus Magnum* that was to have treated almost every conceivable aspect of human life from man's relation to the universe, to learning and wit, "Civil and Religious Society", and "private Ethics or practical Morality"'.[1] This book describes the details, problems, and fluctuations of that ambitious and comprehensive project, which was to occupy Pope centrally from late 1729 to 1735 and sporadically thereafter until his death in 1744. Before plunging *in medias res*, let us try to establish the immediate context of the plan. Pope left no account of the circumstances surrounding the genesis of his ethic scheme, and I shall therefore do no more than provide a hypothetical sketch of the way in which various elements in Pope's background and immediate circumstances combined to urge him to begin his ethic scheme and give it epistolary form.

Pope first referred to working on his project in November 1729, and the *Epistle to Burlington*, the first epistle to be published of the eight comprising *An Essay on Man* and the *Moral Essays*, appeared in December 1731. If one had to date the moment when, according to Pope's self-portrait in the *Epistle to Arbuthnot*, he 'stoop'd to Truth and Moraliz'd his song', either of those dates would be a good choice. 'By "moraliz'd his song"', Geoffrey Tillotson wrote in 1946, 'Pope means his writing of *An Essay on Man*, the *Moral Essays*, the *Imitations of Horace*, the epitaphs.'[2] Yet in beginning his lecture on 'The Moral Poetry of Pope', Tillotson says he will 'be speaking of [Pope's] poetry as a whole. . . . In his later poems . . . Pope did not "stoop to Truth" for the first time, but stooped only to more of it.'[3] Although Tillotson is right to insist upon the continuity of Pope's

[1] Reuben Brower, *Alexander Pope: The Poetry of Allusion* (Oxford: Clarendon Press, 1959), p. 241.

[2] Geoffrey Tillotson, *The Moral Poetry of Pope* (Newcastle upon Tyne: Literary and Philosophical Society, 1946), pp. 1–2.

[3] Ibid., pp. 1, 2–3.

concern with morality throughout his literary career, there is no doubt of a decided change in Pope's writing after 1729.

Between April 1729 and December 1731, Pope, hard at work on his ethic scheme, published no new major works. In the years immediately preceding this period, his major publications were his six-volume edition of Shakespeare (1725), his translation of the *Odyssey* (1725, 1726), three volumes of *Miscellanies* (the misleadingly titled 'Last' containing *Peri Bathous* (March 1728)), the *Dunciad* (May 1728), and the enlarged *Dunciad Variorum* (April 1729). This group of publications itself calls out for division between Pope's editorial and translating activities on the one hand and his creative writing on the other, and Robert W. Rogers with considerable persuasiveness suggests 1726 as the real point at which Pope began to think of committing himself to a great moral work. Rogers feels that Pope was then diverted from his plans 'to attempt poetry of an exalted character' because 'in 1726 irresistible incentives to satire occurred' in the form of Swift's three-month visit at Twickenham and the publication of both Curll's *Miscellanea* (containing some early and indiscreet letters by Pope) and Theobald's *Shakespeare Restored*.[4] Rogers points out that work upon the *Miscellanies* and the *Dunciad*, though temporarily deflecting Pope's attention from his ethical commitment, ultimately had the effect of intensifying it, partly because of the pamphlet war started by his satiric work, partly through the counter-reaction of Pope's friends:

> . . . much of his later poetry reflects his desire to correct the portrait of his moral character to which the dunces had given currency. Most important of all, his respectable critics having deplored a waste of talent upon fools whose follies were obvious, whose dullness was manifest in their decision to attack Alexander Pope, he was stimulated to strenuous efforts to create a lasting monument to his genius. Such stimulation largely made possible the *Essay on Man*, the *Ethic Epistles*, and the *Imitations of Horace*.[5]

[4] Robert W. Rogers, *The Major Satires of Alexander Pope* (Urbana: The University of Illinois Press, 1955), p. 7.

[5] Rogers, *Major Satires*, pp. 30–1. Rogers gives more weight to the importuning of Pope's friends than would seem to be warranted. A number of these are conventional verse tributes, and his quotation (p. 29) from Bishop Atterbury's letter telling Pope to 'Employ not your precious moments and great talents on little men and little things; but choose a subject every way worthy of you' seems in context to be Atterbury's response to a letter from Pope in which he has told Atterbury of his ethic scheme after already having begun it. (See *Correspondence*, iii. 76–8, Atterbury to Pope, 20 November 1729.)

One may wish to see Pope's work on the *Miscellanies* and the *Dunciad* not as a detour from the high road to morality so much as a resumption and completion of long-abandoned Scriblerus projects and a belated and honorable entry into the contemporary Battle of the Books, after the very long and arduous period of involvement in his translating and editorial projects. (As later chapters will show, Pope did not like loose ends; in the last years of his life, he similarly undertook projects that had their inception a decade or more earlier.) Nevertheless, Mr. Rogers's sense of Pope's mood in 1729 seems correct: Pope had reached the age of forty, had long held for himself the high ideal of modelling his career on those of Virgil, Spenser, and Milton, and wished for a firmer claim to the grudging rewards of Prince Posterity than would be likely to come his way from engaging in Wars with the Dunces.

At around the same time, other contributing influences seem to have conspired to help turn such nebulous aspirations into more specific plans for a poetic project of considerable weight and magnitude. One of these was undoubtedly the influence of Pope's friend Henry St. John, Lord Bolingbroke. A mention of his influence is, in fact, the sole general conjecture Maynard Mack hazards to dispel the obscurity surrounding the history of the composition of *An Essay on Man*:

> The conditions favourable to its conception were probably established with the return of Bolingbroke from exile in 1723–4, when it is evident from the correspondence that the poet was beginning to toy with ethical speculation and the statesman to assign himself the role of guide, philosopher, and friend.[6]

Without reopening the question of the extent of Bolingbroke's specific influence on the *Essay*,[7] we can say with some assurance that Bolingbroke stood in relation to Pope's *opus magnum* at its earliest stages as Swift had stood in relation to the *Dunciad* and as Warburton was to stand to the *New Dunciad*. 'The inscription to the Dunciad is now printed and inserted in the Poem', wrote Pope to Swift in October 1728. 'Do you care I shou'd say any thing farther how much that poem is yours? since certainly without you it had

[6] Twickenham, III: i, p. xii and n. 5.
[7] Ibid., pp. xxix–xxxi; *Anecdotes*, ii. 632–3.

never been.'[8] 'The Encouragement you gave me to add the fourth book, first determind me to do so', wrote Pope to Warburton in December 1742, '& the Approbation you seemd to give it, was what singly determind me to print it.'[9] In the great tribute that closes the *Essay on Man*, Pope similarly acknowledges Bolingbroke as the 'master of the poet, and the song' upon whose urgings he 'turn'd the tuneful art / From sounds to things, from fancy to the heart', and Bolingbroke himself wrote to Swift in August 1731, 'does Pope talk to you of the noble work which, att my instigation, he had begun, in such a manner that He must be convinced by this time I judged better of his tallents than He did?'[10] Acting as godfather and mentor, Bolingbroke encouraged Pope to give a more central and fundamental place in his poetry to the philosophical and ethical reflections that had long characterized portions of his work.

Pope's plan to write in an elevated, abstract, and overtly moral vein is accompanied by his decision to cast his work in epistolary form. This characteristic, too, is a reflection of both immediate circumstances and long-held tendencies. Pope himself alludes to the first of these in the note to the reader prefacing the anonymous early issues of Epistle I of *An Essay on Man*: '*As the Epistolary Way of Writing hath prevailed much of late, we have ventured to publish this Piece composed some Time since, and whose Author chose this Manner, notwithstanding his Subject was high and of dignity, because of its being mixt with* Argument, *which of its Nature approacheth to Prose*.'[11] In the *Poetical Career of Alexander Pope*, R. K. Root similarly notes that the early 1730s 'produced a large harvest of ethical epistles, published like those of Pope in slender folios with large and handsome type', and lists a number of them by various authors.[12]

The 'Epistolary Way of Writing' has a significance far greater than its immediate vogue in the early 1730s, for it is also the Horatian way of writing, and following the work of Reuben Brower and Maynard Mack, one does not need to document the significance of the Horatian model for Pope. Horace not only provided Pope with congenial models for writing, but also helped provide him with

[8] *Correspondence*, ii. 522.
[9] Ibid. iv. 434.
[10] Ibid. iii. 213.
[11] Twickenham, III: i, p. 6.
[12] R. K. Root, *The Poetical Career of Alexander Pope* (Princeton: Princeton University Press, 1938), pp. 238–9, n. 2.

'a place to stand', in Maynard Mack's phrase. Mack agrees with Reuben Brower's description of Pope's career as 'progressively an *Imitatio Horati*', a development that begins well before 1730.[13] As Brower writes, 'with the noble *Epistle to Robert Earl of Oxford* (1721), Pope reached maturity as a poet of Horatian "moral song", if he was not yet in Warton's unsympathetic phrase, "a moral, a satiric, and a didactic poet"'.[14] Pope's full commitment to Horace comes in 1729. In that summer, Fenton wrote to Broome, 'I saw our friend Pope twice when I was at London. . . . He told me that for the future he intended to write nothing but epistles in Horace's manner, in which I question not but he will succeed very well.'[15] Although this remark does not imply that Pope has committed himself to a comprehensive ethic scheme, by November of the same year, in a letter to Swift, Pope refers to his work as 'a system of Ethics in the Horatian way'.[16] Although Chapter II will argue that the *Essay on Man*, the most systematic portion of the scheme, owes at least as much to Lucretius as to Horace, the over-all and fundamental influence of Horace upon Pope's general plan is indisputable.

The many influences coalescing in 1729, when with the completion of the *Dunciad* 'Pope asked himself to what he was to turn his hand',[17] make his decision to construct an ethic scheme readily comprehensible, even if they do not fully account for it. One cannot determine what precise weight to give any of these elements, yet in combination they gave Pope the incentive to carry the war against vanity, pride, and the debasement of national and cultural standards on to a new and more elevated plane in which satire joined with moral philosophy in a series of epistles that affirm 'That REASON, PASSION, answer one great aim; / That true SELF-LOVE and SOCIAL are the same; / That VIRTUE only makes our Bliss below; / And all our Knowledge is, OURSELVES TO KNOW.'

[13] Maynard Mack, *The Garden and the City* (Toronto: University of Toronto Press, 1969), pp. 232, 234.

[14] Brower, p. 165.

[15] *Correspondence*, iii. 37.

[16] Ibid. 81.

[17] Bonamy Dobrée, *English Literature in the Early Eighteenth Century, 1700–1740* (New York and London: Oxford University Press, 1959), p. 535.

CHAPTER I

POPE'S PLANS FOR HIS 'ETHIC WORK' 1729–1735

POPE was most deeply engaged in planning and executing his ethic scheme in the years 1729 to 1735. That scheme, not outlined fully until 1734, in an 'Index' prepared for appearance in the 1734 folio edition of *An Essay on Man*, was to include many more epistles than the eight composed in this period and published together in 1735 as Books I and II of *Ethic Epistles*. These eight epistles, four constituting *An Essay on Man* and the four *Moral Essays* (or *Epistles to Several Persons* as they are sometimes alternatively called), are parts of what Pope, also in 1734, called 'my *Opus Magnum*' in a letter to Swift. Although most of the remarks about the plan dating from the period 1729 to 1735 are fragmentary, vague, and unsystematic, taken together they testify to Pope's concentration upon the development of this project. Although not his sole literary undertaking in this period, it was by far the most extensive one, and the one to which he devoted the major amount of attention. Under survey in this chapter is all surviving evidence other than the poems themselves: Pope's correspondence, Spence's *Anecdotes*, notes in the *Essay on Man* manuscripts, and the notes to and format of collected editions of *An Essay on Man* and the *Moral Essays* falling within these dates. The survey, a chronological one where at all possible, shows that the plan existed from the very outset and that the conception helped to shape the composition of *An Essay on Man* as well as the *Moral Essays*.

Publication and Composition

The first three epistles of *An Essay on Man* were published respectively in February, March, and May of 1733. Epistle IV appeared in January of 1734, and the four were published together in April 1734. All these editions appeared anonymously, although by the time of the appearance of the collected edition, Pope's authorship was an open secret. An outline of the 'Contents' for Epistles I to III appears in a re-issue of Epistle I in April of 1733, that is, even before the first edition of Epistle III. In the first printing of Epistle IV a 'Contents' page precedes the text; and in the collected edition of the *Essay*, the 'Contents' outlines for the four epistles are grouped together preceding Epistle I. This last pattern is followed in all the later editions under discussion. In 1735 *An Essay on Man* became part of the collected *Works*, Volume II, first in the quarto and folio editions in April, and next in the octavo editions in July. The octavo editions, which are discussed in the final section of this chapter, are the first to carry substantial footnoting.

The publishing history of the early editions of the four *Moral Essays* is rather more complicated than that of *An Essay on Man*. The first to appear, over a year before Epistle I of *An Essay on Man*, was the *Epistle to Burlington*, now known as Epistle IV, in December 1731. It was reissued twice in January 1732, the only significant difference from the original being the half-title, which changed from 'Of Taste' to 'Of False Taste'.[1] Next to be published, in January of 1733 (that is, a month before *An Essay on Man*, Epistle I), was the first edition of the *Epistle to Bathurst*, which later became Epistle III of the *Moral Essays*. On this occasion, Pope wrote to Swift:

I have declined opening to you by letters the whole scheme of my present Work, expecting still to do it in a better manner in person; but you will see pretty soon that the letter to Lord Bathurst is a part of it, and you will find a plain connexion between them, if you read them in the order just contrary to that they were published in.[2]

[1] The change of title seems not to have been dictated by the general requirements of the larger project but by a suggestion of Aaron Hill to Pope. See *Correspondence*, iii. 257, 260, 268.

[2] Ibid. 348. Sherburn's note to this passage reads, 'He is thinking of his four "Moral Essays" which were published in an order opposite to that in which he intended to and did arrange them when they were collected.' This statement may not be precisely true, as our survey of publishing shows. Pope may have been thinking of Bathurst and Burlington in relation to the *Essay on Man* epistles rather than to the epistles to Cobham and to a Lady, since the former were appearing the same spring, the latter not until a year and two years later.

To Cobham, now Epistle I of the *Moral Essays*, appeared in January of 1734, a full year later than *Bathurst* and a week before the first publication of *An Essay on Man*, Epistle IV; and the *Epistle to a Lady* appeared last of this group thirteen months later still, in February of 1735. The *Moral Essays* never appeared separately as a group, but joined *An Essay on Man* in the publication of *Works*, Volume II, in April and July of 1735.[3] This edition of *Works*, Volume II, also contained the 'Contents' outlines of the four epistles together immediately after the half-title, 'Ethic Epistles, the Second Book'.

The dates of publication of these eight epistles do not, as we shall see, entirely reflect the time and order in which they were written. The publication dates do, however, help to highlight a feature of considerable significance about the relationship among the *Moral Essays* which Pope himself has obscured: notice that the original editions of the epistles to Burlington and Bathurst precede publication of the *Essay on Man* epistles, whereas the epistles to Cobham and to a Lady appear well after the publication of the first three epistles of the *Essay*. The epistles to Bathurst and Burlington on the one hand, the epistles to Cobham and to a Lady on the other, are linked only by way of *An Essay on Man*: at this stage they are not grouped together. The implications of this distinction will emerge as the analysis continues.

The history of the composition of the eight epistles cannot be entirely reconstructed because the sources of information—Spence's notes and Pope's and Bolingbroke's letters—are themselves fragmentary and unobjective in various ways. Although Spence is the major source and is generally reliable, his collection of notes is nevertheless of limited value, partly because he was abroad and hence out of touch with Pope for long periods (in the time under immediate survey, he was away for two and a half years—from December 1730 to July 1733); and partly because, as Professor

[3] This is the octavo edition of July 1735, in Twickenham III: i termed '1735b', and in Twickenham III: ii termed '1735c'. The discrepancy arises from the fact that in the folio edition of *Works*, Volume II in April 1735, the *Essay on Man* section is composed of remainder sheets from the 1734 edition of the poem; the folio edition is therefore without significance in the *Essay*'s textual history and is omitted from the critical apparatus of Twickenham III: i.

Sherburn has suggested, it is possible that Spence's notes are not a transcription of Pope's conversations in their entirety or even a précis of their central themes, but a record of the passages that Spence himself found most memorable when jotting them down soon afterwards.[4] Pope's letters, too, must be read *cum grano salis*, for he was often careless, particularly in dating letters, and often disingenuous or secretive about what he was writing and what progress he was making with a given work. Furthermore, a great many letters are no longer extant; there are tantalizing remarks to and from correspondents referring to fuller remarks in private letters we do not have. Nevertheless, after all such distorting factors have been taken into account, these sources provide invaluable and indisputable information, enabling us to piece together much of the progress of the *opus magnum*.

The first specific mention of the 'Ethic system' occurs in Bolingbroke's letter to Swift, 19 November 1729: 'Bid him [i.e. Pope] talk to you of the Work he is about.'[5] Pope amplified this extremely vague reference slightly by his remark, 'The work he [Bolingbroke] speaks of with such abundant partiality, is a system of Ethics in the Horatian way', in the letter he added to Bolingbroke's and sent off, together with it, nine days later.[6] During the following year (1730), Pope remained at work on his ethic scheme, as Spence's entries of May and November attest. The first entry reads as follows:

> The first epistle is to be to the whole work what a scale is to a book of maps, and in this, I reckon, lies my greatest difficulty—not only in settling and ranging the parts of it aright, but in making them agreeable enough to be read with pleasure. POPE *1–7 May 1730*
>
> This was said in May 1730, of what he then used to call his 'Moral Epistles', and what he afterwards called his *Essay on Man*. He at that time intended to have included in one epistle what he afterwards addressed to Lord Bolingbroke in four. SPENCE[7]

Even at this early stage, Pope seems to have had moments in which he considered abandoning the scheme, as Spence's parenthetical

[4] George Sherburn, 'Pope at Work' in *Essays in the Eighteenth Century Presented to David Nichol Smith*, ed. John Sutherland and F. P. Wilson (Oxford: Clarendon Press, 1945), p. 51.

[5] *Correspondence*, iii. 71.

[6] Ibid. 81. Bolingbroke had sent his letter to Swift by way of Pope.

[7] *Anecdotes*, i. 129–30, no. 294.

comment on Pope's words in the following entry, also from the first week of May 1730, indicates:

Perhaps we flatter ourselves when we think we can do much good. 'Tis mighty well if we can just amuse and keep out of harm's way. (After he had been speaking coldly of his moral work, and had been pressed to go on with it, on account of the good it might do to mankind.)[8]

Six months later Spence noted,

Mr. Pope's poem grows on his hands. The first four or five epistles will be on the general principles, or of 'The Nature of Man', and the rest will be on moderation, or 'The Use of Things'. In the latter part, each class may take up three epistles: one, for instance, against avarice, another against prodigality, and the third on the moderate use of riches; and so of the rest.

These two lines contain the main design that runs through the whole:

Laugh where we must, be candid where we can;
But vindicate the ways of God to Man.

POPE *28 or 29 November 1730*[9]

Spence's entries thus attest what the manuscript notes will corroborate, that there are epistles (here, presumably, versions of those to Bathurst and Burlington) envisioned beyond those making up *An Essay on Man*, even when the *Essay* was in the earliest stage of composition.

Other Spence entries for the year 1730 also attest to Pope's conception of *An Essay on Man* and the *Moral Essays* as forming a single moral scheme. The first of these makes its initial appearance in print in Mr. Osborn's recent edition:

Mr. Pope is now employed in a large design for a moral poem. There will be several behaviours of men flung into fables: one in particular on

[8] *Anecdotes*, i. 131, no. 298.

[9] Ibid., no. 299. Also of interest is Osborn's footnote, p. 131: 'The original notes of this conversation read "five or 6" epistles, indicating Pope's early design.' Mr. Osborn's editorial decision to print the latest text in Spence's own hand ensures a smoother reading than would be possible if Spence's earliest, often jumbled, notes were chosen as copy text. The increase in coherence, however, sometimes tends to obscure evidence about the dating and nature of Pope's works in progress. See, for instance, the references to the date of Pope's epic plan in Chapter VII below.

Further confirmation, if so terse and belated a reference can be considered a confirmation, of Pope's occupation with the ethic work during the summer of 1730 is provided by Atterbury's remark in a letter of 23 November 1731: 'Do you pursue the moral plan you marked out, and seemed sixteen months ago so intent upon?' (*Correspondence*, iii. 247).

the misery of affluence (planned just like that of Job, only with the contrary point in view), which Mr. Pope says he foresees already will take up at least a thousand verses. As he can't read by candlelight, he makes lines towards this design every evening that he is without company.

COLONEL HAY *early 1730*[10]

This third-hand report may suggest that at an early stage what is now the concluding part of the *Epistle to Bathurst*, the tale of Sir Balaam, was to have been an independent poem, yet still an integral part of the greater whole. Perhaps the Man of Ross section of the *Epistle to Bathurst* was to have the same quasi-independent existence. At least such would be a possible interpretation of the following few lines of a 1730 Spence entry from which grew notes that Mr. Osborn prints as separate items. The passage reads in part, 'The first Ep: to ye whole, w^t^ a Scale of Miles to a book of Maps. ye Man of Ross: Sr Balaam: fire, meat & drink: ye Dying Courtier &c.'.[11] The first part of this memorandum appears in expanded form as the first of the Spence entries quoted above. The second part also achieves separate and expanded existence as entry no. 316 in Mr. Osborn's edition, and the final phrase, a references to the *Epistle to Cobham*, ll. 252–5, is entry no. 318. Their consecutive appearance here is an important corroboration in more specific form of Spence's note quoted above, beginning 'Mr. Pope's poem grows on his hands'.

Spence's conversations for the year 1730 furnish the only clues to Pope's composition plans during that year. In addition to references to work upon what eventually were to be *An Essay on Man* and the epistles to Bathurst and to Cobham, there is an anecdote of May 1730:

Mr. Pope has very large prose collections on the happiness of contentment. Prodigality (in his piece) flings away all in wrong tastes. 'Tis thus in particular that some of the gardening poem will be of service.[12]

[10] *Anecdotes*, i. 129, no. *293*. I think it likely—especially in view of the third-hand derivation of this entry—that the parentheses are wrongly placed here. According to the entry as it stands, Colonel Hay is reporting that Pope is planning a fable on the misery of affluence which will take up at least a thousand lines. Such a plan is extremely unlikely, especially in view of Pope's general tendency to underestimate the length of proposed works. To place the opening parenthesis at the beginning of the second sentence would yield the more plausible reading, 'Mr. Pope is now employed in a large design for a moral poem . . . which Mr. Pope says he foresees already will take up at least a thousand verses.'

[11] Ibid. ii. 709 (textual note to no. *295*).

[12] Ibid. i. 138, no. *310*.

The 'gardening poem' would seem to be an early version of the *Epistle to Burlington*.[13] That Pope must have been working on the *Epistle to Burlington* at this time is clear also from the first datable document for 1731, a letter of April in which Pope refers to sending the Earl of Burlington the epistle addressed to him;[14] although the first published edition was not to appear until December 1731. By the end of July 1731 Pope had finished the third epistle of *An Essay on Man* and was working on the fourth, as is clear from his words to Bethel in a letter of 28 July: 'I have just finished an Epistle in Verse, upon the Nature & Extent of Good nature & Social affection; & am going upon another whose subject is, the True Happiness of Man.'[15] A few days later, in a letter to Swift of 2 August, in which he outlines the main topics of *An Essay on Man* in his usual rambling fashion, punctuated by some specific facts, Bolingbroke confirms that this stage has been reached: '. . . these three Epistles I say are finished. The fourth he is now intent upon . . . the Epistles I have mentioned will compose a first Book. the plan of the Second is settled.'[16] The next clear indication of progress[17] is in a letter from Pope to Fortescue in March 1732 where reference is made to sending Fortescue Epistle III of the *Essay* ('the third of the first part, relating to society and government') for transcription, and requesting the return of the portion of his 'large and almost boundless work' previously sent, providing that it has been transcribed.[18]

Pope's other project of 1732 was to make final preparations to publish the *Epistle to Bathurst* although the poem had clearly been

[13] For further detail on this point see *Anecdotes*, ii. 631, Appendix A to no. *310*.

[14] See Pope to the Earl of Burlington, 4 April (*Correspondence*, iii. 187–8). Pope had a purpose quite distinct from his moral scheme in preparing this epistle for publication so far in advance of the others. He thought it might serve as a preface to the second volume of Burlington's work on Palladio's designs. This immediate purpose, however, need not preclude the notion that it was composed with an eye to the moral scheme as well. See Chapter V.

[15] *Correspondence*, iii. 209.

[16] Ibid. 213–14. That Bolingbroke is not imposing order upon Pope's disorder is clear from Spence's earlier statements, and will become clearer in the discussion of the manuscript notes below.

[17] Through this period there are vague statements of progress in various letters, some stressing the inchoate nature of the work, others emphasizing the finished nature of certain (unspecified) fragments. See letters to Caryll (6 Dec. 1730), to Bethel (8 Sept. 1731), and to Hill ([4] Oct. 1731), ibid. 155, 227, 232, respectively.

[18] Ibid. 271.

in Pope's thoughts since early May 1730.[19] In June 1732 Pope sent his thanks to Jacob Tonson, Sr. for verifying facts about the Man of Ross, writing that 'I have no thoughts of printing the poem (which is an epistle on the *Use of Riches*) this long time, perhaps not till it is accompanied with many others'.[20] But by October Harley had seen part if not all of this epistle, by November it had gone to press, in December Pope was fretting over printing delays, and in January it was in print.[21]

In the same month, that is January 1733, Pope was apparently writing the *Epistle to a Lady*,[22] and by 16 February he could write to Swift,

> Your Lady friend is *Semper Eadem*, and I have written an Epistle to her on that qualification in a female character; which is thought by my chief Critick in your absence to be my *Chef d'Œuvre*: but it cannot be printed perfectly, in an age so sore of satire, and so willing to misapply characters.[23]

Although Pope may have vacillated over whether and what to omit in the first printing, and was occupied in seeing the epistles of the *Essay on Man* through the press in the spring of 1733, it is hard to see why there should have been a two-year delay between the completion of the epistle and its publication in February 1735. On Warburton's testimony, this epistle was written very quickly.[24] Possibly, Pope chose to delay publication until after the *Epistle to Cobham* was ready for print. In April 1733 Pope wrote again to Swift, saying,

[19] See Spence's notes, as reported above, and see also Chapter IV, p. 82. Pope also tells Caryll in early March 1733 that the poem 'was the work of two years by intervals' (*Correspondence*, iii. 353). One of the reasons for postponing publication of it was the outcry that met the publication of the *Epistle to Burlington*. (See Pope to the Earl of Oxford, Jan. 1732. 'The Noise which Malice has raisd about That Epistle has caused me to suppress a much better, concerning The *Use of Riches* . . .', *Correspondence*, iii. 267.)

[20] Ibid. 291.

[21] Sherburn's inference that Pope has enclosed at least a part of the *Epistle to Bathurst* in his letter to the Earl of Oxford of 22 Sept. 1732 (*Correspondence*, iii, 315) is supported by references in the exchange of letters between Pope and the Earl of Oxford in October (ibid. 324–6). The printing delay is referred to in Pope's letter to Caryll, 14 Dec. 1732 (ibid. 337).

[22] Apparently, that is, if one assumes that this is the work referred to in Pope's remark to Caryll, 'I believe you will receive from the care of your poor god-daughter a prettier poem [than the Epistle to Bathurst]' (ibid. 340). See Twickenham III: ii, pp. xxxv–xxxvi.

[23] *Correspondence*, iii. 349.

[24] So Ruffhead (presumably via Warburton) and Warburton himself in his notes to the 1751 edition, both quoted in Twickenham, III: ii, pp. xxxvi and 47, respectively.

'I have but last week finished another of my Epistles, in the order of the system; and this week (*exercitandi gratia*) I have translated, or rather parody'd, another of Horace's . . .'[25] Unless Pope is being careless in his use of the phrase 'last week', the epistle he alludes to cannot be *To a Lady* but must be either *An Essay on Man*, Epistle IV, or the *Epistle to Cobham*.[26] Yet it is not until the following autumn that references in the letters make clear that these two epistles are in the process of final revision.[27]

In the autumn of 1733 the *Epistle to Cobham* was completed and revised, and it was published in January of 1734 as was Epistle IV of *An Essay on Man*. When sending these to Swift, Pope wrote a covering letter, using the phrase adopted as the title of this study: 'You'll have immediately by several franks (even before 'tis here publish'd) my Epistle to Lord Cobham, part of my *Opus Magnum*, and the last Essay on Man.'[28] Three months later, in a letter to Swift of April 1734, Bolingbroke wrote: 'you have seen I doubt not the Ethic Epistles: and tho' they go a little into metaphysicks I perswade myself that you both understand and approve them. the first Book being finished, the others will soon follow for many of them are writ or crayoned out.'[29] The open-ended character, yet distinct evidence of the planning, of 'Ethic Epistles' Book II at this time,

[25] *Correspondence*, iii. 366.

[26] Whether or not Pope is being careless here is a somewhat tangled question. The Horatian work, mentioned as composed 'this week', has presumably already been mentioned as 'done' in a letter to Caryll of 20 March (ibid. 358). Pope's letter to Swift is dated by Pope as 2 April, which would make the references to 'last week' and 'this week' at least venial sins, but Mr. Sherburn (following Ball; see note, ibid. 365) amends the date to 20 April which, if correct, stretches the point considerably, and Pope's references to 'weeks' might be better read as 'months'.

[27] By 23 October Caryll had seen at least the portion of the *Epistle to Cobham* containing the 'character' of Wharton. See *Correspondence*, iii. 390. By 1 November Cobham had seen the epistle dedicated to him and had made suggestions for revision, and by 8 October had seen the revised portions. See the letters from Cobham to Pope (ibid. 391–2, 393). The letter to Caryll also contains a possible oblique reference to revision of Epistle IV of *An Essay on Man*, and there are clear references to its revision in letters to Bethel (9 Aug.) and Fortescue (13 Nov.), *Correspondence*, iii. 381, 395.

[28] Ibid. 401 (Pope to Swift, 6 January 1734). After citing this letter in his Introduction, Bateson goes on to say that the *Epistle to Cobham* was the poem meant to be 'what a scale is to a book of maps' (Twickenham, III: ii, pp. xxxiv–xxxv). The poem Pope must mean is *An Essay on Man*.

[29] *Correspondence*, iii. 404–5. As Sherburn notes, by the term 'Ethic Epistles' Bolingbroke presumably means the *Essay on Man*.

clearly apparent in Bolingbroke's letter, will also be supported by information other than that provided by letters and reports of conversations.

The available evidence describing planning and composition reflects the publication process in associating the epistles to Bathurst and Burlington and disassociating these two from the epistles to Cobham and to a Lady, and in distinguishing between epistles that are part of the system and those that are not. Although the *Epistle to Bathurst* was published during the same month and year (January 1733) that the *Epistle to a Lady* seems to have been composed in, the former seems to have been completed many months earlier. None of the evidence presented so far suggests that Pope thought of the four Moral Essays as constituting a separate, unified book, although each of them (and no others) is considered a part of the *opus magnum*. Other poems outside the system intervene between the earliest and latest of the epistles within the system. During the period so far surveyed, Pope also wrote at least two Horatian satires—the Imitations of Horace, *Satires* II, i (published in February 1733) and II, ii (which must be that meant in the April 1733 letter to Swift, and which was published in July 1734). However, when mentioning them in letters Pope consistently prides himself on how speedily he composed them,[30] so we may legitimately assume that their composition cannot have deflected him from his serious concentration upon *An Essay on Man* and the *Moral Essays*. The sentence in the April 1733 letter to Swift, moreover, illustrates well the continuous and consistent distinction Pope draws throughout this period between those epistles that are part of his 'system' and those that are not.[31]

Plans for Ethic Epistles Books I and II: Unpublished Material

There are two extant manuscript versions of Pope's *Essay on Man*, one in the Pierpont Morgan Library in New York, one in the Houghton Library of Harvard University. They have lately become somewhat more accessible through reproduction in the handsome limited edition printed in 1962 for members of the Roxburghe

[30] See *Correspondence*, iii. 348, 350, 353, 358.

[31] See, for instance, passages in ibid. 316, 348, 351, 362, 401.

Club and containing an introduction by Maynard Mack.[32] Both are working drafts, undated and perhaps undatable. The earliest possible date must be some time after the beginning of May 1730, the time Spence recalled when he wrote, 'He at that time intended to have included in one epistle what he afterwards addressed to Lord Bolingbroke in four.' For although marginal notations at many points in the manuscripts reveal Pope's uncertainties as to how many epistles there were to be and what each was to include, the *Essay* had clearly grown beyond the one-epistle stage. And the two drafts, one of which began as a direct copy of the other, soon begin to show a more complicated relationship. Maynard Mack says that the Harvard manuscript, 'though plainly intended to have been a fair copy of the Morgan Manuscript when the poet made it, soon turned under his relentless revisions into a working manuscript in its own right'.[33] A description of the appearance of the manuscripts will be a useful introduction to the manuscript marginalia that refer to the plans for epistles beyond those in the *Essay*.

Epistle I in both manuscripts is copied in Pope's neat hand, and is very close to the published version. The Harvard manuscript is clearly a direct transcription of the Morgan manuscript. The same appearance and relation between manuscripts holds true for most of Epistle II as well. Pope's practice, here as in the composition of the *Epistle to Bathurst*, was to transcribe sections—usually verse-paragraphs—down the inside halves of each opening, leaving wide margins at the outer edges of each page for annotations, alterations, and new composition. Yet whereas an examination of the later of the two manuscripts of the *Epistle to Bathurst* shows that all the verse in the central block derives without exception from either the central block or the marginal additions of the previous manuscript, so straightforward a relation is not characteristic of later portions of the *Essay on Man* drafts, whose variants suggest that some records integral to the composing process—perhaps only scraps of paper (or

[32] This edition has helped make possible two excellent doctoral dissertations on the nature of Pope's manuscript revisions, Dennis Roland Hoilman, 'Alexander Pope's Revisions of *An Essay on Man*', University of Utah doctoral dissertation, 1968 (Ann Arbor, University Microfilms), and Sylvia Sidwell Leonard, 'Wit and Judgment: Pope and the Art of Revision', University of Maryland doctoral dissertation, 1971 (Ann Arbor, University Microfilms).

[33] *Reproductions*, pp. xi–xii.

backs of envelopes)—have been lost. Towards the end of Epistle II, for instance, lines appear in the centre block of the Harvard draft that are found nowhere in the Morgan manuscript (for instance, lines 241–4, 283–6).

Annotations at the end of Epistle II in both manuscripts raise the possibility that Pope may at one point have thought of the *Essay on Man* as a two-epistle work. In the Morgan manuscript, there is a line drawn beneath the concluding lines (291–4) of Epistle II, followed by the note, 'Finis'. This note may refer solely to the drafting of the epistle, especially since a similar 'Finis' appears also at the end of the Morgan draft of Epistle III. But on the final page of the Harvard draft of Epistle II, after a line drawn across the page under the concluding lines of the epistle, there is first a subsequently marked-out phrase reading, 'Come then my friend &c. to last. / Oh when along ye Stream of Time &c. to know his God. / To end Lib. 1.', a version of Epistle IV, 373 ff., with the marginal note, 'Peroratio Lib. 1.', and another note at the bottom right-hand corner of the page reading, 'Finis Lib. Prim'. These may seem to be significant pointers to a conception of the *Essay* as a two-epistle work, but the actual appearance of the Harvard page suggests that this may not be so. The notations and verse separated from the original (and final) conclusion of Epistle II by a line extended across the page are in a different ink and slightly different hand, suggesting that like the extant early versions of the Man of Ross portrait and the tale of Sir Balaam in the set of *Epistle to Bathurst* drafts (described in Chapter IV), the peroration was to be a part of the poem that Pope worked on separately from the continuous portions. Indeed, to call it a peroration is misleading, for it may not have been so considered at this stage of composition: many versions of it appear in the manuscripts, and its first appearance is in the margin of the Morgan manuscript opposite the *opening* of Epistle II.[34]

A sure indication of the unsettled structure of the poem accompanies the passage in the Harvard manuscript equivalent to Epistle II, lines 249–60. It has a broken line vertically down the margin,

[34] The lines are next transcribed into the central block of verse in the Harvard MS. at the opening of Epistle II, but a marginal note there reads 'Incipit III. Dele.'. For further details on this complicated issue, see *Reproductions*, pp. xiii–xiv; Leonard, 'Wit and Judgment: Pope and the Art of Revision', pp. 117–18, 229–34.

a delete sign, and the phrase, 'postpone to ye third'. Later, Pope crossed through the last phrase and replaced it with 'Stent'. Similar uncertainty marks the drafting of Epistle III. Near the opening of Epistle III in the Harvard draft, a marginal note reads, 'Incipit 3. Learn then thyself, & end it with Come then my Friend &c. to——', again referring to the concluding passage of the poem, the verse-paragraph that is now Epistle IV, 373 and following. This may signal a point when the *Essay* was thought of as a three-epistle work. Towards the end of Epistle III, again in the Harvard manuscript, there are twelve lines crossed through with the notation, 'haec omnia ? in epist. sequent.'. These lines, considerably revised, become Epistle IV, 361–72.[35] This passage is followed by four more lines (not crossed through) surrounded by a wavy line beside which Pope notes, 'Postpone to end ye following Epistle.' The second couplet of this passage corresponds to Epistle IV, 339–40 in the printed version. The six lines following it are unannotated and become the concluding lines of Epistle III in printed form.

The appearance of the handwriting in the drafts also reflects the evolving state of the poem. The central block of text in the (later) Harvard manuscript is uniformly neat, although in Epistles II and III marginal additions increase in length and number. The earlier Morgan manuscript shows much greater variation from epistle to epistle. Pope transcribed Epistles I and II very neatly from a previous draft, but in Epistle II added in the margin large blocks of poetry which become progressively more of a scrawl and more tentative. He began to copy Epistle III in a more hurried script and then began to transpose, cancel, rewrite, and compose lengthy sections of verse. Finally, the draft of Epistle IV records a significantly earlier stage of composition. The Harvard manuscript does not

[35] Some readers (see Sherburn, 'Pope at Work', p. 59; Hoilman, 'Alexander Pope's Revisions', p. 195 n. 11; Leonard, 'Wit and Judgment: Pope and the Art of Revision', pp. 190–1, 227–8) have been confused by a misplacement of the equivalent of this passage in the Morgan MS. It is on a small page that follows after the draft of Epistle IV but should appear as the last page of the draft of Epistle III. That it belongs at the end of Epistle III is clear from its small size and its page number (11), which relate it to the little sheet folded to make four pages numbered 7, 8, 9, and 10, which contain Epistle III, 216–310. Even more conclusively, the catchword at the bottom of p. 10 is 'Pa' and p. 11 begins 'Parent or Friend . . .' (a variant of IV, 367–8) and continues with an early version of IV, 361 ff., which, as the Harvard version makes clear, originally appears as the conclusion of Epistle III.

contain any part of Epistle IV; the Morgan manuscript takes us only about half way through it, and the characteristic pattern of neat central block with wide margins has vanished. The Morgan version of Epistle IV is clearly a record of composition at a much earlier stage than the manuscript versions of the first three epistles. Pope is no longer transcribing from an earlier draft to the Morgan draft; instead, he is apparently hurriedly jotting down his first trial couplets, frequently crossing out and rephrasing first attempts. Interspersed with these snatches of verse are many examples of what Pope called his 'prose collections', also jotted down in a small and hurried hand. Maynard Mack places these in the first of his five categories of manuscript marginalia. He is primarily interested in the evolution of the poem, whereas we are studying the evolution of the *opus magnum*. His divisions are helpful ones, however, and, with different emphasis, I use them in the following examination of Pope's manuscript notations.

The first group of marginalia, the prose propositions of Epistle IV, takes us, in Mack's words, 'about as close to the actual processes of composition as we are likely to get'[36] and sometimes shows 'verse sucking prose into its own vortex'.[37] This stage of composition is a fascinating one, but peripheral to our immediate purpose of tracing the interconnectedness of the ethic epistles. (Its closest analogues among Pope's working papers are the transcript of a portion of the *Dunciad* manuscript and the plan for Pope's projected epic, which are described in Chapters VI and VII, below.) A second type of marginalia throws light on the evolution of the *Essay on Man* to its four-epistle form. Several illustrations of this type have been given above; another, referring to the abortive 'Epistle on the Limits of Reason', will be considered in relation to Walter Harte's poem on reason in which Pope showed a marked interest.

The three remaining kinds of marginalia correspond to those found in the published text. One kind, as Mr. Mack points out, have the character of editorial annotations. They name an authority or supply an analogue for what is being attempted in verse.[38] Another

[36] *Reproductions*, p. xvii. Mack gives illuminating examples of this process, pp. xviii–xxiii.

[37] Ibid., p. xx.

[38] An instance is '*Vide* Oppian Halieut. Lib. I', the Harvard MS. note to Epistle III,

group of notes, writes Mack, 'supply simply a running précis of the poem's thought such as was used to compose the "Argument"'.[39] He notes that this kind of notation appears especially in the Harvard manuscript, whereas scrutiny reveals that they are in every instance also in the earlier Morgan manuscript. (In neither manuscript are there any such notes to Epistle I.) Because they are in a much more cramped and written-over scrawl, they are less easy to detect in the Morgan manuscript. Mack's remark conveys the suggestion that the running notes to *An Essay on Man* are a development from the verse, yet the appearance of these notes in the manuscripts, especially the Morgan draft, suggest that they, like the poetry itself, grew out of Pope's prose collections, were integral to the creative process, and helped to shape the final stabilization of the parts of the poem.[40]

The remaining variety of notes are those, as Mr. Mack states, that make cross-reference to other parts of the poem, or to other poems originally projected for the large ethic work to which the *Essay* itself was to be 'what a scale is to a book of maps'. In accordance with his separate interests, Mr. Mack simply mentions this category in passing, but the few notes of this sort supply the most specific and significant basis for suggesting the scope of the plan and the interconnection among the ethic epistles at a stage that, although undatable, must nevertheless precede publication of the *Essay*. Of particular value are those notes that relate to the first few lines of Epistle I in each manuscript. These are first set out below and then compared.

The notes to the opening of Epistle I in the earlier (Morgan) manuscript are marginal, and are keyed to the lines of verse as follows:[41]

	opposite line:
Inconsistencys of Character, ye Subject of Ep. 5	6 'A mighty maze . . .'

177–8. Such notes seem to be characteristic of the earliest stages of composition, since similar 'editorial' annotations appear in Pope's epic outline. See Chapter VII.

[39] *Reproductions*, p. xii.

[40] See an expanded version of this point in Hoilman, 'Alexander Pope's Revisions', pp. 232–49.

[41] The notes to the Morgan MS. exordium were also transcribed by Sherburn, 'Pope at Work', p. 59, except that Sherburn omits the final note. He transcribes the MS. version of the opening lines; I give the printed version. Revisions in the transcription are Pope's. See also Hoilman, p. 131.

Passions, Virtues &c. ye Subject of Ep. 2	7 'A Wild, where . . .'
The Use of Pleasure, in Lib. 2.	8 'Or garden, . . .'
Of the Knowledge of Mankind	
~~The Characters~~ λ [?]λ Epistle 1st of Book 2.	10 'Try what the open . . .'
Learning & Ignorance, Subject of Epist. 3 of Book 2.	11 'The latent tracts, . . .'
The rest λIn general	13 'Eye Nature's walks, . . .'

The Harvard manuscript exordium notes appear at the bottom of the opening page of the draft of Epistle I. There are only ten lines of verse on the page and, commencing with line six, Pope has numbered them. The prose notes are in two sections, one immediately below the other, and the appearance of the handwriting and their placement on the page seems to indicate that the lower group of notes was written first. This second section reads as follows:[42]

oposition. 6th verse, alludes to ye Subject of this first Epistle, ye State of M[
& hereafter, disposed by Providence, tho to him unknown.

7th verse, to ye Subject of ye Second, ye Passions, their good or evil.

8th verse, to ye Subject of ye 4th, of mans various pursuits of Happiness or Pleasure.

epistle of ye second, the
10th verse, to ye Subjects of ye Second λ book, λ Characters of Men & Manners.

13. 14. of ye first Epistle of
11. & 12th verse, to ye subject λ ye Second book, The Limits of Reason, Learning & Ignorance

16 Verse, to ye Subject wch runs thro ye Whole Design, the justification of ye Methods of Providence.

In the small space remaining between the block of verse and the notes given above, Pope apparently decided to write a more general note to introduce the section given above. He wrote it once, crossed out phrases and added alterations, and then, as his working space became impossibly cramped, tore off a piece of the outer margin

42 A verbatim transcript (see frontispiece). Each notation occupies only one line in MS. The omission signified by the square bracket in the first line is caused by Pope's having torn away part of the page here.

and pasted in another fragment of paper containing what seems to be his final version of the first section of the exordium note. It reads as follows:[43]

This Exordium relates to the whole work. The 6th, 7th, & 8th lines allude to ye Subjects of This Book, the General Order & Design of Providence; the Constitution of the human Mind, whose Passions, cultivated, are Virtues, neg[lecte]d, Vices; the Temptations of misapplyd Selflove & wrong pursuits of Power, Pleasure and false Happiness. The 10th, 11th, 12th, &c. allude to ye [sub]jects of ye following books; the [various?] characters and capacities of Men, of Learning & Ignorance, [the?] Knowledge of Mankind and the Manners [of the a]ge. The last Line sums up the moral & main Drift of ye whole, [the?] Justification of ye Ways of Provi[dence.]

Both sets of notes agree in their purpose, to relate the lines of the exordium to various parts of the *Essay on Man* and to successive epistles of the following book or books. Both agree in many of the topics listed—Passions, Pleasure, Human Character, Learning and Ignorance—though not in their positions in the 'whole work'. Only in placing a consideration of 'Passions' in Epistle 2 is there an exact agreement of number and order. Both agree that the Knowledge of Mankind and a consideration of Learning and Ignorance will be major topics of Book 2, but the Harvard notes reverse the order proposed by the Morgan notes. Neither set of exordium notes mentions 'Society', the subject of Epistle 3. Further along in the Morgan manuscript, a note to Epistle I, line 88 ('A hero perish, or a sparrow fall'), reading 'Vid. Epist. 3 of animals Verse . . .' (with a space after 'Verse' suggesting that a specific line number was to be supplied later) may refer to the printed Epistle III, which has many references to animals, and in manuscript form has even more.

The implications of Book and Epistle numbering are, in my view, the following: the Morgan manuscript notes belong to a stage of composition in which the number and order of epistles in the moral scheme have not as yet been fixed. At first sight, the notes would seem to reflect a two- or three-epistle stage in the evolution of the

[43] This note also appears in Twickenham, III: i, p. 12, but the notes at the bottom of the MS. page are not mentioned. The tipped-in note may be linked to the poetic text by a faint dagger which may possibly correspond with the double dagger opposite line 4. The left part of this note has faded considerably.

Essay on Man; for the note, 'The Use of Pleasure', which appears to refer to what later was to become Epistle IV of Book I, is here given as the subject of 'Lib. 2'. As a possible explanation, one may conjecture that the terms 'Book' and 'Epistle' are used carelessly and interchangeably, but such a solution will not suffice here, since 'Ep. 2' has just been mentioned; 'Lib. 2' must therefore refer to something quite distinct from it. Moreover, Pope seems to have made a distinction between the *Essay* as abstract philosophy, and the epistles to follow as applied philosophy, consistently employing the word 'Use' only in the titles of the latter.

The very first of the Morgan exordium notes, 'Inconsistencys of Character, ye Subject of Ep. 5', raises even more complications. Mr. Sherburn says that 'This might well refer to the first Moral Essay'. Although certainly an acceptable observation on the ordering we are familiar with from printed editions, it is not one that is helpful in recreating what Pope may have meant at this particular stage before completing the poem. If one assumes that 'Ep. 5' refers to Book I, this note may belong to that stage of planning marked by Spence's entry of late November 1730, cited above, beginning 'Mr. Pope's poem grows on his hands. The first four or five epistles will be on general principles, or of "The Nature of Man," and the rest will be on moderation, or "The Use of Things"'. (Mr. Osborn's footnote to this entry tells us that in a Spence jotting earlier than the one used as a copy text for the same note, Spence wrote 'five or six' rather than 'four or five'.) Alternatively, one may posit the notion that the note refers to a running tally of epistles that in this particular case does not indicate the separation of Book II from Book I. In this case, one would assume a three-epistle *Essay*, and then a new book with a fourth epistle ('Epistle 1st of Book 2') 'Of the Knowledge of Mankind', a fifth epistle (the second of Book 2, not otherwise accounted for) on 'Inconsistencys of Character', a sixth ('Epist. 3 of Book 2') on 'Learning & Ignorance', and perhaps further epistles on 'The Use of Pleasure'. This is a very tenuous hypothesis indeed, but not, I think, wholly to be dismissed. It accords with the eventual titling and order of the *Epistle to Cobham* and the *Epistle to a Lady*, although, of course, they may not have been thought of as separate poems at this stage.

Neither the note itself nor either of the hypotheses about it is reflected at all clearly in the manuscript notes to the *Essay* as distinct from its exordium. Although it is impossible to determine the time relation between poetic composition and prose notes, this note does locate the Morgan manuscript as dating significantly earlier in time than the Harvard manuscript, whose exordium notes clearly refer to the final four-epistle form of the *Essay*. These notes may help to date the Harvard manuscript at some point nearer to the summer of 1731, when Pope's letter to Bethel and Bolingbroke's to Swift support one another in specifying that the third epistle has been finished, the fourth and final one begun, and the plan of the whole settled.

This manuscript evidence linked with Spence's jottings and Pope's correspondence illuminates another important aspect of the process of composition. The early-1730 references to part of Book II, Sir Balaam, the Man of Ross, 'fire, meat & drink', and 'the gardening poem', suggest that the final shaping of the *Epistle to Burlington* and the *Epistle to Bathurst* certainly preceded and are likely to have conditioned the shaping of Epistle IV of *An Essay on Man*, and perhaps even the other epistles that were to be composed as part of the scheme. In their recent study of Pope's health, Nicolson and Rousseau conjecture that the first three epistles of *An Essay on Man* took final shape while Pope was recuperating from illness under Bolingbroke's roof during April and May of 1731.[44] Pope had then not yet proceeded to Epistle IV, but well before that had made many concrete references to parts of the epistles to Bathurst and Burlington, and in April of 1731 he had sent some version of the latter poem to Burlington himself.

With one exception, all the topics given in the manuscript exordium notes are developed in the eight completed epistles. The exception is the Epistle on the 'Limits of Reason, Learning & Ignorance'. This particular topic does however recur in the period 1729–35. Two such occurrences are in the Harvard manuscript. In the margin, stretched vertically down page 16, opposite thirty-six lines of text, twenty-four of which become Epistle II, lines 19–42 of the printed version of *An Essay on Man*, is the note, 'postpone all

[44] Marjorie Nicolson and G. S. Rousseau, '*This Long Disease My Life*', *Alexander Pope and the Sciences* (Princeton: Princeton University Press, 1968), pp. 36–47.

these to the Epistle on the Use & Extent of Learning'. And after several blank pages following the end of Epistle III of the Harvard manuscript of *An Essay on Man*, there is an inserted leaf containing only the following heading and eight lines of verse:

Incipit Liber Secundus.
Epist. I. of Y^e Limits of Reason

And now, transported O'er so vast a Plain,
While the free courser flies with all the Rein;
While heav'nward, now his mounting Wings he feels,
Now stoops where Fools fly trembling from his heels;
Wilt thou, my Laelius; keep ye Course in sight,
Or urge the Fury, or assist ye Flight?
Laelius, whose Love excus'd my labours past,
Matures my present, & shall bound my last.

These lines, obviously part of the exordium, and showing parallels in tone and metaphor to the opening of *An Essay on Man*, give no clue to the treatment of the subject.[45]

Our perusal of the manuscript notes is over, but the Epistle on Reason lingers on. In May or June of 1734, Pope wrote to Mallet:

You will order Gilliver accordingly, & upon the whole let Mr Harte give him directions. I fancy the Title of an *Essay on Reason* is the best, & am half of opinion, if no Name be set to it, the public will think it mine especially since in the Index, (annext to the large paper Edition of the Essay on Man) the Subject of the next Epistle is mentioned to be *of Human Reason* &c. But whether this may be an Inducement, or the Contrary, to Mr Harte, I know not: I like his poem so well (especially since his last alterations) that it would no way displease me.[46]

Walter Harte's *Essay on Reason* was published by Gilliver anonymously at the beginning of 1735. As the letter to Mallet suggests, Pope was willing that the public should think it his. For a time, too,

[45] 'Laelius' is the pseudonym given to Bolingbroke in the first line of Epistle I of the *Essay* in the first two editions (1733). The first 6 lines of this patch of verse appear first in rougher form in the margin on the Harvard MS. page concluding Epistle II. The final couplet appears first in both MSS. as part of Epistle IV, 373 ff., and achieves printed form as the opening couplet of *The First Epistle of the First Book of Horace Imitated* (1738).

[46] *Correspondence*, iii. 408–9.

he seemed willing to deceive his personal circle as well, as a letter of 8 February 1735 to Caryll suggests:

> I send you constantly whatever is mine. The ludicrous (or if you please) the obscene thing you desired me to send, I did not approve of, and therefore did not care to propagate by sending into the country at all. Whoever likes it so well as to think it mine, compliments me at my expense. But there is another piece, which I may venture to send you in a post or two, *An Essay on Reason* of a serious kind, and the intentions and doctrines of which I think you will not disapprove.[47]

However, if there is deliberate ambiguity about authorship intended in the linking of the offer to send 'another piece' with the opening sentence of the paragraph, 'I send you whatever is mine', it lasts three months at most. For in May 1735 Pope, writing to Caryll once more, spoke again of the *Essay on Reason*, commenting, 'I was not sorry many people took Mr Hart's poem for mine.'[48] Furthermore, other evidence suggests that Pope was not entirely without some claim upon the poem. Casting more light on the final sentence of the letter to Mallet, quoted above, is Joseph Warton's note, 'Pope inserted many good lines in Harte's *Essay on Reason*.'[49] Alexander Chalmers similarly notes that Pope had a considerable share in it, 'although no part of his share can be exactly ascertained, except the first two lines'.[50] A close reading of Harte's poem shows some

[47] *Correspondence*, iii. 450. [48] Ibid. iii. 455.

[49] J. Warton, *Essay on the Genius and Writings of Pope*, Vol. II (1782), 154 n. On Warton's authority, Griffith assigned Harte's poem, published anonymously in February 1735, a number, though numbers are regularly reserved for Pope's works alone. See R. H. Griffith, *Alexander Pope: A Bibliography*. In Two Parts (Austin: University of Texas Press, 1922–7), ii. 275.

[50] Alexander Chalmers, ed., *Works of the English Poets from Chaucer to Cowper* (1810), xvi. 312. Harte's poem opens as follows:

> From Time's vast Length, eternal and unknown.
> Essence of God, coeval REASON shone;
> Mark'd each recess of Providence and Fate,
> Weighing the present, past, and future state:
> 'Ere Earth to start from Nothing was decreed,
> 'Ere Man had fal'n, or God vouchsaf'd to bleed!

There seems to me nothing so specially distinctive about the opening couplet as to stamp it as Pope's contribution without Chalmers's remark. Chalmers also says (p. 316) that Harte's 'attachment to Pope led him to an imitation of [Pope's] manner, particularly in the Essay on Reason and that on satire'.

Since Harte's poem is rather easy to come by, interested readers may wish to compare some closely similar passages. Instances are Harte, 15–22 and *Essay* III, 151–60 (Harte

passages bearing marked affinities with the subject-matter and style of *An Essay on Man*, but no contemporary evidence exists to determine Pope's part in the poem, which, as Chalmers notes, 'might with more propriety be called a fine Christian poem [than a fine philosophical poem], as it has more of religion than philosophy, and might have been aptly entitled An Essay on Revelation'.[51]

In the letter to Mallet quoted above, in which Pope spoke of the printing of Harte's poem, he also referred to an 'Index (annext to the large paper Edition of the Essay on Man)'. According to Spence, this Index was included in only about a dozen copies of the 1734 quarto edition of the poem, most of which were later called back. Spence then offers a full transcription of the Index, but, as Mr. Osborn explains, it is not in Spence's hand, and, as printed, it obscures the relationship between the particular epistles of Book I and the corresponding units of Book II.[52] As the Index of 1734 is the single most reliable and ample extant source of information about Pope's plans for his ethic system when the scheme was at its freshest and most ambitious, it is transcribed here (below, p. 28) not from the *Anecdotes* but from the Scolar Press facsimile reproduction of the only known printed copy of the Index leaf.[53] The Index of 1734 is consistent with the Harvard manuscript notes to the Exordium of *An Essay on Man*, although of course it considerably extends the number and topics of the Ethic Epistles, Book II. In both outlines, the ordering of the first two sections of Book II, 'Of the Use of Things', is the same: the first is to be 'Of the Limits of Human Reason' (including 'Of the Use of Learning'

is describing life in Eden; Pope is describing 'the State of Nature'); Harte, 49–58 and *Essay* I, 121–30 (on men aspiring to be Gods); Harte, 137–42, 149–52, 169–74 and *Essay* II, 19–22, 29–42 (the last passage is the one Pope annotated in the Harvard MS. for postponement 'to the Epistle on the Use & Extent of Learning'). Harte's poem is consistently less harsh in tone and more explicitly Christian.

[51] Chalmers, xvi. 316. In *The Works of Alexander Pope* (1797), iii. 10–11, Joseph Warton records the following anecdote: 'Mr. Harte more than once assured me, that he had seen the pressing letter Dr. Young wrote to Pope, urging him to write something on the side of revelation; . . . And when Harte frequently made the same request, he used to answer, "No, no! You have already done it;" alluding to Harte's Essay on Reason, which Harte thought a lame apology, and hardly serious.'

[52] See *Anecdotes*, i. 132; ii. 710 (no. 300 and its textual note).

[53] Appendix, *An Essay on Man. Alexander Pope. 1734* (London: Scolar Press, 1969). See also D. F. Foxon's 'Introductory Note' to this facsimile edition.

INDEX
TO THE
ETHIC EPISTLES.

The FIRST BOOK. Of the NATURE and STATE of Man.	The SECOND BOOK. Of the USE of THINGS.
EPIST. I. —With respect to the *Universe*.	Of the Limits of Human Reason. —Of the Use of Learning. —Of the Use of Wit.
EPIST. II. —As an *Individual*.	Of the Knowledge and Characters of Men. Of the particular Characters of Women.
EPIST. III. —With respect to *Society*.	Of the Principles and Use of Civil and Ecclesiastical Polity. —Of the Use of Education.
EPIST. IV. —With respect to *Happiness*.	A View of the Equality of Happiness in the several Conditions of Men. —Of the Use of Riches, &c.

and 'Of the Use of Wit') which obviously corresponds closely with the Harvard note referring to 'The first Epistle of ye Second Book, the Limits of Reason, Learning & Ignorance'; and the second, 'Of the Knowledge and Characters of Men', just as obviously corresponds closely to the Harvard reference to 'ye Second Epistle of ye second book, the Characters of Men & Manners'. Yet the format raises a problem that Mr. Osborn outlines:

> The 'Index,' here printed from the original paper, bears the same words printed by Singer, but raises one important question—was the Second Book to consist of nine epistles, or five? Singer's printer set the sub-headings equal with the headings, but the original seems to indicate only five epistles.[54]

[54] *Anecdotes*, i. 133.

Mr. Osborn proffers the solution to this problem by way of a related entry by Spence that reads:

> The four first epistles [the *Essay on Man*] are the scale for all the rest of the work, and were much the most difficult part of it. 'I don't know whether I shall go on with the Epistle on Government or that on Education.' ⌜Mr. Pope's plan would take in an Essay on Government, and on Education, among the mezzo-subjects.⌝ POPE *1734*
>
> He spoke a little warmer as to the use of it, but more coldly as to the execution. SPENCE[55]

To this entry, Mr. Osborn appends a note, reading in part, 'Pope's use of the term "Mezzo-subjects" indicates that "Of the Use of Education" was definitely a sub-heading'. Yet two details suggest that this was not quite the case. First, the use of parentheses suggests that 'mezzo-subjects' is not Pope's term, but Spence's, and may apply to all parts of the second book, whose *main* 'subject' is 'Of the Use of Things'. Secondly, Mr. Osborn singles out 'Of the Use of Education' for comment, presumably because the format of the original copy of the index suggests that it might be a subsection of the larger unit 'Of . . . Civil and Ecclesiastical Polity'. But this last unit must be the one Spence refers to as 'an Essay on Government'. 'Essay' is again Spence's term; in the direct quotation by Spence of Pope's words, the term is 'Epistle' and Pope speaks of the epistles on Government and Education on equal terms, rather than subordinating the latter to the former. Although Mr. Osborn's solution does not I think fit the case, no greater certainty attaches to any other solution based on the format of this Index alone.

The epistles on government and education are the only portions of Book II not previously alluded to by Pope. One can, I think, feel confident in assuming that Pope meant them to be 'applied' extensions of the 'abstract' treatment of 'Man with respect to Society' in *An Essay on Man*, Epistle III. Since even Epistle III of the *Essay* itself was not included among the cross-reference notes to the exordium of the poem, we cannot infer that the epistles of Book II were conceived later than Epistle III of the *Essay*. Possibly their

[55] Ibid., no. 301. The phrase in brackets is Osborn's; the sentence in half-brackets, Spence's.

conception was at least partly responsible for Pope's decision to extend the *Essay* beyond its earlier one- or two-epistle form.

The format and spacing of the printed Index of 1734 clearly indicate that Pope envisioned the other units in Book II as having a direct correlation with the individual epistles of Book I comparable to that which I have just described in connection with Epistle III of the *Essay*. That is, 'Of the Limits of Human Reason', 'Of the Use of Learning', and 'Of the Use of Wit' form a group closely tied with the themes of *An Essay on Man*, Epistle I, 'Of the Nature and State of Man, with Respect to the Universe' whose subject is man as a rational being and which emphasizes the vital importance of an awareness of the limits of his reasoning power. Next, the two epistles 'Of the Knowledge and Characters of Men' and 'Of the particular Characters of Women' clearly form a unit and stem in particular from *An Essay on Man*, Epistle II, 'Of Man as an individual'. All the epistles in this group emphasize the psychology of man, offering the principle of the Ruling Passion as an explanation of human behaviour. We have already noted the group on 'Society'. The units in the fourth and final group, 'A View of the Equality of Happiness in the several Conditions of Men' and 'Of the Use of Riches' are, correspondingly, direct developments of *An Essay on Man*, Epistle IV. This appears to be a straightforward and workable outline and one which shares many of the features of outlines of the moral scheme after 1735, which we shall consider later.

Why then did Pope call back this Index? In general, one supposes, because he was not far enough advanced with drafts of subsequent poems to wish to commit himself publicly to parts of the *opus magnum* project that were ill-defined and that he might not finish. In particular, because, in his words, 'I don't know whether I shall go on with the Epistle on Government or that on Education'. Spence himself speculates that this is the reason why Pope said 'I have drawn in my plan for my Ethic Epistles much narrower than it was at first'.[56] This is the opening line of the entry that also contains the Index, and it is on account of the remark that Spence offers the Index as a straightforward description of the plan before Pope

[56] *Anecdotes*, i. 132, no. 300.

'drew it in'. Later Spence also added the query, 'Why? Frō his ment^{g} the heads of Ecc^{l} and Civil Polity wch he aft^{ds} resolv'd not to touch upon in y^{t} Poem?'[57] Spence presumably refers to Pope's declaration in April 1744 that 'I could not have said what I *would* have said without provoking every church on the face of the earth, and I did not care for living always in boiling water', and the further remark that the material originally intended for the book on civil and ecclesiastical government would appear instead in his epic on Brutus.[58] In addition to wishing to avoid becoming embroiled in controversy, Pope may in 1734 have been experiencing difficulties in drafting this work, as the excerpts from letters quoted in Chapter VI suggest. By this time too, he may have become more interested in planning the unit on 'the Limits of Human Reason', which he outlines in some detail in a letter to Swift in 1736 (also quoted in Chapter VI), and into which he may have planned to absorb some of the material originally conceived of as part of the Epistle on Education. Instead of advertising the uncompleted parts of the *opus magnum* by specific title, Pope chose instead to refer to them very casually in the prefatory 'Design' in the 1734 edition of *An Essay on Man* and to give the appearance of tight organization to those epistles already completed when he published them together in 1735.

Notes and Format of Collected Editions, 1734 and 1735

From this time forth until the advent of Warburton, Pope, as Spence relates, drew in the plan for his Ethic Epistles. The 1734 folio edition of *An Essay on Man*, from which Pope withdrew the Index, was the first to carry a prefatory note, headed 'The Design'. Its opening and closing paragraphs read:

Having proposed to write some pieces on Human Life and Manners, such as (to use my lord Bacon's expression) *come home to Men's Business and Bosoms*, I thought it more satisfactory to begin with considering *Man* in the abstract, his *Nature* and *his State*: since, to prove any moral duty, to enforce any moral precept, or to examine the perfection or imperfection of any creature whatsoever, it is necessary first to know what *condition* and *relation* it is placed in, and what is the proper *end* and purpose of its being . . .

[57] Ibid. ii. 710 (textual note to no. 300).
[58] Ibid. i. 134, no. 302. (Also see Chapter VII.)

What is now published, is only to be considered as a *general Map* of MAN, marking out no more than the *greater parts*, their *extent*, their *limits*, and their *connection*, but leaving the particular to be more fully delineated in the charts which are to follow. Consequently, these Epistles in their progress (if I have health and leisure to make any progress) will be less dry, and more susceptible of poetical ornament. I am here only opening the *fountains*, and clearing the passage. To deduce the *rivers*, to follow them in their course, and to observe their effects, may be a task more agreeable.

The vague references to 'some pieces on Human Life and Manners', 'the Charts that follow', and 'these Epistles in their progress (if I have health and leisure to make any progress)', represent a commitment less firm than the specific titles in the Index, to continuing the ethic scheme on a grand scale and with specific constituents. Nevertheless, 'The Design' does make public and authoritative the conception of *An Essay on Man* as a foundation for other epistles. And the very phrasing of the conception in the first sentence of the final paragraph associates it with Pope's remarks to Spence in 1730 and 1734 that the *Essay on Man* was to be to the whole work 'what a scale is to a book of maps'. The notes making cross-references that first appear in the octavo edition of Pope's *Works*, Volume II, of 1735, stress the interdependence of the eight epistles comprising the *Essay on Man* and the *Moral Essays* as we know them.

In addition to cross-reference notes, there are three other kinds of notes. These are, first, the notes comprising the running argument and, second, the notes that name an authority, examples of which were evident in the *Essay on Man* manuscripts. A third sort, prominent only in the *Moral Essays*, is the species of note that identifies contemporary persons or events, partly as a way of establishing a basis for Pope's moral indignation. The longest of this sort is the note to the *Epistle to Bathurst*, line 20, elaborating upon the careers of Ward, Chartres, and Waters. Similarly, the note to *Bathurst*, ll. 65–8, for instance, begins, 'This is a true story'; and the note on the Man of Ross (*Bathurst*, l. 250) stresses that he 'actually lived'. Such notes appear in all the *Moral Essays* except the *Epistle to a Lady*, where Pope later wrote (note to ll. 7–13), 'The poet's politeness and complaisance to the sex is observable in this instance, amongst others, that, whereas in the *Characters of Men* he has sometimes made use of real names, in the *Characters of Woman* always fictitious.'

Heralding the more extensive annotation to appear in July 1735, is a 'Postscript' to the quarto and folio editions of April 1735 in which Pope gives a number of notes for *Bathurst* and *Arbuthnot* and a group of textual emendations of *An Essay on Man* and the *Moral Essays*, under the following heading:

> It was intended in this Edition to have added *Notes* to the *Ethic Epistles* as well as to the *Dunciad*, but the book swelling to too great a bulk, we are oblig'd to defer them till another Volume may come out, of such as the Author may hereafter write, with several Pieces in Prose relating to the same subjects.
>
> In the meantime, that nothing contained in the former Editions may be wanting in this, we have here collected all the *Variations* of the separate Impressions, and the *Notes* which have been annexed to them, with the additions of a few more which have been judg'd the most necessary.

Cross-reference notes, then, first appear in the first octavo edition of 1735, which is also the first edition to employ a running 'Argument'. As the running argument contains no significant differences from the outline of contents, and as neither changes in any marked way from the original folio editions in the early 1730s to the version of 1734, I shall discuss only the cross-reference notes.[59] There are altogether fifteen of these in the 1735 octavo editions. Eight are attached to the *Essay on Man*, and all of them point forward rather than back, all but two to later epistles of the *Essay*. The exceptions, as might be expected, are notes on the Ruling Passion. Both are in Epistle II. The first of these, alluding to the passage beginning 'As Man, perhaps, the moment of his breath' (II, 133 ff.), reads '*The* Predominant Passion, *and its* Force. The use of this doctrine, as apply'd to the Knowledge of mankind, is one of the subjects of the second book.' The second note, appended to the line, 'A mightier Pow'r the strong direction sends' (II, 165), reads as follows:

165 ff. *Its* Necessity, *in directing men to different purposes*. The particular

[59] Mack's transcription of the *Essay on Man* notes and their variants until 1743 is complete, but Bateson excludes all notes except those in the 1744 Pope–Warburton edition, so his textual policy (Twickenham III: ii, pp. lv–lvi) is not helpful in tracing the progress of those notes that do not appear in 1744. This seems the logical place to quote these notes, but their importance is further amplified by comparison with later versions, quoted in Chapter VI.

application of this to the *several Pursuits* of Men, and the *General Good* resulting thence, falls also into the succeeding books.[60]

The terms 'use' and 'application' here remind us of the phrasing in Pope's Index of 1734. 'Books' in this case may conceivably mean 'epistles'; even so, the term must refer to the *Moral Essays* as well as to later epistles of *An Essay on Man*.

Of the remaining six notes in the *Essay on Man*, five are attached to Epistle I, one to Epistle II, all directing the reader to later epistles within the *Essay*.[61] Such notes, interconnecting the four epistles of the *Essay on Man*, serve as a reminder that these epistles are not independent and self-sufficient units, but ones which depend for their full meaning and power upon their position in the whole book.

Of the seven notes in the *Moral Essays*, two (in *To a Lady* and *Bathurst*) lead us to *Cobham*, two in *Burlington* lead to *Bathurst*, another two in *Burlington* lead to both *Bathurst* and the *Essay*, Epistle II, and a note in *Bathurst* itself also leads to the *Essay*, Epistle II.[62] The note in *To a Lady* is attached to its title, and links this epistle to that to Cobham. It reads, 'Of the Characters of Women [a Corollary to the former Epistle], *treating of this Sex only as contra-distinguished from the other.*' (square brackets in the original). Parallel to it is the note to the title of *Burlington*, linking it with *Bathurst*: 'This Epistle is a Corollary to the preceding: As that treated of the Extremes of *Avarice* and *Profusion*, this takes up one branch of the latter, the Vanity of Expence in people of Quality or Fortune.' This note essentially repeats the opening sentence of the 'Argument' to *Burlington*. Similarly, the note to *Burlington*, l. 169 ('Yet hence the Poor are cloath'd, the Hungry fed') expands on the same theme as the note following the penultimate sentence of the 'Argument'. The note to the text reads:

V. 169 &c. The *Moral* of the whole, where Providence is justified in giving Wealth to those who squander it in this manner. A Bad taste employs more hands, and diffuses Expence more, than a good one. This

[60] Here, as elsewhere throughout, all line references are to the Twickenham text. Observe that the first sentence of each note is part of the running argument.

[61] These are the notes to i. 79, 94, 170, 185, 265; ii. 291–2.

[62] Two of the *Burlington* notes are in its 'Argument'.

recurs to what is laid down in Book I. Epist. II V. 240---7 [the 'happy Frailties' passage], and in the Epistle preceding this, V. 161 &c.[63]

Of the two notes in *Bathurst*, one (to l. 86, 'Unhappy Wharton . . .') is of no special significance, simply directing us to the character of Wharton in the *Epistle to Cobham*. This is the only note that directly links the first pair of epistles with the second. The other is a companion to the line reference (V. 161 &c.) in *Burlington* given directly above. To that line, 'Hear then the truth: 'Tis Heav'n each Passion sends', is atttached the note (not in the Twickenham edition):

V. 161 &c. *That the Conduct of Men with respect to Riches, can only be accounted for by the Order of Providence, which works the General Good out of* Extremes, *and brings all to its* Great End *by perpetual Revolutions.* See Book I Epist. 2 v. 165 &c. 207.

In addition to being indirectly related to the *Burlington* notes, this note connects *Bathurst* directly to the *Essay on Man*, Epistle II, once again specifically repeating the reference to line 165, on the ruling passion directing men to different purposes.

The common purpose of these notes is to interconnect the eight epistles to form a unit to 'justify ye Methods of Providence' (as the manuscript note phrases it), especially by linking the epistles of Book II to the second epistle of Book I. This direct relationship with Epistle II is in one sense only a confirmation of what we already know about Pope, that he is especially interested in Man 'As an Individual'. However, the notes do introduce a complicating factor to the pattern we discerned in the Index of 1734 and in all previous evidence of plans for the *opus magnum*, and which seems to result from Pope 'having drawn in the plan for his Ethic Epistles much narrower than it was at first'. The Index divides the first two *Moral Essays* from the last two, by the inclusion of works on civil and ecclesiastical polity and education, and appears to suggest that only the first pair were to be directly associated with Epistle II of Book I. The Index is thus consistent with all other available evidence up to 1734. Yet the cross-reference notes of 1735 also link the last pair directly to Epistle II instead of to Epistle IV of *An Essay on*

[63] Bracketed reference mine. This note appears in Twickenham III: ii, p. 153, without line numbers altered from the 1735 octavo edition, which in the case of *Essay* II are, compared with the 1744 text, ten lines out.

Man. As in the case of the withdrawal of the Index from circulation, this effort to make the epistles on the use of riches a development from the *Essay*, Epistle II, strongly suggests a desire by Pope to make the *Moral Essays* appear to be a completed part, instead of a fragmentary assemblage of parts, of a larger scheme.

The format of the 1735 octavo volumes of the *Works* also deliberately encourages the reading of the eight epistles as a unit, tied to one another and distinct from Pope's other works. The whole volume falls into five units, containing, respectively, *An Essay on Man*; the *Moral Essays*; seven other epistles (the major one being that to Arbuthnot); imitations of Horace and Donne satires; and eleven Epitaphs. There is no initial table of contents covering the whole volume; however, all but the group of epitaphs are introduced by individual half-title pages (though that to the *Essay* is omitted in the first octavo edition). The half-title for the *Essay on Man* reads, 'Ethic Epistles, The First Book, to Henry St. John L. Bolingbroke, Written in the Year 1732'. It is followed by the 'Design' and the 'Contents' for all four epistles. The half-title of the *Moral Essays* reads, 'Ethic Epistles the Second Book', also followed by the 'Contents' for all four epistles. The next group is preceded by a half-title page reading, 'Epistles, the Third Book. To Several Persons'. Observe, then, that only the first two groups of epistles are designated *ethic* epistles, and are thus carefully marked off from the following ones.

I stress this point because the quarto and folio editions of the same year (1735) do not make so sharp a distinction. In both of them the half-title beginning the second group reads, 'Ethic Epistles, the Second Book. To Several Persons'.[64] Then follows a heading, 'The Contents of the Second Book', introducing, like the octavo edition, the 'Arguments' of the four *Moral Essays* all grouped together. However, following the *Epistle to Burlington*, with neither half-title nor any other division, appear in order the following poems: 'Epistle V. to Mr. Addison', 'Epistle VI to Robert Earl of Oxford,

[64] The title-page for the *Essay on Man* section varies from folio to quarto (see n. 3 above). In the folio edition there is a rather elaborate title-page reading 'An Essay on Man, Being the First Book of Ethic Epistles. To Henry St. John, L. Bolingbroke'. The quarto edition has a far less elaborate title-page for the *Essay on Man* section, reading only 'Ethic Epistles, to Henry St. John, L. Bolingbroke. Written in the Year 1732.', omitting, that is, both the specific title and the phrase 'the First Book'.

and Earl Mortimer with Dr. Parnel's Poems', 'Epistle VII to Dr. Arbuthnot'. This grouping of seven 'ethic' poems, contrary to the reiterated assumption and manifold evidence presented so far, that Pope consistently kept his 'ethic system' distinct from his other writing, is anomalous. It suggests, as does the Index of 1734 and Spence's *Anecdotes* of the same period, that Pope was still very indefinite about the scope of his system, and may have felt that the other three epistles might be drawn into the plan to substitute for those projected but unwritten. In any case, the blurring of the distinction was a very temporary expedient, for three months later, with the octavo editions, Pope revised the groupings in the manner described above, designating only the *Essay on Man* and the *Moral Essays* as 'Ethic' Epistles.

The three major subdivisions of this chapter correspond roughly to the three stages of Pope's authorial activity. The first is the planning stage, during which Pope conceived of his scheme as a whole and gathered together 'prose collections'; the second is the composition of the poetry; the third, the supervision of the printed versions. The process is, of course, not anywhere so neat as this, largely because Pope's plans for the *opus magnum* shifted and changed, displaying greater or less clarity, broader or narrower scope, throughout the entire time under survey. Nevertheless, for the period 1729–35, during which all eight epistles moved through these stages, evidence suggests that the composition of each epistle was significantly affected by Pope's efforts to see it in relation to the larger *opus magnum* scheme. Each epistle was in large part conceived, written, revised, and eventually printed with others (some never written) in mind. The final, that is the 1735, two-book plan represents a shrunken and somewhat misleading version of Pope's plans and ambitions during the period in which he was most deeply engaged in this project. In the following four chapters we shall examine parts of the manuscript drafts and final form of the poetry itself with the hope that by applying the conclusions of this chapter, we shall be able to suggest a more satisfying interpretation and one more faithful to Pope's intentions than is to be had by reading the epistles in isolation from one another.

CHAPTER II

AN ESSAY ON MAN

As a long, complex, and uneven poem, *An Essay on Man* has received extensive scholarly and critical attention. Some scholars concentrate on the poem's ideas; others focus almost entirely on its rhetorical patterning; even those attempting an overview often find it most convenient to illustrate their points from a single epistle.[1] The *Essay* tends to resist integrated analysis. The experience of reading the poem is markedly different from the experience of reading about it, even when the interpreter is as sensitive and knowledgeable as Martin Price or Maynard Mack.[2] One feels that such interpretations are a good deal more coherent, more consistent, more fully integrated than the poem itself.

One perspective that seems not to have been sufficiently explored is that of the poem's genre and poetic models.[3] In Maynard Mack's well-known comparison, we are told what the poem is not: it is not narrative or mythic history like *Paradise Lost*; it is not introspective autobiography like Wordsworth's *Prelude*.[4] Critics agree that it is clearly a didactic and philosophic poem, with a dramatic awareness of audience, and it has been compared with Horatian epistles, the epistles of St. Paul, and Lucretius' *De Rerum Natura*. But such suggestions are rarely developed very far, and *An Essay on Man* is the only poem of Pope that we attempt to interpret without sustained

[1] Recent examples of each approach are: Douglas H. White, *Pope and the Context of Controversy: The Manipulation of Ideas in 'An Essay on Man'* (Chicago: University of Chicago Press, 1970); Martin Kallich, *Heav'n's First Law: Rhetoric and Order in Pope's 'Essay on Man'* (Dekalb, Illinois: Northern Illinois Press, 1967); Thomas R. Edwards, Jr., 'Visible Poetry: Pope and Modern Criticism', *Twentieth-Century Literature in Retrospect*, ed. Reuben Brower (Harvard English Studies, 2, 1971), pp. 299–321.

[2] See Martin Price, *To the Palace of Wisdom* (Garden City, New York: Doubleday, 1964), pp. 129–42; Maynard Mack, 'Introduction', Twickenham, III: i.

[3] Yet few would quarrel with Rebecca Price Parkin's statement that 'of all the traditional factors which shaped Pope's career as a poet, none was more powerful than the neoclassical concept of genre', *The Poetic Workmanship of Alexander Pope* (Minneapolis: University of Minnesota Press, 1955), p. 160.

[4] Twickenham, III: i, pp. lxxii–lxxviii.

reference to specific classical antecedents. Although *An Essay on Man* draws on many sources for its range of ideas and tone, several kinds of evidence both external—in correspondence, manuscript drafts, and Spence's *Anecdotes*—and in the poem's tone and structure combine to suggest the predominant influence of *De Rerum Natura* upon the *Essay*.

The same evidence suggests that the poem's relation to the larger scheme, the *opus magnum*, was also a significant factor in determining the poem's development, its subjects, and the arrangement of its parts. The manuscript annotations cited in the preceding chapter indicate that the composition of the poem was attended by considerable uncertainty about its divisions and its length. At various stages the poem was to have been one epistle, possibly two, perhaps three, then four or five, five or six, before it settled into its final four-epistle form. Blocks of poetry were tested in one position, then marked for inclusion elsewhere within the *Essay* or for transposition into poems that were to follow it. And all evidence points to a significant hiatus between the completion of the first three epistles and the fourth. These uncertainties in planning seem partly to be the result of Pope's efforts to anticipate the ultimate form of the *opus magnum* for which the *Essay* was to be only the first stage, the '*general Map* of MAN', which would be more fully delineated in subsequent 'charts'. The strengths and weaknesses of the poem in final form may have at least a partial correlation with the clarity or haziness with which other parts of the scheme were conceived.

The question of the poem's formative antecedents and that of its function as a foundation for other 'Epistles in their progress' are closely connected, and such evidence as there is about one often relates also to the other. I propose to examine the poem from both perspectives as a way of placing it in a larger and more accurate context that will allow us to see its organization and direction in a clearer light. Such an investigation cannot be definitive, for Pope's allusions to his conception both of the *Essay* itself and of his larger plan are scanty, casual, and fragmentary, and it is hard to determine which allusions are merely passing remarks and which should be interpreted as significant clues to his plans. Moreover, even though Pope always transforms his models radically, the *Essay*'s relation to

De Rerum Natura is considerably more obscure than is characteristic of the relation between his other works and their major models. And the *Essay*'s function as a foundation for other works tends to be forgotten in the absence of a completed *opus magnum*. But since these interrelated clues to the *Essay*'s conception have more frequently been brushed aside than gathered together and probed for meaning, they seem due for close and careful attention.

'*The same grave march like Lucretius*'

Soon after the publication of all parts of *An Essay on Man* as a single poem, Pope commented on its tone and style in a letter to Swift, in which he himself refers to the poem's Lucretian gravity:

> The design of concealing myself was good, and had its full effect; I was thought a divine, a philosopher, and what not? and my doctrine had a sanction I could not have given to it. Whether I can proceed in the same grave march like Lucretius, or must descend to the gayeties of Horace, I know not, or whether I can do either?[5]

Although this passage is well known, the tendency has been to dismiss its implications in favour of considering the *Essay* as a variation upon Pope's later Horatian poems. After quoting the passage above, Reuben Brower suggests that Horace rather than Lucretius 'won the day in the completed poem', citing sections throughout the four epistles that convey 'the illusion of well-bred good talk'. Mr. Brower notes departures from 'the usual conventions of intimacy and politeness' in passages that marvel at the universe in tones ranging from 'the grandly solemn to the rudely ironic' or that cast scorn on pride and folly in varying tones and modes of address. Nevertheless, reminding us of Horace's own wide range of tone, he concludes that 'the *Essay on Man* appears as a free and original variation on the Horatian diatribe-epistle. The source of its life and of its limitations are alike Horatian.'[6]

Certainly one would not want to deny Horatian influence upon *An Essay on Man*, particularly in its introduction and conclusion, yet the claim for Lucretian influence seems even stronger. Lucretius,

[5] *Correspondence*, iii. 433. Pope and Bolingbroke to Swift, 15 Sept. 1734.

[6] *Alexander Pope: The Poetry of Allusion* (Oxford: Clarendon Press, 1959), pp. 207, 214, 233–4, 239.

too, masters a wide range of tones, and although he is most frequently described as 'grave', 'austere', and 'chaste', he can also be urgent, ardent, and scornful. In a recent essay, William Bowman Piper describes Pope's manner in the *Essay* as one of 'confident assertiveness',[7] and Dryden offers an ample and complimentary characterization of the same mode in Lucretius:

If I am not mistaken, the distinguishing Character of *Lucretius* (I mean of his Soul and Genius) is a certain kind of noble pride, and positive assertion of his Opinions. He is every where confident of his own reason, and assuming an absolute command not only over his vulgar Reader, but even his patron *Memmius*. For he is always bidding him attend, as if he had the Rod over him; and using a Magisterial authority, while he instructs him . . . he seems to disdain all manner of Replies, and is so confident of his cause, that he is before hand with his Antagonists; Urging for them, whatever he imagin'd they cou'd say, and leaving them as he supposes, without an objection for the future. All this too, with so much scorn and indignation, as if he were assur'd of the Triumph, before he enter'd into the Lists.[8]

Modern critics have suggested that both in his prefatory remarks and in the five major passages Dryden translated from Lucretius, he made Lucretius over in his own image, intensifying the scornful tone and minimizing the 'atheistical' implications.[9] Even if this suggestion is true, Dryden's tribute, his modifications of the tone of the original, and his choice of passages for translation exerted considerable influence both directly and indirectly through their insertion and praise in the two-volume edition of the Creech translation of 1714.[10] And Dryden was only the latest of a line of great poets indebted to Lucretius, beginning with Virgil and Ovid, and

[7] 'The Conversational Poetry of Pope', *SEL* x (1970), 513. Mr. Piper links this characteristic with the 'incomplete conversational responsiveness' typical of the first three epistles, but not the fourth.

[8] John Dryden, 'Preface' to *Poems from Sylvae* in *The Poems of John Dryden*, ed. James Kinsley (Oxford: Clarendon Press, 1958), i. 391.

[9] Dryden translated *De Rerum Natura* i. 1–25; ii. 1–61; iii. 830–1094; iv. 1052–287; v. 222–34. On his translations see Mary Gallagher, 'Dryden's Translation of Lucretius', *Huntington Library Quarterly* xxviii (1964–5), 19–25; Norman Austin, 'Translation as Baptism: Dryden's Lucretius', *Arion* vii (1968), 576–602; *The Works of John Dryden III: Poems 1685–1692*, ed. Earl Miner (Berkeley and Los Angeles: University of California Press, 1969), pp. 277–8.

[10] The first edition of Thomas Creech's complete translation appeared in 1682. Dryden's translations appeared in 1685, and many extracts appear in the heavily annotated, posthumous 6th edition of Creech (1714), from which I quote.

extending through Spenser, Milton, and Cowley, with all of whom Pope would have been pleased to associate himself. Despite his notoriety (which may account in part for the paucity of Pope's allusions to Lucretian influence), Lucretius was by Pope's time becoming more widely accepted at his own estimate, as a poet who might properly hope for great renown, 'primum quod magnis doceo de rebus et artis / religionum animum nodis exsolvere pergo, / deinde quod obscura de re tam lucida pango / carmina, musaeo contingens cuncta lepore'.[11]

Certainly much of the *Essay on Man* is more consonant with the hortatory, 'magisterial' mode generally associated with Lucretius than with one of 'well-bred good talk'. Although the introduction to Epistle I of *An Essay on Man* has a genial tone that is often remarked upon, it is a rather deceptive opening,[12] for immediately thereafter the poem rapidly assumes and maintains the 'absolute command' and scornful note Dryden attributed to Lucretius. Even the opening of the poem differs from that of the epistles that follow the *Essay*, where one has a sense of having broken into an ongoing intimate conversation.[13] Pope's over-all efforts to create a suitable voice for the poem, as described by Maynard Mack, can be illustrated from the manuscript revisions of the second line of the poem. Mack writes:

as the poem moved from the Morgan state to the Harvard state and on toward print, . . . the poem gradually found its decorum. In the *Essay on*

[11] *De Rerum Natura* i. 931–4. This and all subsequent Latin quotations of Lucretius come from the edition by Cyril Bailey (Oxford: Clarendon Press, 1947). For assessments of Lucretian influence in the late 17th and early 18th century, see W. B. Fleischmann, *Lucretius and English Literature 1680–1740* (Paris: Nizet, 1964); C. T. Harrison, 'The Ancient Atomists and English Literature of the Seventeenth Century', *Harvard Studies in Classical Philology* xlv (1934), 1–79; T. F. Mayo, *Epicurus in England (1650–1725)* (Southwest Press, 1934); T. J. B. Spencer, 'Lucretius and the Scientific Poem in England', in *Lucretius*, ed. D. R. Dudley (London: Routledge and Kegan Paul, 1965), pp. 131–64.

[12] 'Thus [Pope] tells Bolingbroke that the *Essay on Man* is to be "a system of ethics in the Horatian way", and a reading of *the first twenty lines* [my italics] shews it to be miraculously such.' Norman Callan, 'Pope and the Classics' in *Writers and their Background: Alexander Pope*, ed. Peter Dixon (Athens, Ohio: Ohio University Press, 1972), p. 247.

[13] Cf. Thomas R. Edwards, Jr., *This Dark Estate: A Reading of Pope* (Berkeley and Los Angeles: University of California Press, 1963), p. 46: 'The opening of the *Essay on Man* seems by comparison [with the *Moral Essays*] rather formal and hortatory.'

Man, this is a decorum of abstractions, universals, types. We are taking a survey. Our view is too wide, too general, and on the whole, despite some lively sallies, too grave, to be often interrupted by contemporary particularities of the kind on which formal satires feed or by an insistently colloquial tone in the speaker.[14]

Line 2 in the Morgan manuscript reads as follows:

> groveling low-thoughted
> To ~~working~~ Statesmen, & ~~ambitious~~ Kings

This rather awkward set of revisions changes in the Harvard version, which reads:

> ~~zled~~ ~~flattr'd~~
> To puzling Statesmen and to blust'ring Kings

This is a much more vivid revision, but still not satisfactory to Pope. The printed form shows significant alteration:

> To low ambition, and the pride of Kings

In the final version adjectives qualifying persons have become abstract nouns. 'Low ambition' still includes 'petty Statesmen' in its meaning, but has become a more general and abstract reference. Similarly, the key word in the second half of the line changes from 'Kings' to 'pride', a movement that creates a more dignified and elevated effect, and also introduces one of the great major motifs in the poem.[15]

After the opening lines, the poet is no longer 'expatiating' with his friend, Bolingbroke; he is excoriating all mankind, whom he addresses in such denunciatory terms as 'Presumptuous Man!' (I, 35), 'wiser thou!' (I, 113), and 'Vile worm!' (I, 258). Although Epistles II and III for the most part eschew the first and second person altogether for detached third-person accounts of the operation of the passions and the growth of society, they too appear to address mankind in general rather than an intimate colleague, and occasionally introduce the berating and scornful tone of Epistle I: 'Go, wond'rous creature! . . . Go, teach Eternal Wisdom how to

[14] *Reproductions*, p. xxx.
[15] See Hoilman, 'Alexander Pope's Revisions of An Essay on Man', pp. 53–60, for a detailed analysis of the revision of this line.

rule— / Then drop into thyself, and be a fool!' (II, 19, 29–30); 'Has God, thou fool! work'd solely for thy good' (III, 27). Not until Epistle IV does the poet once again explicitly address Bolingbroke, first in the conclusion to the paean to Happiness ('And fled from Monarchs, ST. JOHN! dwells with thee' [IV, 18]), then in two parenthetical phrases (IV, 240, 260), and finally in the great concluding tribute (IV, 373 ff.).

As Dryden remarks, *De Rerum Natura* also displays many features of this peremptory tone and mode of address. Lucretius writes to and for Memmius as one who is Nature's 'most deserving Favourite' (I, 26–7; Creech i. 41) and as one for whom it is worth the effort 'fit Words to find, / To make Things plain, and to instruct your Mind' (I, 140–1; Creech i. 173–4). He sometimes uses the first person plural, but more frequently uses the first and second person singular, addressing himself particularly to Memmius more consistently and explicitly than Pope addresses *his* Memmius, Bolingbroke. Despite his apparent regard for Memmius, Lucretius keeps him firmly in hand, exhorting him to follow by the use of many direct questions and by the frequent use of constructions following the phrase 'Nunc age': 'Now what remains, observe; distinctly mark: / I know 'tis hard; 'tis intricate and dark' (I, 921–2; Creech i. 927–8); 'Now farther learn, what I with Toil and Pain, / With many a careful Thought, and lab'ring Brain, / Have sought to teach thee' (II, 730–1; Creech ii. 684–6). In general, the earlier portions of the poem address Memmius more specifically and directly than do later portions, which possess much more of the impersonal quality that characterizes parts of Epistles II and III of *An Essay on Man*.

An early manuscript variant indicates that the equation of Bolingbroke with Memmius originates with Pope himself. In the final version of the poem, Pope addresses Bolingbroke by name twice— in the poem's opening line, 'Awake my ST. JOHN!' and in Epistle IV, 18, 'And fled from Monarchs, ST. JOHN! dwells with thee'. In early printed editions, he is called LAELIUS at these points. But of special significance is Pope's earliest choice of address. In the Morgan manuscript the opening line of Epistle I reads 'Awake my Memmius', and a couplet inserted and subsequently excised following what is now Epistle IV, 372 reads, 'Let us, my Memmius! this great Truth confess / One is our Duty, & Our Happiness'. This explicit borrowing from *De Rerum Natura* anchors our exploration of Pope's indebtedness to Lucretius firmly to the realm of fact.

Reuben Brower also notes that *An Essay on Man* is marked by 'rather too insistent questions as if to keep the reader's attention from wandering'.[16] This characteristic too seems clearly to be an inheritance from Lucretius:

> What MIND's unshaken, and what SOUL not aw'd,
> And who not thinks the angry GODS abroad,
> Whose Limbs not shrink, when dreadful THUNDER hurl'd
> From broken Clouds, shakes the affrighted WORLD?
> What, do not CITIES, do not NATIONS fear,
> And think their dismal DISSOLUTION near?
> Why, do not TYRANTS then, and mighty Lords,
> Recall their wicked Deeds, and boasting Words,
> And fear, that now REVENGE is surely come?
> Do they not tremble at approaching Doom?
> (Creech v. 1298–1307; cf. *DRN* v. 1218–25)

De Rerum Natura, like the *Essay*, contains numerous scornful and sarcastic passages. Among the best known are the section of Book II's exordium (40–53) on 'the mimicry of war', parts of the end of Book III on the terrors of death, including the passage on man restlessly fleeing from himself and his boredom (III. 1060–70); the end of Book IV on the Power of Love (1058–1191); caustic verses like that at V. 1009–10 in the description of primitive times ('Then POYS'NOUS HERBS, when pluck'd by Chance, did kill; / Now POYSON's grown an ART, improv'd by Skill' (Creech v. 1071–2)); and in the same book, the passage on the effects of envy (V. 1120–35). Although not a large proportion of the whole poem, such passages are among the most memorable, partly because their intensity contrasts with Lucretius' more typical expository style and partly because the longer passages occupy stressed positions near the beginning and end of books.[17] Lucretius reserves most scorn for those who persist in superstitious delusions about man's afterlife or the gods' interest

[16] Brower, *Alexander Pope*, p. 214.

[17] See D. R. Dudley, 'The Satiric Element in Lucretius', in *Lucretius*, ed. D. R. Dudley, pp. 115–30. The fact that Dryden's translations incorporate the first three passages above may have added to their general recognition in the early 18th century.

in the human universe. When translating such passages Creech often interpolates phrases of direct address as intensifiers of Lucretius' third-person references that sound like those in Pope's *Essay*. 'Plain nonsense!', 'fond Fool!', 'Fools!' are examples of interjections from Creech's translation of Lucretian passages describing those who cling to belief in immortality (III. 800 ff.; Creech iii. 773, 859, 865, 905); 'Deluded Ignorants!', 'Absurd and vain!' are Creech's terms for those who believe that 'heav'nly tyrants' cause natural phenomena like lightning, thunder, heat and cold (see VI. 52–5, 853; Creech vi. 59, 847). By no means all such interjections, however, originate with Creech. In the exordium of Book II, for instance, Lucretius bemoans those who choose worldly goals of riches and power instead of detachment and serenity: 'O miseras hominum mentis, o pectora caeca!' (II. 14; 'Blind wretched man!' (Creech ii. 16)). And in Book III, Lucretius has Nature ask 'cur non ut plenus vitae conviva recedis / aequo animoque capis securam, stulte, quietem?' (III. 938–9).[18]

Examples like these make it clear that Lucretius and his English translators provided Pope with specific precedents for his manner of address and his range of tone from magisterial through scornful to urgent and colloquial. Pope, of course, also drew on other appropriate sources. Horace, as we have noticed, is an obvious influence. Another obvious model is the Book of Job, particularly Chapters 38 to 42, the voice speaking from the whirlwind, which was a favourite choice for paraphrase among Pope's contemporaries. Maynard Mack's citations from the Book of Job in the Twickenham volume concentrate heavily on analogues from Job 38–41, and are appended to those portions of the *Essay*, Epistles I and II, that chastize man for striving to explore the cosmological universe instead of seeking to know himself and pursue moral ends. The effect of such passages (*Essay* I, 21–8, 247–58; II, 19–36), like the scornful irony of God's answer to Job, is to accentuate man's littleness in relation to God's greatness. They contrast not only man's ignorance with God's wisdom, but also man's impotence with God's omnipotence. These allusions may help to account for what Rebecca Parkin describes as a relation between preacher and congregation. She continues, 'It is

[18] Creech (iii. 925–7) does not here directly translate 'stulte' ('thou fool').

important to emphasize that the speaker's tone is closer to that of a great evangelical preacher . . . than to the lucid didacticism of a Lucretius'.[19] However, she herself notes, 'The *Essay on Man* is didactic, but its didacticism is not that which advises turnip planting in the dark of the moon or moderation in judging literature. It is more like the didacticism of a Lucretius speaking of first and last things.'[20] Though she is undoubtedly thinking here of a Lucretian weightiness of subject and tone, we have also indicated examples of Lucretius' scathing intensity, and if in portions of the *Essay* Pope has echoed the Book of Job, such indebtedness need not suggest the abandonment of the Lucretian model. The two works are in many ways compatible in mood and effect. As. W. Y. Sellar notes, *De Rerum Natura* shows Lucretius' 'deep sense of the littleness of human life'.[21]

Lucretius has yet another significant variant in tone, that in which he pays ardent tribute to Venus (I. 1–61), and to Epicurus (I. 62–79; III. 1–30; V. 1–54; VI. 1–42). For the most part, Pope avoids or mutes this tone of religious exaltation, though at one stage in his plans he considered including a direct imitation of it. Quoting Pope, Spence records, 'In the Moral Poem I had written an address to our Saviour, imitated from Lucretius' compliment to Epicurus, but omitted it by the advice of Dean Berkeley'.[22] Some of the characteristics (though not the awesome attribution of divinity) of Lucretius' tributes to Epicurus appear also in Pope's great closing tribute to Bolingbroke, his 'guide, philosopher, and friend':

> Come then, my Friend, my Genius, come along,
> Oh master of the poet, and the song!
> And while the Muse now stoops, or now ascends,
> To Man's low passions, or their glorious ends,

[19] Parkin, *Poetic Workmanship*, p. 19. See Leonard, 'Wit and Judgment: Pope and the Art of Revision', pp. 108–10, and the references on p. 110, for additional attention to Pope's biblical borrowings.

[20] Parkin, *Poetic Workmanship*, p. 165.

[21] W. Y. Sellar, *The Roman Poets of the Republic* (Edinburgh, Edmonston and Douglas, 1863), p. 271.

[22] *Anecdotes*, i. 135, no. 305 (1734). Note that while Pope eschews a direct imitation, he adopts the phrasing of lines 6 ff.—the repetition of 'te, dea, te . . . te'—in two very effective scathing passages of the *Essay*: I, 132–40 (Pride's assertion that Nature does all 'for me. . . for me . . . for me . . .') and III, 27–42 ('Hast God, thou fool! work'd solely for thy good, / Thy joy, thy pastime, thy attire, thy food? . . .'). See also Mack's note to I, 131 ff.

Teach me, like thee, in various nature wise,
To fall with dignity, with temper rise;
Form'd by thy converse, happily to steer
From grave to gay, from lively to severe;
Correct with spirit, eloquent with ease,
Intent to reason, or polite to please . . . (*Essay*, IV, 373–82)

Maynard Mack notes that lines 379 and following are modelled on Horace's *Satire* I, x, 9–14, which Pope later used as a motto for the title page of *Epistles to Several Persons*.[23] But like the introduction, the peroration is more formal and elevated than is true of a purely Horatian close, and it appears also to owe much to Lucretius. In particular, Pope seems to have combined in the image of Bolingbroke both Memmius and Epicurus. Just as Pope here speaks of Bolingbroke not merely as his companion, his Memmius, but also as 'master of the poet, and the song', so Lucretius speaks of deriving his truths and inspiration from his master, Epicurus:

tu pater es, rerum inventor, tu patria nobis
suppeditas praecepta, tuisque ex, inclute, chartis,
floriferis ut apes in saltibus omnia libant,
omnia nos itidem depascimur aurea dicta,
aurea, perpetua semper dignissima vita. (*DRN* iii. 9–13)

THOU, PARENT of PHILOSOPHY, has shown
The Way to TRUTH by Precepts of THY own.
For, as from sweetest Flow'rs the lab'ring BEE
Extracts her precious Sweets, Great Soul! from THEE
We all our Golden Sentences derive;
Golden, and fit eternally to live. (Creech iii. 9–14)

Like the opening, the conclusion combines Horatian echoes and tones with Lucretian formality, intensity, and high seriousness. It is fitting that as part of his closing summary, Pope not only alludes to the precepts that are central to the poem, but also to the range of tones, styles, and moods that the poem has displayed, and it seems clear that *De Rerum Natura* has contributed significantly to this range.

[23] See Mack's note to IV, 379 ff. The couplet 379–80 is a rendering of 'sermone modo tristi saepe jocos', and seems to derive also from *The Art of Poetry* (1683), the Soames–Dryden translation of Boileau, lines 75–6, 'Happy, who in his Verse can gently steer, / From Grave to Light; from Pleasant to Severe' (noted in *The Satires of Horace*, ed. A. Palmer [London: Macmillan, 1964; 1st edn., 1883], p. 230).

'*Lucretius of death reverst*'

Like *An Essay on Man*, *De Rerum Natura* is a long, complex, and uneven poem. It is, in fact, something like five times the length of the *Essay*. Each book is several times longer than each epistle of the *Essay*, and there are six books. It is different from the *Essay* not only in its greater length, but in such obvious characteristics as its explicitly pedagogical procedure, its careful summaries of argument, and its abrupt (perhaps uncompleted) close. Moreover, the fundamental philosophic ideas and thematic patterns of the two poems are dissimilar, as are the dominant directions of each. The Lucretian poem has a falling movement that concentrates on materialism and harsh reality and that repeatedly emphasizes death, decay, and destruction. Each book moves *from* creation *to* destruction, as does the whole poem. In contrast, the *Essay* has a rising pattern. It begins with emphasis upon man's pride, vanity, and capacity for error, but by focusing from the start on man's littleness, teaches him how to accept his limitations, recognize the providential order, and achieve virtue and future bliss by imitating God's benevolence.

Once we look beyond these obvious differences, however, there are striking structural similarities. Dr. Johnson described the *Essay on Man* as a 'metaphysical morality', and the phrase is highly appropriate to *De Rerum Natura* as well: both poems expound the nature of things and man's relation to them so that man may overcome error and be free to pursue real virtue, genuine happiness, and higher ends. Modern critics have described *De Rerum Natura* in ways that make clear its appropriateness as a general model for Pope's *Essay*. Gordon Williams writes:

> What makes Lucretius' poetry outlive the shortcomings of his physics and cosmology is his capacity to see through the simple events of life and discern behind them a system of relations that carries conviction without being tied to this or that way of expressing the physical nature of the universe. No Roman poet better expresses the *sub specie aeternitatis* viewpoint.[24]

And Elizabeth M. McLeod writes:

> Lucretius, having examined the discontent evident among his contemporaries, concluded that men were frustrated and despairing because they

[24] *Tradition and Originality in Roman Poetry* (Oxford: Clarendon Press, 1968), p. 718.

lacked self-knowledge. Their patent ignorance led them to misinterpret the purpose of their existence to such an extent that they could not discharge adequately their duties as human beings. Lucretius proposed to offer a remedy based on Epicurean atomism, first by demonstrating the existence of natural laws which governed all created things, and then by showing how these laws applied specifically to human beings. When men had thus come to realize the true nature of the universe and their own position in it, they would understand the meaning of human life and would be able to conform to the limitations imposed by their human nature.[25]

A closer look first at some sections of the two poems and some poetic devices they share, and then at their similar pattern of organization, will suggest that the Lucretian model may be responsible not only for major elements in the *Essay*'s tone but also to a considerable extent for its ordering of parts and its division among epistles.

Pope's annotation 'Lucretius of death reverst. Lib. 3. fine.' appears in the margin of the Morgan manuscript keyed to the couplet,

> The blest today is as completely so
> As who began a thousand years ago.
> (*Essay* I, 75–6)

As the Twickenham edition indicates, this couplet is 'reversed from Lucret. III 1087–94', the concluding lines of Book III, as translated by Dryden (iii. 319–21):

> The Man as much to all intents is dead,
> Who dyes to day, and will as long be so,
> As he who dy'd a thousand years ago.

In many ways the phrase, 'Lucretius of death reverst' (with and without the pun) is an appropriate motto not just for this echo but for the entire *Essay*.

The whole passage of which the couplet is a part is, of course, a reversal of Lucretius. Where Lucretius insists on the 'nothingness' that follows death, Pope reminds man that he possesses the hope of future bliss. Pope's emphasis on this idea is even clearer in earlier orderings of the sections of Epistle I, in which these lines follow immediately after the verse-paragraph on hope (I, 91–8), as the textual note to line 98 in the Twickenham edition makes clear. Also

[25] 'Lucretius' *Carmen Dignum*', *The Classical Journal* 58 (1962–3), 145.

part of this verse-paragraph at the same stage was another couplet that is a direct reversal of a fundamental Lucretian theme:

> Safe in the hand of one disposing Pow'r,
> Or in the natal, or the mortal hour.
> (*Essay* I, 287–8)

Whereas Lucretius insists upon the serene detachment of the gods and their lack of both interest in and power over humans, *An Essay on Man* here and throughout asserts a providential universe.

Another striking instance of 'Lucretius reverst' is the passage that immediately follows the exordium to *An Essay on Man*:

> Thro' worlds unnumber'd tho' the God be known
> 'Tis ours to trace him only in our own.
> He, who thro' vast immensity can pierce,
> See worlds on worlds compose one universe,
> Observe how system into system runs,
> What other planets circle other suns,
> What vary'd being peoples ev'ry star,
> May tell why Heav'n has made us as we are.
> (*Essay* I, 21–8)

Noting that the 'He' of line 23 may be properly interpreted to mean that there is no such man, Maynard Mack continues, 'Pope's passage is implicitly a reply to Lucretius' celebration of Epicurus (i. 62–79) as a mortal whose mind, defying religion, did pierce through vast immensity (*omne immensum*, 74) and beyond the universe (*flammantia moenia mundi*, 73) to reach a godlike knowledge of why we are as we are. Pope's [Morgan] MS. version of 23–4 [He who can all the flaming limits pierce / Of worlds on worlds that form one Universe] explicitly echoes the Lucretian passage.'[26] The Lucretian passage reads:

> ergo vivida vis animi pervicit, et extra
> processit longe flammantia moenia mundi
> atque omne immensum peragravit mente animoque,
> unde refert nobis victor quid possit oriri,

[26] Twickenham, III: i, p. 15 n. See also Leonard, 'Wit and Judgment: Pope and the Art of Revision', pp. 78, 87–8. The same Lucretian passage is evoked in Rochester's 'Satyr against Reason and Mankind' in the defence of Reason by the speaker's complacent clerical adversary. Reason, he says, enables us to 'Dive into mysteries, then soaring pierce / The flaming limits of the universe, / Search heaven and hell, find out what's acted there, / And give the world true grounds of hope and fear' (ll. 68–71).

quid nequeat, finita potestas denique cuique
quanam sit ratione atque alte terminus haerens.
quare religio pedibus subiecta vicissim
opteritur, nos exaequat victoria caelo.
(*DRN* i. 72–9)

His vigorous and active Mind was hurl'd
Beyond the flaming Limits of this WORLD
Into the MIGHTY SPACE, and there did see
How Things begin, what can, what can not be:
How All must die, All yield to fatal Force;
What steady Limits bound their nat'ral Course.
He saw all this, which others sought in vain,
Thus by his Conquest we our Right regain;
RELIGION he subdu'd and WE now reign.
(Creech i. 96–104)

Pope appears to be indebted to this passage for more than the single couplet explicated by Maynard Mack. Like Creech he follows the Lucretian passage in its emphasis on 'he' and 'us', its emphatic repetition of indirect questions, and its focus upon the conquest of knowledge. But where Lucretius exhorts man to use his reason to the uttermost as a way to escape the burdens religion imposes and to achieve true understanding, Pope, in contrast, derides reason and repeatedly emphasizes its limitations, as in the lines that immediately precede the Lucretian echo:

Say first, of God above, or Man below
What can we reason, but from what we know?
Of Man what see we, but his station here,
From which to reason, or to which refer?
(*Essay* I, 17–20)

In the following reversal of Lucretius in Epistle I of the *Essay*, the middle section (lines 251–6) appears neither in manuscript draft nor in the first published version of the epistle. Pope writes:

From Nature's Chain whatever link you strike,
Tenth or ten thousandth, breaks the chain alike,
And if each system in gradation roll
Alike essential to th' amazing whole;
The least confusion but in one, not all
That system only, but the whole must fall.
Let Earth unbalanc'd from her orbit fly,
Planets and Suns run lawless thro' the sky.

> Let ruling Angels from their spheres be hurl'd,
> Being on being wreck'd, and world on world,
> Heav'n's whole foundations to their centre nod,
> And Nature tremble to the throne of God:
> All this dread ORDER break—for whom? for thee?
> Vile worm!—oh Madness, Pride, Impiety!
> (*Essay* I, 245–58)

Lucretius, especially as translated by Creech, writes of the world's disintegration in remarkably similar terms:

> dictis dabit ipsa fidem res
> forsitan et graviter terrarum motibus ortis
> omnia conquassari in parvo tempore cernes.
> quod procul a nobis flectat fortuna gubernans,
> et ratio potius quam res persuadeat ipsa
> succidere horrisono posse omnia victa fragore.
> (*DRN* v. 104–9)

> And yet I'll sing: perchance the foll'wing Fall
> Will prove my Words, and shew 'tis Reason all:
> Perhaps thou soon shalt see the sinking WORLD
> With strong Convulsions to Confusion hurl'd;
> When ev'ry rebel ATOM breaks the Chain,
> And all to prim'tive NIGHT return again:
> But CHANCE avert it! Rather let REAS'N shew
> The WORLD may fall, than SENSE should prove it true:
> (Creech v. 111–18)

The rhyming of 'World' and 'hurled', 'all' and 'fall', the references to 'confusion' and 'Chain', the rare and effective use of enjambement, are common to Creech's and Pope's passage, as is the picture of the whole interdependent order of the world. For Lucretius, there is no doubt that the world will end this way—the only question is when. Reason shows that despite the appearance of order, the universe is compounded of disorder, chance, accident. His picture of inevitable collapse is a logical deduction from his materialist premisses. Pope uses the same description to make precisely the opposite point: despite proud man's egocentric and limited view, reason shows that beyond apparent disorder, there is universal order. The *Essay*'s picture of catastrophe is a logical absurdity based on man's false belief that the universe does or should revolve around him. The

Lucretian passage is profoundly pessimistic; the Pope passage ultimately optimistic.

Many other passages may be singled out as major instances of 'Lucretius with a difference'. A final example of this kind is from the beginning of Epistle III of the *Essay*:

> Look round our World; behold the chain of Love
> Combining all below and all above.
> See plastic Nature working to this end,
> The single atoms each to other tend,
> Attract, attracted to, the next in place
> Form'd and impell'd its neighbour to embrace.
> See Matter next, with various life endu'd,
> Press to one centre still, the gen'ral Good.
> See dying vegetables life sustain,
> See life dissolving vegetate again:
> All forms that perish other forms supply,
> (By turns we catch the vital breath, and die)
> Like bubbles on the sea of Matter born,
> They rise, they break, and to the sea return. (*Essay* III, 7–20)

The Twickenham notes cite Ovid and a number of seventeenth-century references, but the passage is reminiscent also of Lucretius:

> Denique iam tuere hoc, circums supraque quod omnem
> continet amplexu terram: si procreat ex se
> omnia, quod quidam memorant, recipitque perempta,
> totum nativo ac mortali corpore constat.
> nam quodcumque alias ex se res auget alitque,
> deminui debet, recreari, cum recipit res. (*DRN* v. 317–23)

> Lastly, look round, view that VAST TRACT OF SKY,
> In whose Embrace our EARTH and WATERS lie:
> Whence all Things rise, to which they all return,
> As some discourse; the same both WOMB and URN:
> 'Tis surely MORTAL all: for that which breeds
> That which gives Birth to other Things, or feeds,
> Must lose some Parts; and when those Things do cease,
> It gets some new again, and must increase. (Creech v. 360–7)

Pope's passage is in fact reminiscent of many in Lucretius, for the movement of the atoms composing all natural things including man in a cycle of creation and destruction is the most fundamental of

Lucretius' themes and organizing patterns.[27] In this particular pair of passages, both Pope and Lucretius take a comprehensive view of the world and all life within it, both use the word 'embrace', both emphasize what seems to be an unending cycle of birth, death, and rebirth. The crucial difference is of course that for Lucretius, ''Tis surely MORTAL all', whereas for Pope, atoms, matter, and men are moved by the non-material power of Love and 'the gen'ral Good':

> One all-extending, all-preserving Soul
> Connects each being, greatest with the least;
> (*Essay* III, 22–3)

The relation between the *Essay* and *De Rerum Natura* is more fundamental than the fact that they both treat of first and last things, and contain many comparable passages; they are patterned along common lines and with the help of similar methods of organization. *De Rerum Natura* has an architectonic pattern that shapes the poem and that is especially emphasized in the opening and closing of each book. The proem of every book (except Book II) is on the theme of creation; the close of every book (except Book V) focuses on the idea of decay or destruction. Of these, the Proem to Book I, praising the creative and generative powers of 'alma Venus', and the conclusion of Book VI, describing the horrible and widespread destruction caused by the plague, are appropriately the most impressive. The cyclical pattern of birth and death, growth and decay, underlies many passages in the poem, but is especially dominant in the openings and closings of books; in most cases these amount to 'set-pieces' that at one and the same time seem detachable and also mark major stages in the poem's development.

The same structural pattern (though an inverse thematic one) marks the movement of *An Essay on Man*. The opening exordium, as the manuscript annotations indicate, is meant like the Lucretian opening to introduce not only Epistle I but the entire poem. The famous opening of Epistle II, though frequently reprinted as a separable passage, firmly relates its argument to the stage arrived at

[27] The most detailed analysis of this informing theme is Richard Minadeo: *The Lyre of Science: Form and Meaning in Lucretius' 'De Rerum Natura'* (Detroit: Wayne State University Press, 1969). See also the note to lines 15–18: 'Pattison compares Lucretius, II, 67 ff.', Twickenham III:i, p. 93.

in the preceding epistle (compare I, 282–3, 'Know thy own point: This kind, this due degree / Of blindness, weakness, Heav'n bestows on thee' with II, 1–2, 'Know then thyself, presume not God to scan; / The proper study of Mankind is Man'). Epistle III, like Epistle II, opens with a back reference, 'Here then we rest', as it summarizes in abstract and impersonal form the movement from individual to society that has taken place at the end of Epistle II, and goes on to change the stress from a negative one upon 'wants, frailties, passions' (II, 253) to the positive facets of mutual interdependence. Finally, Epistle IV opens with the great address to Happiness that begins an exploration of 'the false scale of Happiness' and the true.

In contrast to the Lucretian pattern of conclusions to each book, reiterating the theme of inevitable decline and disintegration, the endings of each epistle of the *Essay*, as Maynard Mack has noted, mark the gradual rising movement of the poem: 'at the close of each [epistle] comes a picture of man reunited with the divine order, and there is an unmistakable progression in these pictures'.[28] The assertion at the end of Epistle I, 'Cease then, nor ORDER Imperfection name: . . . One truth is clear, "Whatever IS, IS RIGHT"' (I, 281, 294) is just that—an assertion—which man cannot yet see, or bring himself to accept. In Epistle II, pride still has the upper hand, as the wry final couplet indicates, 'See! and confess, one comfort still must rise, / 'Tis this, Tho' Man's a fool, yet GOD IS WISE' (*Essay* II, 293–4). 'In the picture of reunion with which the third epistle closes [writes Mack], man is no longer diminished or even deluded; he is a creative agent reproducing in his society the harmonies of God's, living "supported" by the Whole, but nevertheless contributing to it. And in the corresponding passage of the fourth (which brings together the leading themes of all: acceptance, self-love, sociality, happiness) man becomes regenerate.'[29] Thus the *Essay*, like *De Rerum Natura*, shows at the openings and conclusions of each epistle a firm demarcation of stages of its argument.

The two poems have structural affinities that relate even more closely to one another than has yet been suggested. That Pope may

[28] Maynard Mack, ed., *The Augustans* (English Masterpieces, Vol. V) (Englewood Cliffs, N.J.: Prentice-Hall, 2nd ed., 1961), p. 28.

[29] Ibid.

have been thinking in a general way of *De Rerum Natura* as a model for his work seems a proper conjecture from Spence's note of November 1730: 'Mr. Pope's poem grows on his hands. The first four or five epistles [Spence's later change from his original note reading 'five or 6' epistles] will be on general principles, or of "The Nature of Man", . . .'[30] An examination of the internal organization of the two poems suggests that far from being an idle remark, Spence's note hints at a significant structural correspondence between the two works. There appears to be a clear correlation between the subjects of Pope's first three epistles and the subjects of the six books of *De Rerum Natura*. The Lucretian poem orders its discussion in pairs of books: the first two explain the physical nature of the universe, the next two the mind and soul of man, the final two describe the origin of the world, the origin and development of society, and the phenomena of the heavens and the earth. This pattern of organization is followed in *An Essay on Man*, in which Epistle I treats '*Of the Nature and State of Man, with respect to the* UNIVERSE', Epistle II '*Of the Nature and State of Man, with respect to* Himself, *as an Individual*', and Epistle III, '*Of the Nature and State of* Man, *with respect to* Society'. Not only is the *Essay*'s ordering of subjects comparable to that in *De Rerum Natura*, but also the focus of each epistle of the *Essay* corresponds to each pair in Lucretius. This correlation, if shown to be convincing, will help to explain not only the general organization of the *Essay* but also some of the reasons for Pope's shifting plans about the number of epistles the *Essay* was to contain and for the fact that Epistle IV seems to have been completed well after the first three and according to a somewhat different pattern.

In the first two books of *De Rerum Natura*, Lucretius expounds the ultimate principles of the atomic philosophy—that the universe consists solely of matter, motion, and void—in order to lay the foundation for the rest of his poem. As W. Y. Sellar points out, 'Although the treatment of his subject may sometimes carry him into greater detail than is necessary for his purpose, yet the key-note to the whole poem is his conviction of the irreconcilable opposition between the truth of nature and the falsehood of the ancient mythology. This thought

[30] *Anecdotes*, i. 131, no. 299.

determines the course of the argument.'[31] If, for Lucretius, man's greatest error was to believe that natural phenomena were attributable to the direct agency of the gods, for Pope man's greatest error was to conceive of the universe as homocentric: 'Ask for what end the heav'nly bodies shine, / Earth for whose use? Pride answers, "'Tis for mine: . . . Seas roll to waft me, suns to light me rise; / My foot-stool earth, my canopy the skies"' (I, 131–2; 139–40). If Lucretius' aim was to demonstrate that universal order and causation required no supernatural agency, whereas Pope wished to demonstrate that the universe had providential design—'All Nature is but Art, unknown to thee; / All Chance, Direction, which thou canst not see; / All Discord, Harmony, not understood; / All partial Evil, universal Good' (I, 289–92)—then Lucretius' starting point was also eminently appropriate as Pope's starting point. This fundamental contrast determines the 'reversing of Lucretius' in individual passages. Epistle I of the *Essay* in fact shows the heaviest dependence of Pope on Lucretius, the greatest number of demonstrable echoes of Lucretian passages. It seems evident that as the conception of the poem and the outlines of Pope's larger scheme grew clearer, he grew less and less dependent on Lucretius, but his early indebtedness seems to have given him a firm starting point.

Because the first pair of books in *De Rerum Natura* lays the foundation for the remainder, the correlation between this pair and the first epistle of the *Essay* may also explain Pope's early conception (reflected in Spence's anecdote recording Pope's conversation of May 1730) of the *Essay* as consisting of only one epistle. After his tribute to Epicurus at the beginning of Book III, Lucretius marks the stage the poem has reached:

> Since then I've taught what SEEDS of BODIES are,
> And how they move, what diff'rent Shapes they wear,
> And how from these all Beings first may spring:
> Next of the MIND, and of the SOUL, I'll sing;
> And chase that Dread of Hell, those idle Fears,
> That spoil our Lives with Jealousies and Cares,
> Disturb our Joys with Dread of Pains beneath,
> And sully them with the black Fear of Death.
> (Creech iii. 33–40)

[31] Sellar, *Roman Poets of the Republic*, p. 226.

Creech's anonymous editor begins 'The Argument of the Third Book' by saying, 'The Poet flatters himself, that in the two former Books, he has fully and rightly explain'd the Nature, and the Properties of his Atoms. In the four remaining Books, he applies himself very attentively to describe the Effects which those Atoms produce. And first, as he had Reason to do, he brings upon the Stage the Parts of the Mind, and of the Soul: And this is the Subject of the Disputation of all this Book.'[32] This firm division between the opening pair of books and those that are to follow sounds like Pope's repeated conception of the *Essay* as treating general principles and the following poems as treating the applications of principles, or 'The Use of Things'. However, if this division has any influence upon Pope's plan to make the *Essay* only a single epistle, it is not reflected in the extant manuscripts, which record a time when the composition of Epistle I, 'Of Man *in the abstract*' (as the opening phrase of Epistle I's 'Argument' reads), seems immediately to have been followed by the composition of Epistle II.

Although most of Pope's references to Epistle II refer to its subject as 'the Passions', one version of the notes to the exordium in the Harvard manuscript refers to 'the Constitution of the human Mind', which makes clearer its likely connection with Lucretius. In Books III and IV, Lucretius speaks primarily of the mind, the soul, and the senses, rather than the passions, but this pair of books has the same focus as Epistle II of the *Essay*. Both concentrate on 'Man as an Individual', his psychology, his drives, his immediate (and misdirected) goals, and his ultimate goals. Although Lucretius naturally describes the mind and soul as material just as are the other parts of man's body, and emphasizes that the mind receives information only through the senses, whereas Pope's epistle describes both reason and the passions as gifts of God, both works stress the ambivalent nature of illusion, both make a harshly realistic assessment of man's behaviour, and both illustrate the driving force of lust, frailty, and mutual needs. Pope develops a theory of the Ruling

[32] *T. Lucretius Carus, Of the Nature of Things, In Six Books, Translated into English Verse; by Tho. Creech* (London, 1715), i. 193. In *A Bibliography of Lucretius* (London: Rupert Hart-Davis, 1962), Cosmo Alexander Gordon notes (p. 179) that in some copies of the 1714 edition, Volume I is dated 1715. He also suggests (p. 171) that the editor was John Digby, translator of *Epicurus' Morals* (1712).

Passion to cover a variety of needs, drives, and ambitions in different individuals; for Lucretius these differences are secondary to the one single 'Ruling Passion' that besets all men—the fear of death. Few passages in Epistle II echo specific passages of Lucretius, for Pope has developed a totally different psychological theory, but the place and focus of Epistle II of the *Essay* clearly parallels the general thrust of Books III and IV of Lucretius.

With Epistle III of the *Essay*, Pope returns to a close correspondence with *De Rerum Natura*, particularly with Book V, which traces the origin and development of society. Many other works also contribute to Epistle III's exposition, but Lucretius figures large among the citations in the Twickenham text.[33] Both poets closely follow the same general pattern tracing the development of society, political organization, religion, chaos, political stability, and the arts of civilization out of the state of nature, although each poet attributes somewhat different characteristics and value to each stage. For Lucretius the state of nature is austere: men, though hardy, lived in a state of ignorance and feared beasts by whom they were mangled and killed, whereas Pope describes the state of nature as an idyllic one, when 'Man walk'd with beast, joint tenant of the shade' and when there was no murder whatsoever either by or of men or beasts. Despite his harsh view of the state of nature, Lucretius shares with Pope the view that the arts of civilization are a mixed blessing, which includes murder, wars, decadence, luxury, and superstition, along with true benefactions.

Pope's description of the change from a state of nature to a civil state (Epistle III, section IV and following) is unsatisfying, and appears to be one of the major instances covered by Maynard Mack's statement (in the note to I, 145–8) that 'Pope's fluency . . . fails him oftener in the *Essay* than in any other poem'. It is, for instance, difficult to determine just when and how Pope (normally so expert in his command of adverbs) thinks the change from a state of nature to a civil state has come about, or when and how a 'restoration of *True Religion* and *Government* on their first principle' (note to 283 ff.) was effected. An explanation for the lack of poetic assurance evident in the central sections of this epistle may lie in Pope's

[33] See the notes to III, 70, 119 ff., 162, 163, 200, 201–2, 207, 249–52, 271–86.

haziness about the role Epistle III was to play in the larger scheme, the *opus magnum*. Neither it nor the epistles that might have evolved from it figure clearly in any of the extant manuscript or editorial notes, anecdotes or letters that date from the early 1730s. Epistle III was published in May 1733, yet the two works that seem to have been planned as expansions of it—'Of the Principles and Use of Civil and Ecclesiastical Polity' and 'Of the Use of Education'—are not mentioned until the Index of 1734. And this belated reference is accompanied by Spence's observation that Pope was 'speaking coldly' about whether he would proceed with composing them. As we shall see, the outline of the epic on Brutus suggests that ten years later Pope was aware of and pondering the problems rather hazily sketched out in Epistle III of the *Essay*.

Pope does not follow Lucretius through the description of awesome natural phenomena culminating in the ravages of the plague described in Book VI of *De Rerum Natura*, though such natural phenomena and their tendency to induce abject superstition seem also to be subjects Pope planned to develop in considerable detail in 'Brutus'. Whether or not the extended description of the plague was to have been the final passage of *De Rerum Natura*, it seems likely to have been close to the poem's end, and such a conclusion would be wholly inappropriate to Pope's work. The *Essay*'s final depiction of the prospect of bliss awaiting man if he accepts his place in the nature of things and attempts to approximate God's benevolence has moved so far from Lucretian concerns that it can have no parallels (even in reverse) with *De Rerum Natura*. Epistle IV of the *Essay* is devoted to a realm of experience unacceptable to Lucretius, who is intent upon laying bare material causes and phenomena and is consistent in advocating withdrawal from human affairs and resigned acceptance of decay and destruction as the way of the world. It scarcely need be said that Epistle IV of the *Essay* shows no connections with or verbal echoes from Lucretius.

There seems to have been a considerable hiatus between the completion of the first three epistles of the *Essay* and the fourth. Although several references in the correspondence of Pope and Bolingbroke to others during the summer of 1731 confirm one another in declaring that Epistle III has been completed and that Pope is hard at work on a fourth and final epistle, there are no further clear references to Epistle IV until August 1733, well after the first three epistles followed one another into print in February, March, and May of 1733.[34] Some manuscript annotations indicate that at a point earlier than the summer of 1731 Pope seems to have contemplated completing the *Essay* in three epistles. The primary evidence for this variant in planning is the note at the beginning of Epistle III in the Harvard draft that reads 'Incipit 3. Learn then thyself, & end it with Come then my Friend &c . . .', the last phrase a reference to the concluding passage of the poem, the verse paragraph that is now Epistle IV, 373 ff. But other notes towards the end of Epistle III record plans for an additional epistle (see page 18). The very tentative draft of Epistle IV in the Morgan manuscript suggests that Pope did not begin to compose Epistle IV until Epistle III was very near completion. The manuscripts thus confirm both one another and the other kinds of external evidence in pointing to a major pause in the composition of the *Essay*.

A possible explanation for this delay may be that in composing the first three epistles of the *Essay*, Pope had found *De Rerum Natura* a useful model for the *Essay*'s tone, structure, expository pattern, and basic order, but for a time found it difficult to organize the material of the final epistle for which Lucretius could not be a guide. Epistle IV has its own set of generic analogues: more clearly than any other part of the poem, it is organized as a dialogue, and its structure is reminiscent of Juvenal X (on the Vanity of Human Wishes) or Boethius' *Consolation of Philosophy*.[35] Its tone, too, as we noticed earlier, is mellower than that characterizing the first three epistles. The development of its themes may also owe a debt to Pope's growing clarity about the relation of parts of the *opus magnum* to one another. In particular, the *Epistle to Bathurst* and the *Epistle to Burlington*, both of which explore the pursuit of true and false happiness, virtue, and vice, seem to have contributed to the composition of the *Essay*'s final epistle.

[34] See Chapter I, pp. 13–14 and note 27.

[35] See, for instance, D. W. Robertson, Jr., 'Pope and Boethius' in *Classical Medieval and Renaissance Studies in Honor of Berthold Louis Ullman*, ed. Charles Henderson, Jr. (Roma: Edizione di Storia e Letterature, 1964), ii. 505–13, which, however, discusses not structure but ideas and figurative language.

The relationship of *An Essay on Man* and *De Rerum Natura* suggested here is obviously based on tenuous evidence. Yet what evidence there is—in the borrowings, tone, and ordering of the *Essay* itself, and in the manuscript notations, correspondence, and anecdotes—suggests such a hypothesis. In planning the *Essay* as a foundation for the other parts of the *opus magnum*, Pope would have found *De Rerum Natura* an attractive and appropriate model. In following 'the same grave march like Lucretius' and reversing 'Lucretius of death', the *Essay* provided a foundation for the 'system of ethics in the Horatian way' that accorded with Pope's conception of it as outlined in his Design: 'to begin with considering *Man* in the abstract, his *Nature* and his *State*' as a way of 'opening the *fountains*, and clearing the passage' for the livelier epistles to follow. The evidence of Pope's dependence upon Lucretius is clearest at the poem's earliest stages of composition—for instance, in the Morgan manuscript's discarded use of the term 'Memmius' and its clearer echoes of the Lucretian passage on the mind of man piercing through vast immensity and beyond the universe, and also in the greater number of closely comparable passages in Epistle I of the *Essay* than in later epistles. As the composition of the *Essay* proceeded, and its conception and that of the *opus magnum* grew clearer to Pope, he seems to have relied less and less upon the Lucretian model to the point where Epistle IV departs entirely from it. So gradual was this movement that Epistle IV, despite its many differences from the first three epistles, appears to be a successful, integrated conclusion to the *Essay*, and throughout catches up words, phrases, and ideas of preceding epistles, firmly grounding the final prospect of bliss in a context of ideas made familiar by the poem's developing pattern.[36] Certainly the *Essay*'s range of tone and its basic 'magisterial' quality, its structural outline and organizational pattern, and its expository and philosophic content are in greater accord with a Lucretian than with a Horatian model. A combination of external and internal clues suggests *De Rerum Natura* as a formative prototype for Pope's *Essay*, a poem which has always seemed to be a peculiarly ill-defined anomaly in an age and for a poet so acutely conscious of genre.

[36] The Twickenham notes to Epistle IV provide helpful cross-references. See, for instance, the notes to IV, 35–8, 55–6, 62, 341, 376.

CHAPTER III

THE *EPISTLE TO COBHAM* AND THE *EPISTLE TO A LADY*

APPARENTLY the last of the moral epistles to be completed, the *Epistle to Cobham* and the *Epistle to a Lady* joined the others in 1735 as the first two in the group of four poems constituting 'Ethic Epistles: the Second Book'. In the absence of a completed epistle or group of epistles on 'The Limits of Human Reason', this pair of poems follows directly after *An Essay on Man*, and stems from the concerns of Epistle II of the *Essay*, '*Of the Nature and State of Man, with respect to* Himself, *as an Individual*'. Of the four epistles in the 'Second Book', the *Epistle to Cobham*'s connection with the *opus magnum* is clearest and is conceded by all; the *Epistle to a Lady*'s faintest—even well-nigh non-existent.[1] The *Epistle to Cobham* seems to have come into existence partly as a response to Epistle II of *An Essay on Man* and partly as a response to the *Epistle to a Lady*, both of which were written before it. So far as the *Epistle to a Lady*'s connection with the *Essay* scheme is concerned, it is primarily via the *Epistle to Cobham*, as is suggested by the note attached to the *Epistle to a Lady*'s title in the collected editions: 'Of the CHARACTERS of WOMEN [a Corollary to the former Epistle] *treating of this Sex only as contradistinguished from the other*'. Considered apart from the

[1] See Twickenham III: ii, 'Introduction', pp. xxxiv–xxxvii, *et passim*. The *Epistle to a Lady* has frequently been interpreted alone and without reference to the *opus magnum*. See, for instance, Jean H. Hagstrum, *The Sister Arts: The Tradition of Literary Pictorialism and English Poetry from Dryden to Gray* (Chicago & London: University of Chicago Press, 1958), pp. 236–41; Irvin Ehrenpreis, 'The Cistern and the Fountain: Art and Reality in Pope and Gray' in *Studies in Criticism and Aesthetics: Essays in Honor of Samuel Holt Monk*, edd. Howard Anderson and John S. Shea (Minneapolis: University of Minnesota Press, 1969), pp. 156–75. In contrast, the *Epistle to Cobham* has never to my knowledge been the subject of separate analysis, but has always been considered together with other ethic epistles. See, for instance, Reuben Brower, *Alexander Pope: The Poetry of Allusion* (Oxford: Clarendon Press, 1959), pp. 240–81; Thomas R. Edwards, Jr., *This Dark Estate: A Reading of Pope* (Berkeley & Los Angeles: University of California Press, 1963), pp. 46–79.

opus magnum, the *Epistle to a Lady*'s history is troubled while the *Epistle to Cobham*'s is straightforward; from the perspective of the scheme, the case is almost the reverse. Let us look first at the finished poems, and then suggest some of the complications that lie behind their relationship.

The 'Epistle to Cobham'

Of the Knowledge and Characters of Men: To Sir Richard Temple, Lord Viscount Cobham was first published in January 1734. It is a conversational poem, yet our sense of Cobham as the second speaker is strong only at the beginning of the poem, where we have a lively sense of his pragmatism and his keen interest in observing human nature, and at the conclusion, where he is (prophetically) praised for dying words which will surely do him credit, in distinct and unique contrast to other characters whose dying words reveal them as consistently and ignobly self-centred. For most of the poem's length we do not, I think, attribute the interjection of questions and suggestions to Cobham in particular, but rather to the poet's sense of speaking to an audience committed to the search for a key to the understanding of human character. This sense of a shared search for truth is closely akin to the manner and method of *An Essay on Man*, Epistle IV. In both epistles, false and partial views—all products of wishful thinking—are raised and rejected in favour of the only possible way of achieving one's goal.

It seems natural that the *Epistle to Cobham* and Epistle IV of the *Essay* should be comparable in manner, since they were published within a week of one another, in January 1734, and were both in the final stages of composition during the late summer and autumn of 1733.[2] In matter, it hardly needs saying that the *Epistle to Cobham* develops primarily from the concerns of Epistle II of the *Essay*. What may need saying is that the *Epistle to Cobham* really develops only one major strand of Epistle II. In focusing on the Ruling Passion, the *Epistle to Cobham* ignores the role of Reason: the 'Thought' of 'Chaos of Thought and Passion, all confus'd' (*Essay*

[2] *Correspondence*, iii. 381 (9 Aug. 1733) and 395 (13 Nov. 1733) for references to final revisions of the *Essay*; 390 (23 Oct. 1733), 391–2 (1 Nov. [1733]), 393–4 (8 Nov. [1733]) for references to revisions of the *Epistle to Cobham*.

II, 13), the 'light' of 'This light and darkness in our chaos join'd' (*Essay* II, 203) are not given attention. And though we hear that 'Man's a fool', we do not hear that 'GOD IS WISE'.

The *Epistle to Cobham* is dedicated to teaching us that there is no easy key to the knowledge of men. The single one of value that emerges is the Ruling Passion, and even its value is highly qualified. Moreover, two-thirds of the poem pass before the Ruling Passion is introduced at all. These first two-thirds of the poem are devoted to two basic themes: the changeability of mankind, and the examination of an apparently overwhelming number of obstacles to and fallacious propositions about the knowledge of men's characters. These themes are specific and detailed extensions of such general truths (adumbrated in *An Essay on Man*, Epistle II) as man's inconsistency, his constant search for pleasure (however benighted), his interest in immediate goals, his egotism. As the *Essay* tells us,

> The rogue and fool by fits is fair and wise,
> And ev'n the best, by fits, what they despise.
> 'Tis but by parts we follow good or ill,
> For, Vice or Virtue, Self directs it still; (*Essay*, II, 233–6)

Yet where a dominant aim of the *Essay* was to urge man to redirect his attention from vanity, pride, and egotism outward and upward to a sense of participation in a divine and beneficent universe, the *Epistle to Cobham* considers man, not as he ought to be, but as he is: restless, obstinate, contradictory, perverse. It is really his perversity that prevents an easy reading of character. As the poem emphasizes, men mask their motives, change them whimsically, act on impulse or from trivial or unguessable urges, lack self-knowledge, and vary infinitely from one another in their aims, views, and actions.

Moreover the subject of the poem, as its full title proclaims, is compound. Men's characters are an object of mockery, to be sure, but so is the notion that anyone can pretend to a knowledge of character. Of both observed and observer it is true that 'What Reason weaves, by Passion is undone'. Observers are blind to the role that their own biases and preferences play in the act of observing (9–14; 23–38) and attach far too much importance to Reason in forming theories of behaviour and in determining the motives behind actions (29 ff.). The heaviest irony in the poem is reserved for the task of demolishing any general theories that purport to read men 'in the gross'—as rational beings or as members of social classes or professions—or that purport to comprehend men either by what they say or what they do or how they do it.

Considerable irony therefore attaches to the bare notion that the Ruling Passion should be advanced as the key to the knowledge of mankind. It, too, is a general hypothesis and presumably has all the weaknesses shared by other general theories—that it is too abstract, that it is subject to the biases of the observer, that it posits in man an unchanging constant after portraying him for two-thirds of the poem as a 'Chaos of Thought and Passion, all confus'd'.

The final third of the poem, however, addresses itself to answering these objections, and does so indirectly and especially by way of individual examples. The use of individual instances is in itself an answer to the major objection to other approaches: that they consider men 'in the gross'. For the theory of the Ruling Passion invariably involves studying the behaviour of every man in isolation as an individual whose follies, caprices, and goals are his own and create their own unique pattern. The poem offers only one extended character for examination, that of the Duke of Wharton. Wharton is so very singular, seemingly capricious and contradictory that, for purposes of rhetoric at least, if the principle of the Ruling Passion is successfully applied to him, its worth will have been triumphantly demonstrated. Wharton is the epitome of the kind of wildly inconsistent behaviour that in the earlier portion of the poem was isolated as unfathomable by conventional theories of character. And the very length and thoroughness of the portrait again appears to be an answer to the kinds of objections registered earlier. In the analysis of Wharton, puzzling dimensions of character are *not* suppressed; no single action or complex of actions has pre-eminence; no talent, or facet of personality, or folly goes unremarked. The behaviour of a lifetime passes in review, and only then is Wharton plain: his Ruling Passion is his 'Lust of Praise'. By means of this portrait, the poem performs its double function: at one stroke it mocks the character of Wharton (and by implication the vanity of all men), and it vindicates the principle of the Ruling Passion.

Following this portrait—the climax of the poem—comes a reminder of the fallibility of the observer even when using the best of tools (210–21), and at this point the poem shifts direction. We now have a series of portraits that continue to illustrate the validity of the principle of the Ruling Passion, but from a different angle. In the concluding portion of the poem, the emphasis is upon the strength and consistency of the Ruling Passion 'ev'n at life's expence', developing the relevant section (161–74) of *An Essay on Man*, Epistle II. In doing so, it also continues the disease motif of Epistle II of the *Essay*, and fulfils the promise of one of Pope's earliest remarks recorded by Spence: '[Mr. Pope has a] new hypothesis, that a prevailing passion in the mind is brought with it into the world, and continues till death (illustrated by the seeds of the illness that is at last to destroy us being planted in the body at our births).'[3]

Yet the change of emphasis reinforces a crucial limitation to the principle of the Ruling Passion as a method of explaining character. It is not predictive. No man's behaviour can be a model for any other man's; no man's behaviour can be examined in part; not until his death can we have sufficient evidence of the strength and consistency of the particular Ruling Passion that sways any particular individual. This is a severe qualification and a frustrating one. But it is also the one that makes the study of character endlessly fascinating and that prevents so-called sages from playing God. In combination with all the other qualifications to its usefulness, this last one effectively enforces the effort—begun in the *Essay*—to undermine man's aspirations to divine omniscience.

Although the poem thus embodies a complex set of injunctions, qualifications, and objections, and certainly functions as a unified poem, it nevertheless appears to assume a previous knowledge of the Ruling Passion. In accordance with the *opus magnum* plans, the *Epistle to Cobham* demonstrates only the utility of the principle.[4] For an understanding of the nature of the Ruling Passion, its strength, violence, capacity for growth and destruction, its origin in self-love, and its resistance to reason, one must read *An Essay on Man*, Epistle II.

[3] *Anecdotes*, i. 130, no. *296*.

[4] See the phrasing in Spence's note of 1730, the Index of 1734, the notes of the 1735 edition, Chapter I, pp. 10, 28, 33–4.

These characteristics are merely alluded to within the *Epistle to Cobham*, most conspicuously in the following passage:

> In this one Passion man can strength enjoy,
> As Fits give vigour, just when they destroy.
> Time, that on all things lays his lenient hand,
> Yet tames not this; it sticks to our last sand.
> Consistent in our follies and our sins,
> Here honest Nature ends as she begins. (222–7)

The 'miniatures' that follow this passage act as exemplifications of its truth. But the background to the comment is to be found in Epistle II of the *Essay*. The *Epistle to Cobham* is not—nor was it meant to be—entirely self-sufficient and convincing without a reading of the *Essay*.

Partly because of its considerable dependence upon the preceding poem, partly because of the extent to which it devotes itself to straightforward pedagogical rejection of alternate hypotheses, the *Epistle to Cobham* seems less rich and colourful, and is less immediately appealing, than the other moral epistles that follow *An Essay on Man*. It is, however, as Mr. Bateson remarks, 'eminently readable', and it frequently achieves the density and metrical virtuosity of Pope's best writing. A good example is the powerful and scathing passage attacking the possibility of judging character by studying those in 'high life':

> 'Tis from high Life high Characters are drawn;
> A Saint in Crape is twice a Saint in lawn;
> A Judge is just, a Chanc'lor juster still;
> A Gownman, learn'd; a Bishop, what you will;
> Wise, if a Minister; but, if a King,
> More wise, more learn'd, more just, more ev'rything.
> Court-virtues bear, like Gems, the highest rate,
> Born where Heav'n's influence scarce can penetrate:
> In life's low vale, the soil the virtues like,
> They please as Beauties, here as Wonders strike. (87–96)

This passage begins so blandly that despite the irregular beat of the first line with its cluster of heavy stresses in mid-line, the regularity and speed of the next two lines may carry us unsuspiciously past the ambiguity of meaning in the second line. We are likely to begin to see the irony only in the middle of the fourth line which forces a strong pause only to be followed by the obvious inadequacy of the colloquial 'what you will'. Similarly, we may not hesitate over the next line, but hard upon it comes the thudding force of the description of the king, 'More wise, more learn'd, more just, more ev'rything', wherein the succession of heavy monosyllables brakes the line, and collapses bathetically in the rushed phrase 'more ev'rything', which parallels the earlier 'what you will'. Two lines further along, 'Born where Heav'n's influence scarce can penetrate', the rhythm of the last half of the line breaks down completely in a mouthful of syllables, and then, as if having dazzled us long enough, both the intense irony and the extreme metrical variation vanish, and the passage concludes in relatively normal metre with a restatement of the theme that has complexity of a different kind.[5]

This passage is a high point in the poem's initial movement, occurring at just about the end of the first third of the poem, the whole of which is an exercise in the demolition of inadequate keys to character. It is not, however, an isolated *tour de force* by any means, and its metrical agility is less often noticed than, for instance, the monologue of Narcissa (242–7) and the dialogue between the miser Euclio and his servant (256–61). The *Epistle to Cobham* has probably suffered from undeserved lack of attention because of its association with the brilliant *Epistle to a Lady*.

It is important also to take note of the kinds of persons alluded to in the poem. With the exception of the central character of Wharton and the concluding dramatic sketches, these are not quite 'portraits', and the many lines of rather prosaic tutelage may overshadow them, although a line count shows that altogether attention to individual figures occupies almost half the number of lines in the poem. (Such a proportion is not far below that of the *Epistle to a Lady*, whose commentary is less conspicuous because clothed in the painting metaphor and other metaphorical patterns.) Moreover, an important pattern in the *Epistle to Cobham* emerges from the very choice of

[5] The 'Gem and Flower' lines (93–100), singled out for admiration by Dr. Johnson, contain not only the allusion to the conventional idea that precious stones and metals are created by the sun's rays, but probably also echoes of Cowley's translation of Virgil. See Maynard Mack, *The Garden and the City* (Toronto: University of Toronto Press, 1969), pp. 83–5.

subjects sketched throughout the poem. The emphasis is upon rulers, kings, statesmen—public and exalted figures of all kinds. The allusions begin with the Emperor Charles V and his son Philip II; the next portrait is of Caesar; then come the Queen (120–1), Patritio (Godolphin, minister of state (140–5)), the Roman Emperor Otho, Cromwell, and a group of seven European monarchs (146–53); 'Scoto', Secretary of State for Scotland (158–61); Catiline, Caesar once more, and Lucullus, the conqueror of Mithridates (212–19); Politicians, Courtiers, and finally Cobham. There are, of course, portraits of other figures who do not fit this category, for the poem is meant to be an all-inclusive survey of both representative types and individuals of every kind, but the proportion of rulers and public figures is so high that the selection is noticeable and significant.

That the figures are primarily men of world renown rather than contemporaries of Pope contributes to the poem's tone of generality. The choice of figures is appropriate both to the claim for the universal validity of the 'New Hypothesis' and to the essentially didactic manner of the poem's first movement. Moreover, this conformity befits a poem that was supposed to effect a transition from the 'grave march like Lucretius' to the 'gayeties of Horace'. The poem embodies this transition within itself, moving from an examination of principles by reference to historical figures of renown and in expository, relatively abstract language to the application of the Ruling Passion to contemporary figures, using, after the two-thirds point, appreciably more colloquial language, and dramatic vignettes. If we read the poems in the order Pope intended, the *Epistle to Cobham* is an appropriate transition between *An Essay on Man* and the *Epistle to a Lady*. Significantly too, the high incidence of references to rulers and political leaders in the *Epistle to Cobham* helps to bind this poem and the *Epistle to a Lady* thematically, as we shall be in a better position to see after discussing the latter.

The 'Epistle to a Lady'

Of the Characters of Women: An Epistle to a Lady was first published in February 1735. The Twickenham text essentially follows the 1744 edition, printing a poem of 292 lines, markedly longer than the original version which omits the portraits of Philomedé, Atossa, Cloe, and the Queen. This poem, like the *Epistle to Cobham*, opens by attributing an opinion to the person being addressed, and closes with a tribute to the same person, in this case Martha Blount. Like the *Epistle to Cobham* too, and even more obviously, the poem is throughout conversational; it is also partly hortatory in tone, for a number of artists are being commanded to 'paint' the series of portraits that make up the first part of the poem.

The structure of the poem appears straightforward. After the opening four lines follows a passage (5–16) displaying three women in pairs of contrasting poses, an adaptation of conventions of seventeenth- and eighteenth-century portraiture.[6] This paragraph is followed by four lines emphasizing, again with the help of the portrait motif, one of the themes of the early part of the *Epistle to Cobham*, the rapid changeability of women. Next (21–52) follows a series of short portraits, varying from three to eight lines, illustrating this theme and continuing the device of the opening group in showing each figure in two opposing moods. There are then four longer portraits (45–100) of Calypso, Narcissa, Philomedé, and Flavia, as examples of 'Wits',[7] and then (101–14) a paragraph of five very short sketches. The long portraits of Atossa and Cloe follow, separated by a passage of generalization (151–6), concluding 'Chameleons who can paint in white and black?', reminding us of the similar sentiment in the *Epistle to Cobham*: 'Life's stream for Observation will not stay, / It hurries all too fast to mark their way' (31–2).

Next comes the section (181 ff.) usually referred to as the 'Queen portrait', but which might as well be described as the 'high Life' passage, for it is parallel to the brilliantly ironical passage in the *Epistle to Cobham*, quoted above, beginning, ' 'Tis from high Life high Characters are drawn'. Much the same theme is present here in the *Epistle to a Lady*, clothed now in the painting metaphor. The passage reads as follows:

[6] See the fine treatments of Pope's use of the painting metaphor in Hagstrum, *The Sister Arts*, and Martin Price, *To the Palace of Wisdom* (Garden City, N.Y.: Doubleday, 1964), pp. 59–63.

[7] The Elwin–Courthope edition notes at line 100: 'The antithesis of these verses resembles that in the character of the Duke of Wharton.' Wharton, like Flavia, is 'A Fool, with more of Wit than half Mankind, / Too quick for Thought, for Action, too refin'd' (*Cobham*, 200–1, cf. *Lady*, 87, 95 ff.).

One certain Portrait may (I grant) be seen,
Which Heav'n has varnish'd out, and made a *Queen*:
The same for ever! and describ'd by all
With Truth and Goodness, as with Crown and Ball:
Poets heap Virtues, Painters Gems at will,
And show their zeal, and hide their want of skill.
'Tis well—but, Artists! who can paint or write,
To draw the Naked is your true delight:
That Robe of Quality so struts and swells,
None see what Parts of Nature it conceals.
Th' exactest traits of Body or of Mind,
We owe to models of an humble kind.
If QUEENSBERRY to strip there's no compelling,
'Tis from a Handmaid we must take a Helen.
From Peer or Bishop 'tis no easy thing
To draw the man who loves his God, or King:
Alas! I copy (or my draught would fail)
From Honest Mah'met, or plain Parson Hale. (181–98)

This passage echoes in diction as well as in thought the 'high Life' passage in the *Epistle to Cobham* about the futility of drawing characters in exalted stations. Note for instance such repetitions and close parallels of words and phrases as 'Gems' (*Lady*, 185; *Cobham*, 93); 'Bishops' (*Lady*, 195; *Cobham*, 90); 'Parson' contrasted with 'Bishop' (*Lady*, 198), 'A Saint in Crape' contrasted with 'a Saint in Lawn' (*Cobham*, 88); 'draw', 'draught' (*Lady*, 196, 197) and 'drawn' (*Cobham*, 87); and the allusions to 'Heav'n' (*Lady*, 182; *Cobham*, 142). Like the *Epistle to Cobham* passage also, the second portion of this passage (193 ff.) is a variant expression of the substance of the first portion.

The painting image attains its deepest significance in the first ten lines of this passage. Up to this point in the poem, many associations have been called upon by the employment of the painting motif: for instance, the use of line and shade (151–4), of colour (3–4, 17, 155–6), and of pose (7–14). The use of costume and properties is another important element in the pattern: Arcadia's Countess is 'in ermin'd pride' (7); Cecilia is 'drest in smiles . . . / With simp'ring Angels, Palms, and Harps divine' (13–14); Rufa is bent over a copy of Locke (23), and Sappho's diamonds are incongruous against her dirty smock (24). This last element pervades the Queen portrait. As

Hagstrum notes, Pope here uses the metaphor 'in a Swiftian manner reminiscent of the clothes philosophy of *A Tale of A Tub*, to deny the possibility of achieving worth in society portraits where neither naked truth, naked Beauty, nor naked virtue can possibly appear'.[8]

The Queen passage is not only the climax and conclusion of the painting motif, but also serves to introduce a new image pattern and new direction to the poem. Along with its personal connotations, the portrait of Queen Caroline also introduces the metaphor of 'Woman as Queen'. The allusion to the Duchess of Queensberry is particularly appropriate in this context, carrying us further along towards the image of 'Queens' as a generic term: 'But ev'ry Lady would be Queen for life' (218), 'Yet mark the fate of a whole Sex of Queens' (219), 'Queens may die a jest' (282).

The significance of 'Queens' recalls that of public men and monarchs in the *Epistle to Cobham*, a connection that is firmly made by the passage of general commentary immediately following the verse-paragraph on the Queen. In it, there is a continuous contrast between men and women:

> But grant, in Public Men sometimes are shown,
> A Woman's seen in Private life alone: (199–200)

> In Men, we various Ruling Passions find,
> In Women, two almost divide the kind; (207–8)

> Men, some to Bus'ness, some to Pleasure take;
> But ev'ry Woman is at heart a Rake:
> Men, some to Quiet, some to public Strife;
> But ev'ry Lady would be Queen for life. (215–18)

The introduction of the Ruling Passion and the accompanying shift in theme and metaphor in this passage make the *Epistle to a Lady* remarkably like that of the *Epistle to Cobham* in structural pattern. The first introduction of the Ruling Passion occurs in both poems at roughly the two-thirds point, and in both the explicit mention of the Ruling Passion serves to mark a distinct change in theme and tone. The passages quoted above, and the couplet 'Our bolder Talents in full light display'd, / Your Virtues open fairest in the shade' (201–2)

[8] Hagstrum, *The Sister Arts*, p. 239.

suggest that the full effectiveness of the *Epistle to a Lady* depends on reading it in conjunction with the *Epistle to Cobham.*

The two Ruling Passions in Women are 'The Love of Pleasure, and the Love of Sway' (210), and each of these master Passions is explored in later passages of equal length. The first develops the idea of 'the Love of Sway' in association with the 'Queen' metaphor together with images of military power and tyrannical rule, thereby suggesting that such a misuse of the Ruling Passion is a distortion of woman's role and a guarantee of a friendless and fearful old age. The second explores the other Ruling Passion, the Love of Pleasure, where the extreme opposite of the desire to dominate in public life, the shallowness and frivolity that mark an inadequate fulfilment of woman's proper private role, is associated with youthful irresponsibility. Both extremes lead to the same end, an 'Old Age of Cards' and an unmourned death. The references to death and old age in this part of the poem evoke the portraits of Flavia and Atossa in the first part of the poem; they also recall the emphasis upon the final moments of life so prominent in the concluding movement of the *Epistle to Cobham.*[9]

Finally, all these patterns are caught up in the sun–moon metaphor of the portrait of Martha Blount. The sun, 'the glaring Orb', is associated with Queens, Rulers, and public life, and excessive love of power and pleasure, while the moon shining 'Serene in Virgin Modesty' is a final symbol gathering up the proper and particular role of woman in private life and underlining the virtue of moderation. The tribute to the 'Lady' is, however, interrupted by a paragraph (269–80) reminding her and the reader that she, like Cobham, is a rarity, an 'exception to all gen'ral rules' (275).

The 'Epistle to Cobham' and the 'Epistle to a Lady' as Companion-pieces

The *Epistle to a Lady* has received much more attention than the *Epistle to Cobham*, not only because readers find it a more successful

[9] This stress in both poems on the growth of the Ruling Passion, followed 'thro life ... e'en at life's expence' (*Essay* II, 171), is, of course, reminiscent of the whole section of the *Essay* (II, 133 ff.), to which Pope appended the note, 'The Use of this doctrine, as apply'd to the Knowledge of mankind, is one of the subjects of the second book.'

poem, but also because it is a more problematic one. Evidence such as the irregular lineation in the 1735 printing, the mysterious editorial note to line 199 that in 1735 declares that 'certain *Examples* and *Illustrations*' are missing and in 1744 declares that though some have been supplied 'others are still wanting', and the variant version of the poem printed for the Prince of Wales in 1738, clearly suggests that even the 1744 version of the *Epistle to a Lady* which contains the portraits of Philomedé, Atossa, Cloe, and the Queen (and altogether 82 more lines than the poem as first published in 1735), does not represent the poem as Pope first wrote it.[10] Many of the portraits of the poem seem to have had independent lives and histories. The pairs of Rufa and Sappho (21–8), Calypso and Narcissa (45–68), for instance, derive respectively from 'Artimesia' and 'Sylvia, a Fragment', short individual poems published in 1727.[11] From Pope's correspondence with Swift and from the editorial note mentioned above, it is also clear that a major reason Pope did not publish the poem until two years after its apparently rapid composition was his concern that some of the portraits would arouse a furore 'in an age so sore of satire, and so willing to misapply characters'.[12]

Pope's references to having composed the *Epistle to a Lady* constitute the one exception to his normal practice of specifying clearly that any particular poem he was working on between 1729 and 1735 was or was not to be a part of the *opus magnum*. He alludes to it only as a poem to Martha Blount.[13] The only possible allusion to it in relation to the ethic system before 1734 is the Morgan manuscript note to the exordium of *An Essay on Man*, connecting line 6 with 'Inconsistencys of Character, Ep. 5', and that note may well refer to what was to become the *Epistle to Cobham*. The most that one can say with any assurance at all is that whatever the circum-

[10] These and related textual details are fully described in Twickenham III: ii, pp. 40–5; Frank Brady, 'The History and Structure of Pope's *To a Lady*', *SEL, 1500–1900*, ix (1969), 439–62; Vinton A. Dearing, 'The Prince of Wales's Set of Pope's Works', *Harvard Library Bulletin* iv (1950), 320–38. The portrait of Cloe does not appear in the version of the poem in the Prince of Wales's edition, and the portrait of Philomedé raises questions (on which also see Benjamin Boyce, *The Character-Sketches in Pope's Poems* (Durham, N.C.: Duke University Press, 1962), Appendix B, pp. 133–5).

[11] See Twickenham III: ii, pp. 51, 53–4, and R. M. Schmitz, 'Peterborough and Pope's Nymphs: Pope at Work', *PQ*, xlviii (1969), 192–200.

[12] *Correspondence*, iii. 349, and Chapter I, p. 13.

[13] Ibid.

stances of its composition, Pope apparently saw that it could be made a part of the system provided that he wrote a poem that would create a link between it and Epistle II of *An Essay on Man*. Some such decision may have contributed significantly to its delay in publication. Once the *Epistle to Cobham* was written and published, both poems were listed as part of the ethic system in the Index of 1734.

From the perspective of the *opus magnum*, it is the *Epistle to Cobham* rather than the *Epistle to a Lady* that raises problems. Despite or because of being written solely to conform to the moral scheme, the *Epistle to Cobham* appears to have been subject to the same kinds of problems of conception, execution, and revision that characterize all other completed epistles (apart from the *Epistle to a Lady*) within the scheme. If we assume that the *Epistle to Cobham* and not the *Epistle to a Lady* or Epistle IV of the *Essay* is the poem meant by Pope when he wrote to Swift in April 1733 that 'I have but last week finished another of my Epistles, in the order of the system', he was at work on it only after the completion of the *Epistle to Bathurst* (published January 1733), the *Epistle to a Lady* (composed February 1733), and the *Essay on Man*, Epistle II (published March 1733). But he had not in fact 'finished' it, for references in Pope's correspondence in the autumn of 1733 indicate that he is then in the process of revising it. Only in November has the poem taken on final shape, and Cobham comments approvingly on the clarity of the final version in contrast to the perplexing 'brouillion' he remembers having seen earlier.[14]

Preceding the April 1733 references, however, there are suggestions that some such poem had been in Pope's mind during the earliest period of planning the *opus magnum*. The exordium notes in the Morgan manuscript, which appear to date well before the summer of 1731, refer to an epistle 'Of the Knowledge' (a phrase careted in over the crossed-out phrase 'The Characters') 'of Mankind' and an epistle on 'Inconsistencys of Character', and the Harvard exordium notes refer to an epistle on the 'Characters of Men & Manners'. Without more ample information, it is impossible to say whether,

[14] *Correspondence*, iii. 391. Cobham may have seen a draft when Pope visited him for several days during the previous July or August. (See *Correspondence*, iii. 375 n., 383.)

despite the obvious similarity in titling, what Pope then had in mind bears any resemblance to the finished epistle. The first phrase in particular is certainly suggestive of the first two-thirds of the *Epistle to Cobham*, and the final poem may even combine the central elements of what Pope recorded in the exordium notes as two epistles, one on the 'Limits of Reason' and one on the 'Characters of Men & Manners'.

Portions of the last third of the poem also seem to have been in Pope's mind during the earliest period of his planning. The most convenient way of illustrating this is by a Spence note that combines in abbreviated form a number of more detailed notes dated 1–7 May:

Mr P. 1730
Montaigne's 1 Es: lib: 2? is ye best in ye whole book. Mr. P^{s} present design wholly upon human actions, & to reform ye mind: A prevailing passion in ye mind brought into ye world with it & continues till death: [This is in his Morals, w^{t} Humor in a Character.] We s^{d} not speak agst Avarice, w^{t} speaking agst Prodigality: & so of ye rest: The middle ye aimable point. L^{d} B: very much assisting in ye Materials. The first Ep: to ye Whole, w^{t} a Scale of Miles to a book of Maps. ye Man of Ross: Sr Balaam: fire, meat & drink: ye Dying Courtier &c.[15]

The third sentence of this note is a shortened version of the one quoted earlier which includes the parenthetical remark 'illustrated by the seeds of the passion that is at last to destroy us being planted in the body at our births'—a reference that seems to apply to what is now the last third of the *Epistle to Cobham*; Mr. Bateson (erroneously, I think) applies the scale-map image at one point to the *Epistle to Cobham* rather than to the *Essay on Man*;[16] and the final phrase is a reference to the vignette at lines 252–5 of the finished *Epistle to Cobham*. Yet one cannot say that Pope at this point had a clear conception of the *opus magnum* or even of the *Essay on Man*, let alone that he saw the *Epistle to Cobham* and the *Epistle to Bathurst* as two

[15] *Anecdotes*, ii. 709, textual Note to no. *295*. The final phrase appears only in this version.

[16] Twickenham, III: ii, pp. xxxiv–xxxv. As Mr. Bateson himself notes in his transcription of a different, extended version of the same note (Twickenham III: ii, pp. xx–xxi), Pope applies the image to *An Essay On Man* in the final paragraph of its printed 'Design'. (See also *Anecdotes*, i. 133, no. 301.) In 1730 Spence also notes that it refers to the *Essay*, which was then to have been a single epistle (*Anecdotes*, i. 130, no. 294).

distinct poems. Given Pope's habits of composition, it would seem likelier that only after the completion of the *Essay*, the *Epistle to Bathurst*, and the *Epistle to a Lady* did he begin to see the way in which his earlier plans and perhaps some fragments discarded from early drafts of the already completed poems could come together to form the foundation for the *Epistle to Cobham*.

Five of the eight vignettes that make up the concluding portion of the poem are mentioned in various contexts separately before the poem's publication. In his second letter to Pope in November 1733, Cobham makes special reference to 'the Leachour' (228–33), which he is pleased to see shortened, and to 'the Glutton' (234–7), which he refers to in a way that suggests that he has not seen it in previous drafts.[17] The Twickenham notes record Jonathan Richardson's recollection that the four verses he once heard Pope recite about the 'frugal Crone' (238–41) were 'designed for his epistle *On Riches*'. Despite Mr. Bateson's scepticism, this may well be an accurate memory, particularly because its reference to 'the hallow'd taper's end' (239) resembles comparable phrases in the latter portion of the *Epistle to Bathurst*.[18] The vignette of 'the Dying Courtier' may also have been originally intended for the *Epistle to Bathurst*, just as are the three immediately preceding phrases in Spence's 1730 note. Of traceable parts of the poem, only the final line, a sentiment Pope had attributed to Atterbury in an epitaph written in 1732, has an existence separate from the *opus magnum* plans.[19] Like the *Epistle to a Lady*, the last third of the *Epistle to Cobham* seems largely to have been composed of fragments. In contrast to the *Epistle to a Lady*, the fragments that entered the *Epistle to Cobham* seem with one exception to have come from within the plans for the *opus magnum*.

The origins of the *Epistle to Cobham*, though obscure, seem to lie almost wholly within the *opus magnum*; the traceable origins of the *Epistle to a Lady* seem to predate and lie almost entirely outside it. Even this brief and highly tentative account of their origins and

[17] 'I like your Leachour better now 'tis shorter and the Glutton is a very good Epigram', *Correspondence*, iii. 393.

[18] Twickenham, III: ii, pp. 35–6. See also the *Epistle to Bathurst*, lines 196, 292, and Chapter IV, p. 86.

[19] Twickenham, III: ii, p. 38; VI, 343–5.

circumstances of composition should make us aware of how remarkable it is that they consort so well together.

The relation of the finished *Epistle to Cobham* and *Epistle to a Lady* depends not of course on their sources or methods of composition nor on any single characteristic or passage, but on a considerable number and variety of common themes and motifs, as the second section of this chapter has sought to show. Both poems begin by describing individuals as contradictory, inconsistent, changeable, and irrational; stress the vast difficulties inherent in the effort to comprehend and judge human character; next invoke the Ruling Passion as the only principle capable of explaining character; and finally insist on the force and strength of its influence 'ev'n at life's expence'. Both use phrasing, diction, and patterning that are remarkably alike and that recall *An Essay on Man*, Epistle II.

These two poems may properly be called 'companion-pieces', yet it may be important to stress that the term in no way demands that the poems be identical in tone, structure, or theme. As we have seen, the first section of the *Epistle to Cobham* examines and dismisses all approaches to the knowledge of human character except the Ruling Passion. In the final third of the poem a single complex 'experiment' illustrates the supreme, if qualified, usefulness of this key to character, and a series of short vignettes follows, in each of which an individual is 'exposed' by reference to the 'New Hypothesis'. Just as the *Epistle to Cobham* assumes a reading of *An Essay on Man*, Epistle II, for an understanding of the general theory of the Ruling Passion, so the *Epistle to a Lady* assumes a reading of the *Epistle to Cobham* for a justification of the utility of the hypothesis. The *Epistle to a Lady* need not traverse the same ground again; with the key to the knowledge of character assumed to be in our possession, this poem places its major series of characters at the beginning, exposing them as it does so,[20] then applies the principle to the characters of women in particular by contrast to those of men, and concludes by focusing on the theme of virtue as a balance between two extremes or Vices—a theme that the following moral essays, already in fact written and published, use centrally. The movement from the *Epistle to Cobham* to the *Epistle to a Lady* is a progressive

[20] Cf. Edwards, *This Dark Estate*, pp. 73–4.

one, not unlike, though not so closely interrelated as, the successive epistles of *An Essay on Man*. *The Epistle to Cobham* and the *Epistle to a Lady* do not 'need' to be read in the light of one another. To do so, however, and to read the pair with a sense of their place in the *opus magnum*, adds an important dimension to our appreciation of their patterns and meaning.

CHAPTER IV

THE *EPISTLE TO BATHURST*

THE *Epistle to Bathurst* was first published as a separate folio in January 1733. Extant manuscript drafts, as well as the contemporary correspondence and conversations outlined in Chapter I, corroborate Pope's later claims that it 'was the work of two years by intervals'[1] and that 'I never took more care in my life of any poem'.[2] Critics have shown commensurate attention: no other 'Ethic Epistle' has been the subject of so much extended discussion in recent criticism. In addition to the discussion in the Twickenham edition, and the chapter sections in the books of Reuben Brower and Thomas R. Edwards, Jr., there are a number of important individual treatments.[3] In this chapter I shall reconsider the poem with special reference to its manuscript sources and its connections with the *opus magnum*. The major discussion of the poem's particular relation to the *Epistle to Burlington* occupies the final section of the next chapter.

The 'Epistle to Bathurst' in Manuscript Form

The extant working drafts of the *Epistle to Bathurst* are Huntington Manuscripts HM 6007 and 6008, and consist of two complete and successive drafts of the poem plus two separate leaves of an earlier draft. By internal references, mainly to the death dates of actual persons named in the poem, Mr. Wasserman dates the two early leaves and the initial transcription of the first of the two complete

[1] *Correspondence*, iii. 353 (Pope to Caryll, 8 Mar. 1733).

[2] Ibid. iii. 348 (Pope to Swift, 16 Feb. 1733).

[3] See, for instance, Paul J. Alpers, 'Pope's *To Bathurst* and the Mandevillian State' in *Essential Articles for the study of Alexander Pope*, ed. Maynard Mack (Hamden, Connecticut: Archon Books, 2nd ed., 1968), pp. 476–97; Earl R. Wasserman, *Pope's 'Epistle to Bathurst': A Critical Reading with an Edition of the Manuscripts* (Baltimore: Johns Hopkins Press, 1960); Howard Erskine-Hill, 'Pope and the Financial Revolution' in *Writers and their Backgrounds: Alexander Pope*, ed. Peter Dixon (Athens, Ohio: Ohio University Press, 1972), pp. 200–29.

drafts as not later than 30 May 1731. Dates of later revisions of the poem are much more difficult to determine, although Mr. Wasserman does establish the summer of 1731 as the period within which Pope made a second copy (numbered '346*') of a heavily revised page of the first full draft.[4] (At the same period, Pope appears to have begun drafting Epistle IV of *An Essay on Man*.) The later of the two complete *Bathurst* drafts is overlaid with a considerable number of revisions, many of which are extremely rough and tentative; and twenty-eight lines of the first printed version appear in none of the manuscripts; at least one more draft must have existed between those we have and the printer's fair copy. We may also posit missing drafts at the earlier end of the process, for the two early leaves in existence represent clean and stable portions of the poem.

Although such gaps in the history of the poem's composition necessarily make observations about the growth of the poem speculative, I think a number of reliable and illuminating conjectures can be made with a fair degree of confidence. The first of these has to do with the controlling theme of the poem, its emphasis on the personal use of riches and the ways in which such use accords with the providential plan.

Among Spence's earliest anecdotes relating to the *opus magnum* is one that gives a number of clear and direct references to what was to become the *Epistle to Bathurst*:

Sir Balaam: The Man of Ross: The standing jest of Heaven. And sure the gods and we are of a mind. The man possessed of debts and taxes clear, children and wife—five hundred pound a year (public buildings, alms houses, walks, road; The Man of Ross divides the weekly bread; public table twice a week for strangers, etc.)—Will give what we desire; fire, meat and drink. What more? Meat, drink and fire.

POPE *1–7 May 1730*[5]

As Mr. Osborn indicates, 'these notes show that Pope early worked out the contrasting characters portrayed in the *Epistle to Bathurst*, the avaricious Sir Balaam and the philanthropic Man of Ross'. The other references are all to specific quotations of lines (4, 8, 80–1) in the finished poem. The manuscript evidence fortuitously agrees with this record of early planning. The first of the two surviving leaves of

[4] Wasserman, pp. 59–60.

[5] *Anecdotes*, i. 140–1, no. *316*. See also no. *293*.

the otherwise lost early draft contains the entire Man of Ross portrait in a fairly clean and final state, down to the couplet 'Blush, Grandeur, blush! proud Courts, withdraw your blaze! / Ye little Stars! hide your diminish'd rays' (281–2).[6] That at this stage the quoted couplet was apparently meant to be the final one of the portrait is indicated by the fact that in this leaf a line is drawn beneath it, with the rest of the page originally left blank. The leaf thus resembles the leaf of the Morgan manuscript draft at the end of Epistle II of *An Essay on Man*. Like the *Essay* leaf, there are later additions beneath the line on this same page, and later drafts show the development of the portrait to include reflections on the Man of Ross's end; these revisions are discussed later below. Similarly, the second of the two early leaves contains the tale of Sir Balaam in very close to final printed form, although the end of the page coincides with the line, 'And one more Pensioner St. Stephens gains' (394), and we therefore do not have in this version the concluding eight lines of the poem and tale. This early stage begins with a version of the couplet, 'There dwelt a Citizen of sober fame, / A plain good man, and Balaam was his name' (341–2).

Unlike these two remarkably stable and fully developed portions of the poem, the notation of Spence about 'Meat, drink, and fire' seems to be a reflection neither of a long passage nor even of a paragraph of the poem, but of a single couplet, 'What Riches give us let us then enquire: / Meat, Fire, and Cloaths. What more? Meat, Cloaths, and Fire' (81–2). In manuscript, this couplet is the only fixed element in its immediate vicinity amid a positive tempest of deletion, interlineation, marginal revision, further deletion, and ink-smudging through two successive manuscript drafts. So heavy are the revisions in this portion of the first complete manuscript, that it is the only example of a leaf requiring rewriting within the same draft. Even in the second transcription of the page within the same draft (MS. HM 6007, page '346*') the 'Meat, Fire and Cloaths' couplet is once again the only one in the passage not corrected; although the passage following it becomes relatively settled in the

[6] Unless otherwise noted, all quotations and line numbers follow the Twickenham edition. Mr. Wasserman, somewhat confusingly, numbers the manuscript lines differently from those in the printed editions.

second complete draft, the passage preceding it is the subject of considerable change and expansion.

These manuscript passages reflecting the earliest recorded remarks on the poem together form a suggestive image of the way in which the *Epistle to Bathurst* developed. Examination of the manuscripts as a whole, with careful attention to changes of ink and handwriting, reveals that the six major portraits in the poem are the most stable parts of it. The final two-thirds of the poem, that is, are clearly settled before the opening third. Even in the relatively rough opening section, however, its major statements—the opening lines and the passages on the Ruling Passion and on the way in which Providence works through extremes—are as stable as the sturdy 'Meat, Fire, and Cloaths' couplet. Spence's notes, then, seem to be an accurate pointer to the basic direction of the poem. The major illustrations and the major moral statements of man's folly and the misuse of riches belong both to the earliest plans for the *opus magnum* and to the most clearly conceived portions of the *Epistle to Bathurst* drafts.

The manuscript drafts also record the complex process by which these elements become effective and integrated parts of the whole poem. The drafts indicate, for instance, that many of the powerful metaphoric patterns develop to their full extent very late in the poem's composition. An example is the passage describing Blunt's vision of universal deluge (135 ff.), given extended discussion by Mr. Wasserman on account of its evocation of Noah's flood, and by Mr. Brower on account of its *Dunciad*-like intensity. Of the particular lines embodying the flooding metaphor,

> 'At length Corruption, like a gen'ral flood,
> '(So long by watchful Ministers withstood)
> 'Shall deluge all; and Av'rice creeping on,
> 'Spread like a low-born mist, and blot the Sun;
> . . .
> 'See Britain sunk in lucre's sordid charms, . . .
> (137–40, 145)

only the first two and a half lines appear in manuscript. This unit, in fact, appears in both manuscripts, while the remaining lines appear in neither.

A more far-reaching example is the repetition of the word 'end', which, as Mr. Wasserman notes, 'runs like a theme through the last section'. Of the five line-references Mr. Wasserman gives, only those in the portraits of Villiers (314) and Cutler (329) appear in the first of the extant full drafts. The entire passage (283–98), contrasting the ends of the Man of Ross and Hopkins, and creating a link between the first and second portrait triads, was not part of the original concept as reflected by the earliest extant manuscripts. The couplet, 'Behold what blessing Wealth to life can lend! / And see, what comfort it affords our end' (297–8), appears first as a rough marginal insert in the first manuscript. Hopkins's end appears marginally only in the second complete draft, where, however, the lines apply to Cotta, an attribution that survives in the printed poem in the link between 'a candle's end' (292) and 'Curse the sav'd candle' (196).[7] The most impressive play on 'ends' is in the couplet 'Enough, that Virtue fill'd the space between; / Prov'd, by the ends of being, to have been' (289–90). Mr. Wasserman writes in praise of this couplet:

> To establish the full ironic sense that 'end' is to carry, the portrait of the Man of Ross concludes with a highly moving play on the word.... In the parish register, only these two terminal dates prove that one has been. But if, like the Man of Ross, one has filled the space between these two ends with virtue, he has fulfilled the 'ends' of man's earthly existence. The record of birth and death alone, which proves that one has been, is the church's testimony to the irrelevance of wealth and earthly fame. For it is the space between these 'ends' that permits one to fulfill his true 'ends'. One's unrecorded virtuous acts are his true fame and the ultimate testimony to his having been.[8]

Although the eight-line extension to the original portrait of the Man of Ross, which this couplet concludes, exists in a cramped, crossed-out and written-over marginal revision, this fine couplet does not appear in any recognizable form within the manuscript jottings.

Other portions of the manuscripts show the difficulties involved in achieving structural coherence. As noted above, for instance, the entire sixteen-line passage contrasting the ends of the Man of Ross

[7] Compare the lines on the 'frugal Crone', *Epistle to Cobham* (238–41), and see Chapter III, p. 79.

[8] Wasserman, p. 43.

and Hopkins (283–98) was a very late manuscript addition. It is a particularly powerful transition passage, yet is typical of Pope's general pattern of composition, wherein 'framing' lines seem consistently to be later additions to the basic draft. This phenomenon is true even of the two early fragmentary leaves that contain the entire Man of Ross portrait and most of the tale of Sir Balaam. On the first of these leaves, the four lines that introduce the Man of Ross eulogy read:

> There gracious x x acting Gods own part,
> Relieves th' Opprest & glads the Widows heart;
> There English Bounty yet a while shall stand,
> And Honour linger, e're it leaves the land.

The last couplet here as in the final printed version immediately precedes the praise of the Man of Ross (247–8). The first couplet is a variant version of the printed lines 243–5. In printed form, the tribute is to Oxford and especially Bathurst; at this early stage, the recipient of the praise is not yet suggested. An examination of this early leaf shows that there is a decided change in the character of the handwriting and the impression of ink or pen between this four-line unit and the portrait of the Man of Ross, showing that even this short 'frame' marks a stage later than the portrait itself. Much the same, and even more conspicuous, is the transition to the tale of Sir Balaam. The four lines, corresponding to the printed lines 335–8, read:

> Say, for such worth are Other worlds prepar'd?
> Or are they both, in *this*, their *own Reward*?
> A knotty Point! on which we now proceed—
> But you are tir'd—I'll tell a Tale—Agreed.[9]

This passage appears twice in the draft stage represented by the two early manuscript pages: both as a later addition to the beginning of the Sir Balaam leaf and at the bottom reverse side of the Man of Ross leaf. In both places, marginal tags key it for insertion between

[9] In the margin opposite there is an alternative to the first couplet, that printed in the Twickenham edition as a textual variant for all editions 1732–43. The lines (339–40) on the monument in memory of the fire of London enter as a rough marginal addition only in the final MS. draft. The variations in pen and ink on the MSS. pages reveal themselves in varying degrees in the facsimile version. The variations in the Balaam introduction are easily seen, but those in the four lines preceding the Man of Ross portrait, though perfectly clear in the original, are less conspicuous in facsimile.

the end of the Cutler portrait and the beginning of the tale of Sir Balaam. These examples suggest the very gradual development of even the simplest of framing and linking passages.

A major example of the same sort is the thirty-line (219–48) tribute to Burlington and those who, like his 'or OXFORD's better part, / . . . ease th' oppress'd, and raise the sinking heart' (243–4). The passage begins:

> The Sense to value Riches, with the Art
> T'enjoy them, and the Virtue to impart,
> Not meanly, nor ambitiously pursu'd,
> Not sunk by sloth, nor rais'd by servitude;
> To balance Fortune by a just expence,
> Join with Oeconomy, Magnificence;
> With Splendor, Charity; with Plenty, Health;
> Oh teach us, BATHURST! yet unspoil'd by wealth!
> That secret rare, between th' extremes to move
> Of mad Good-nature, and of mean Self-love. (219–28)

In the apostrophe as a whole, Pope gathers up, first of all by a series of negative statements ('Not meanly, nor ambitiously pursu'd, / Not sunk by sloth, nor rais'd by servitude' (221–2)), strands of the previous depiction of the Cottas, turns them into the positive virtues of the golden mean in the use of riches, most particularly the virtue of philanthropy, applying them to Bathurst as an epitome of such virtue, and leads us forward to the Man of Ross, who with even more limited means, is an even more bountiful philanthropist. The placement of the apostrophe to Bathurst thus appears very apt. The rarity of Bathurst's 'Sense', 'Art', and 'Virtue' in the use of riches (219–20) gains emphasis by appearing after the couplet introducing the portrait of Cotta's son: '(For what to shun will no great knowledge need / But what to follow is a task indeed' (201–2)). The passage gives no particularities of Bathurst's use of riches, yet the abstract nouns juxtaposed in balanced lines (223–6) ring out with a sonority that justifies the following wish that 'To want or Worth well-weigh'd, be Bounty giv'n, / And ease, or emulate, the care of Heav'n' (229–30), and the later (punning) prayer that 'Where-e'er he shines, oh Fortune, gild the scene, / And Angels guard him in the golden Mean!' (245–6). Were the praises of Bathurst to be particularized or were the eulogy of him to follow the more concretely detailed eulogy of the Man of Ross, the Man of Ross might easily eclipse Bathurst as a fit object of praise.

However, these lines settle together and into final place only after considerable shifting throughout the manuscript drafts. The original patches of verse (with lines 231–4 preceding 219–20, 223–8) follow the Man of Ross portrait in the early single leaf. These are copied on to the first of the complete drafts of the poem, but the first portion (as quoted above minus the second couplet) is tentatively shifted to the earliest portion of the poem, immediately preceding the 'Meat, Fire and Cloaths' couplet (80–1), contributing to the density of revision there which required a second copy of the page within the same draft. This second copy records Pope's further thoughts in a query about whether to postpone these lines, and in the second complete draft they re-enter the poem just before the Man of Ross passage. Here they join up with additional couplets including the passage now referring to Bathurst and Oxford, but which, as was earlier mentioned, originally applied to an anonymous philanthropist, and then Oxford and Chandos. The final organization and disposition of the thirty-line passage clearly gives it a prominence and unity more appropriate to the poem's addressee than did the scattered couplets.

Yet the passage in final form still reflects some of its uneasy patchwork growth, and does not have the air of inevitability and ease characteristic of Pope's best poetry. One wonders, for instance, what significance to give the qualified compliments ('*yet* unspoil'd by wealth' (226), 'Your's or OXFORD's *better part*' (243); my italics) or the ambiguities in the references to 'gild', 'Angels', 'golden' which suggest a monetary as well as a spiritual reward for the virtuous use of riches. It is surprising, too, to find Bathurst directly addressed (225, 243) in this passage, when he has not seemed to be an active auditor since crying 'All this is madness' (153), and even there is not clearly identified. And the thirty-line passage, though appropriately placed, is not linked to the surrounding portraits by the integrated transitional passages that we noticed Pope developing in other sections of the poem.

These glimpses into the difficulties involved in creating the final poem give one the sense that the *Epistle to Bathurst* is a hard-won and precarious achievement. This may be a false impression, which says less about the finished poem than it does about the manner of approaching it. As Pope himself said, perhaps about this very poem, '[There is] no judging of a piece from the scattered parts'.[10] Yet in writing to Jacob Tonson in June 1732, Pope expressed hesitation about publishing it until it could be accompanied by others, and when he did publish it, assured Swift that he would see 'pretty soon that the letter to Lord Bathurst is a part of the whole scheme of my present work and you will find a plain connexion between them, if you read them in the order just contrary to that they were published in'.[11] Although one ought not to invest such remarks with undue significance, they seem to imply that Pope does not feel that the poem can or should stand on its own. It is paradoxical that the poem that seemed clearly in Pope's mind at the very earliest stages of planning the *opus magnum* should, when finally completed, appear to him to be only a qualified success.[12]

On the other hand, one may see the difficulties of composing the poem and its final lack of independent status as stemming from precisely these early beginnings. The 1730 note quoted above and others from the same date suggest that if the *Epistle to Bathurst* was clearly defined in skeleton form, it was also conceived as a much more ambitious poem, one which, as the preceding chapter suggested, may have contributed passages of verse to the *Epistle to Cobham.* The final section of this chapter suggests that it may also have contributed to the *Essay* itself, especially Epistle IV. And it was written after the *Epistle to Burlington*, and apparently tailored to fit it. If these hypotheses are correct, then we can see that the poem was so inextricably bound up with other parts of the ethic scheme that it is no wonder that Pope should feel that it needed to be read in relation to the others.

The extant manuscripts of the *Epistle to Bathurst* date from too far along in the composition process to reflect these connections. They

[10] *Anecdotes*, i. 168, no. *385* (1–7 May 1730).

[11] See Chapter I, pp. 7, 10–11, 13, and references there. Pope's letter to Swift also mentions that 'I never took more care in my life of any poem than of the [Epistle to Bathurst]'.

[12] See *Anecdotes*, i. 139, no. 312 and its annotation for additional reasons for Pope's difficulties and delay.

do, however, remind us of the way the poem developed around the firm skeleton of the 1730 remarks. A look at the finished poem will indicate the suggestiveness and potential implicit in these few phrases.

The Themes and Structure of the 'Epistle to Bathurst'

The opening portion of the *Epistle to Bathurst* focuses on riches and their effect on society, especially when in the hands of those whose schemes result from corruptions and inversions of virtuous and charitable motives. The first clear unit of the poem consists primarily of an exordium and three fantasies, and ends with the ironic comment on Blunt's vision and the 'sober sage's' cry, 'All this is madness' (153). Madness it is indeed, yet the obvious escape route, suggested in Bathurst's response 'Why take it, Gold and all' (80), is no solution, for the whole section proclaims the inextricable permeation of society by riches. The over-all vision is totally negative: it is the ultimate inundation of society through the misuse of riches by mad individuals. Once the 'disputing Doctors' have both owned 'Riches in effect / No grace of Heav'n or token of th' Elect' (17–18), the poetic argument is so structured at this point that wealth appears to be given only to 'the Fool, the Mad, the Vain, the Evil' (19). All the figures described in this section of the poem are 'standing jests of Heav'n', mad visionaries, who are foolish, vain, and corrupt. Of the remainder of this verse paragraph, Mr. Wasserman writes,

> Beginning with the quasi-scriptural line, ' 'Tis thus we eat the bread another sows,' the speaker examines with considerable gravity and without a hint of satire the equal capacity of riches for good and evil. The paragraph (21–34) has the neatly systematic organization that has always characterized the sermon form, progressing from the individual to society to the nation: riches may preserve life or hire the assassin, help trade or lure the pirate, extend society or corrupt a friend, raise an army or betray the nation.[13]

By concentrating only on the second half of the paragraph (29–34), Mr. Wasserman makes the passage appear rather more 'neatly systematic' than the whole suggests. Pope has not just catalogued a

[13] Wasserman, p. 24.

balanced list of positive and negative uses of riches; he has clearly loaded the dice, by focusing upon the misuse of riches in the preceding half-dozen lines. The neutral, and even Biblically elevated, verbs 'eat' and 'sows', in the line (22) that Mr. Wasserman quotes above, devolve rapidly and disconcertingly into the verbs 'riot' and 'starve' (24) and make this transition from neutrality to irresponsibility and injury by way of a line explicitly describing 'commodious Gold' as 'unequal'. Rather than being of 'considerable gravity and without a hint of satire', the next four lines seem to me to be heavily sarcastic:

> What Nature wants (a phrase I much distrust)
> Extends to Luxury, extends to Lust:
> And if we count among the Needs of Life
> Another's toil, why not another's Wife? (25–8)

Pope appears here to be adopting the voice of a facile and untrustworthy debater, and by tone and phrasing is suggesting that the man who says 'What Nature wants' (25) as an axiomatic, factual statement really means, as Pope's extensions ironically imply, '*I* want', and his wants are endless.

To curb the endlessness of this immorality and selfishness, Pope humorously proposes 'bulky bribery' as a fanciful panacea, whereby 'Poor Avarice one torment more would find; / Nor could Profusion squander all in kind' (47–8). But this last couplet suggests that the vices themselves are in any event ineradicable; even this visionary scheme could do no more than set some few limits upon their destructive effects. And the scheme itself is as hypothetical as it is humorous, even if it is wryly or wistfully so. Such fantasies are consistently mocked, whether they be Blunt's or Unhappy Wharton's or those of other madmen—and poets. They are always 'Some Revelation hid from you and me' (116), a comment that classes visionary economic schemes with the private visions of religious enthusiasts as false, egotistic, unrealistic, mad.

Pope's powerful visions of the pervasive corrupting power of wealth function in the poem as a method of showing the rare virtuous man how careful a course he must steer in the fallen world, and as a way of stressing the exceptional nature of such virtue in this meed-ruled state. The corrective force of the satire is directed not at society in general, but at the few individuals within it whose moral alertness and soundness of principle will lead them to 'ease the care of Heav'n' and achieve a virtuous life and personal salvation. The section's fantasies—of villainy 'incumber'd' by a return to the barter system (35–64), of invisible paper credit lending 'corruption lighter wings to fly' (65–78), and of 'Corruption, like a gen'ral flood . . . deluging all' (135–52)—all relate to the effects of riches on society in general, and form a pattern of increasingly apocalyptic intensity. Even after the reassuring description of the workings of Providence by extremes in both Man and Nature, there is another grotesque and fantastic vision, intertwining Man and Nature, Avarice and Profusion:

> Who sees pale Mammon pine amidst his store,
> Sees but a backward steward for the Poor;
> This year a Reservoir, to keep and spare,
> The next a Fountain, spouting thro' his Heir,
> In lavish streams to quench a Country's thirst,
> And men and dogs shall drink him 'till they burst. (173–8)

This vision shifts the scene from city to country, emphasizing, through the Cotta portraits, the pervasiveness of the 'deluge'. This section from the Cottas through the Man of Ross portrait (which in turn links with the final section of the poem) mediates between the opening and closing sections by combining the social theme with the personal theme. The Cotta portraits pick up particulars of the lines just quoted and illustrate the working of extremes through time. A 'violent oscillation' (Mr. Alpers's phrase) rather than a comforting balance, the working of extremes through time is merely one way in which Providence works. The reservoir–fountain conceit not only provides a parallel to the portraits of Cotta and son, but is used again in describing the mean between extremes, the Man of Ross making 'the waters flow . . . clear and artless, pouring thro' the plain' (254–8). The reconciliation here is not dependent upon a time-sequence.

Cotta's miserly use of riches is judged by a number of standards: by those of *true* 'Bramins, Saints, and Sages' (a standard Mr. Wasserman elucidates well); implicitly by the standard of country-house behaviour most forcefully represented in immediate poetic tradition by Jonson's 'To Penshurst',[14] and by the philanthropic mean as illustrated by Bathurst and the Man of Ross. At the other extreme of Profusion, the activities of Cotta's son are also weighed against the portrait of the Man of Ross. Where Cotta's son rashly cuts down trees and sells his lands, the Man of Ross plants trees and cultivates the plain. However, Cotta's son is most scathingly indicted not only for senseless profusion, but for the senseless cause of Whig patriotism. Zeal for 'George and Liberty' is not only stupid, but personally catastrophic, for his 'thankless Country' deserts him in his bankrupt condition.

As several critics have pointed out, the Cottas are moral grotesques. The poetic context reduces them to subhuman level. In contrast, the Man of Ross is superhuman. Unlike the Cottas who are unnatural in their mad extremes, the Man of Ross, as Mr. Edwards emphasizes, is a 'version of the magical sympathy of nature with man . . .'. He 'lives in a natural world, and nature echoes his praises in contrast to the Lord whose music and praise come from Fiddlers and Flatterers. . . . He re-enacts, with his dependents and with the landscape, the loving dealings of God with nature and of Christ with men.'[15] Mr. Wasserman, in his turn, stresses the Christlike quality of the Man of Ross: 'the essence of the wifeless, childless Man of Ross's portrait is that beneath the surface language is a current of references to Christ's life and miracles'.[16]

After this portion of the poem comparing the mad extremes of the Cottas' use of riches to the golden mean exemplified by Bathurst and the Man of Ross emulating 'the care of Heav'n' (230), the focus shifts from the effects of the use of riches upon others to its far more important effect upon the users (or rather misusers) themselves. The

[14] Cotta's portrait is convincingly analysed in relation to the 'country-house-poem' tradition by Maynard Mack in *The Garden and the City* (Toronto: University of Toronto Press, 1969), pp. 98–100. For specific suggestions of earlier sources see also Rachel Trickett, *The Honest Muse: A Study in Augustan Verse* (Oxford: Clarendon Press, 1967), pp. 119–20; Sylvia Leonard, 'Wit and Judgment: Pope and the Art of Revision', University of Maryland doctoral dissertation, 1971 (Ann Arbor: University Microfilms), 250–2.

[15] Thomas R. Edwards, Jr., ' "Reconcil'd Extremes": Pope's *Epistle to Bathurst*', *Essays in Criticism* xi (1961), 301–2. This is an earlier and lengthier version of the section on the epistle in *This Dark Estate*.

[16] Wasserman, p. 42. The Man of Ross also has numerous connections with the Augustan *beatus vir* tradition.

middle section of the poem is more optimistic in tone and theme than the opening and closing sections, for it provides insistent reminders of the providential plan. From this perspective, 'Wealth in the gross is death, but life diffus'd' (233), the hoarder simply 'a backward steward for the Poor' (174). Providence oversees and reconciles the general effects of wealth; the individual's misuse of wealth can do irreparable harm only to himself. Man's concern is with virtuous living and, by implication, virtuous dying. It is 'Enough, that Virtue fill'd the space between; / Prov'd, by the ends of being, to have been' (289–90). From the divine perspective it is clear that worldly memorials, like worldly wealth, are inconsequential, and that enshrinement in marble, like heaping up or squandering wealth, is a grotesque substitute for living and dying well.

Via the final group of portraits, we are invited to 'Behold what blessings Wealth to life can lend: / And see, what comfort it affords our end' (297–8). This couplet is ironic in so far as it points forward, for the portraits to follow dwell on the uncomfortable ends of Villiers, Cutler, and Sir Balaam. But the couplet points in two directions, and in its backward reference it is not ironic: virtuously used, Wealth does lend blessings to life, most particularly the most comfortable end of all, a hope of salvation so secure that he 'Who builds a Church to God, and not to Fame' need 'never mark the marble with his Name'.

The three portraits that conclude the poem both parallel and invert the preceding three in many ways, but also dwell so exclusively on 'dying ill' as to bear a marked resemblance to early Renaissance morality plays. Villiers, in particular, is, like Everyman, deserted at the last by health, fortune, friends, and fame. He is 'Victor' (313) in that he has consumed them all in his life of prodigality. Villiers and Cutler are the proper names of actual people, unlike the Cottas upon the identity of whose real-life models much unrewarded scholarship has been expended. The mad, fantastical quality of Cutler's and Villiers's ends (in the double sense) corresponds to Pope's earlier couplet on the Ruling Passion, 'Less mad the wildest whimsey we can frame, / Than ev'n that Passion, if it has no Aim' (157–8), and this link helps us to see how exclusively Pope has come to concentrate on individual morality and psychology rather than on general social corruption. Pope had attributed to the Cottas motives—respectively an emulation of saintliness and patriotism—which, however perverse or self-deluding, partake in some sense of rationality. For Villiers and Cutler, however, he offers no such explanation, even of distorted reasoning. Villiers is simply totally blind and without foresight about his end; and Cutler appears to be wholly in the grip of mad obsession.

We might expect a positive portrait to follow those of Villiers and Cutler and conclude the poem, in the manner of the other ethic epistles. Instead we have something that in theme, content, form, appears quite different from the rest of the poem. We have the fable, not the portrait, of the rise and fall of Sir Balaam. This form is unique to the *Moral Essays*. Yet Mr. Alpers's title for it, in comparing it to Swift's mode, is 'the progress of a soul',[17] and this epithet suggests its appropriateness to the morality-play quality of the last section of the poem.

The essence of Sir Balaam lies in his utterly plodding unimaginativeness. In the early part of his rise, he confines his use of his new-found riches to doubling whatever had been his previous expenditure: he eats two puddings instead of one; he gives sixpence instead of a groat; he goes to church twice instead of once. He continues to be 'Constant at Church, and Change'. Sir Balaam has none of what Dr. Johnson would call moral or religious 'bottom', as the line 'Religious, punctual, frugal, and so forth' (343) clearly conveys. As Mr. Wasserman describes it, 'the shrug with which the line ends make Balaam's virtues rest so indifferently upon him that they are nearly unseated'.[18]

Even the second stage of Balaam's rise, when 'The Tempter' wholly 'secures his soul', shows him as appallingly banal as before. In his social-climbing ambitions for himself and his family, he now (347) 'lives like other folks'. And dies like other folks, too. He is totally corrupted and destroyed by wealth that he has neither sought nor enjoyed nor 'used' in any personal way. And he is so totally without moral or religious strength that no struggle characterizes his

[17] Alpers, 'Pope's *To Bathurst* and the Mandevillian State', p. 493.

[18] Wasserman, p. 47. The poetic strategy of this line is precisely that of lines 90, 92 of the 'high Life' passage in the *Epistle to Cobham*, analysed in the last chapter.

'capture' by the Devil, who cannot have found the task very stimulating. In an important sense, that of the divine perspective, Sir Balaam's wealth is really irrelevant; already *before* it showered upon him, 'his word would pass for more than he was worth' (344). The distinction between moral and economic worth is the ultimate point not only of this fable but also of the poem as a whole, for it emphasizes again and finally that individual morality is the theme and the lesson of the poem, and swings us back to the first section where, though the fantasies of madmen had confused moral and economic 'riches', Bathurst and Pope had firmly agreed that 'Riches in effect' were 'No grace of Heav'n or token of th' Elect' (17–18).

In his parody, Pope is of course mocking neither the Bible nor its *dramatis personae*, but Sir Balaam and his religious and moral inadequacies. So weak are Sir Balaam's religious tenets that unlike Blunt and the elder Cotta, who at least continue to *call* their acts religiously motivated, Sir Balaam,

> now a man of spirit,
> Ascribes his gettings to his parts and merit,
> What late he call'd a Blessing, now was Wit,
> And God's good Providence, a lucky Hit. (375–8)[19]

Sir Balaam, that is, denies the existence of a moral universe. Where the Man of Ross symbolizes the mean as a harmonious resolution of extremes, Sir Balaam symbolizes the discord of the misuse of riches by combining within himself thoughtless frugality and thoughtless expense. Despite Sir Balaam's ignorance, however, the universe is moral, and Sir Balaam represents a moral vacuum within it. Into this hollow,

> the Daemon makes his full descent,
> In one abundant show'r of Cent. per Cent.,
> Sinks deep within him, and possesses whole,
> Then dubs Director, and secures his soul. (371–4)

At the same time as he gives his anti-hero the name of Balaam, Pope is also of course evoking another biblical story, that of Job, both explicitly ('And long'd to tempt him like good Job of old' (350)) and implicitly, by a number of verbal echoes and allusions. This modern counterpart of Biblical figures has clearly fallen far

[19] Howard Erskine-Hill (*N. & Q.*, N.S. xiv. 407–8) elucidates the religious associations of the phrase 'a lucky Hit'.

below the stature of both his prototypes. Although the New Testament authors saw Balaam as 'one who loved the wages of unrighteousness' (2 Peter 2:15) and as one who erred in being motivated by reward (Jude, v. 11),[20] the Old Testament tale has Balaam repeatedly remind Balak, king of the Moabites, that even 'if Balak would give me his house full of silver and gold, I cannot go beyond the word of the Lord my God' (Numbers 22:18; see also Numbers 22:38, 23:8, 24:13). In contrast Pope's Sir Balaam, given a house full of silver and gold, conveniently forgets there is a Providence, a Sabbath Day to keep holy, or a God to worship.

Similarly, Pope's echoes of, and allusions to, the Book of Job ask us to see the deliberate contrasts between the 'Religious, punctual, frugal' Sir Balaam, and the man who 'was perfect and upright, and one that feared God, and eschewed evil'. Mr. Wasserman notes the contrast between commercial ethics and true virtue created by Pope's formulaic opening, as well as other specific contrasts: both the Biblical and the modern Satan initiate temptation by calling down a whirlwind, but the earlier destruction is of Job's children, creating 'poverty', whereas the later destruction is of Sir Balaam's father, creating 'wealth'; Job, holding fast to his integrity, scorns his wife's evil advice to curse God and die, whereas Balaam, lacking all integrity, takes his wife's advice to 'Live like other folks'; Job, the richest of men in the east, not only constantly worships God, but carefully supervises and encourages his children's religious devotion, whereas Sir Balaam conspicuously does neither.[21]

The effectiveness of these references to the original tale lies not only in the damning contrast evoked by each individual allusion and the original context it conjures up, but also in the accumulation of echoes which reach a climax in the last line of Pope's tale and poem: 'And sad Sir Balaam curses God and dies.' The striking point is precisely that this *is* the last line of the tale and poem, whereas in the original, the corresponding words of Job's wife, 'dost thou still retain thine integrity? Curse God and die' (Job 2:9), climax only the *prelude* to the tale. Because Job retains his integrity, he does not curse God and die. There can be no such tale of the modern Job; the

[20] On Biblical commentaries to this effect, see Wasserman, pp. 45–8.
[21] Ibid., pp. 49–52.

final line proclaims him to be totally without integrity. The fact that all the allusions to the Book of Job fall well within the two introductory chapters of a forty-two-chapter book tellingly points to Sir Balaam as an unworthy nonentity. Paradoxically, this is not only the 'pseudo-conclusion' to the poem that Mr. Alpers notices, it is also, in isolation, a 'pseudo-tale'.[22] In contrast not only to Job, but also to the Man of Ross, Sir Balaam has no virtue, no religious beliefs, no moral principles with which to fill 'the space between' birth and death; he has markedly *not* 'Prov'd, by the ends of being, to have been'.

The 'Epistle to Bathurst' and the Opus Magnum

Because of its close connections with preceding themes and phrases in the poem, and because of its abrupt ending, we do not realize, until we stand away from our experience in reading it and consider the poem as a whole, that the fable of Sir Balaam is what Mr. Alpers calls a 'pseudo-conclusion'. The abruptness of the close of the *Epistle to Bathurst* might seem to be a sign of Pope's increasing pessimism about eighteenth-century society. Such a view, however, would depend upon a false premiss: that Pope not only wrote the poem late, but wrote the conclusion last. Yet the manuscript evidence presented earlier in this chapter and the evidence given in Chapter I suggest that the opposite is true: that the tale of Sir Balaam was the kernel round which the rest of the poem grew, and that this poem was the second of all eight epistles in the moral scheme to be completed and published.

One might be particularly disposed to feel that the poem is attenuated when comparing its ending with those of the other *Moral Essays*. Of all four poems, the *Epistle to Bathurst* is unique in *not* concluding with an apostrophe to its eponymous recipient. As we

[22] Alpers, 'Pope's *To Bathurst* and the Mandevillian State', p. 492. The one allusion that falls outside the first two chapters of the Book of Job obeys the same principle. The Lord's blessing of 'the latter end of Job more than his beginning' (Job 42:12) takes the form of precisely doubling his livestock (cf. Job 1:3). This appears to be the source of Balaam's double intake of puddings and double church attendance. Whereas in Job's case material prosperity *is* a token of his election, in the case of Sir Balaam material prosperity and the unimaginative use to which he puts it symbolize spiritual impoverishment.

saw, the eulogistic apostrophe was a matter of considerable uncertainty to Pope in composing the poem, in regard to both its content and its disposition; it forms part of the thirty-line section that becomes lines 219–48 of the printed poem whose patchwork growth and migration we mentioned earlier in this chapter. Were one tempted to adopt a Warburtonian stance, one might consider 'improving' the poem by shifting all or part of this apostrophe, which gathers up a number of the themes and complexities of the poem and corresponds to the conclusions of the other *Moral Essays*, to a position following the Sir Balaam passage and concluding the poem. The fact remains, however, that Pope chose to conclude the *Epistle to Bathurst* with the uncompromising negative picture provided by the modern city knight. That in doing so Pope did not mean the reader to see this as an independent and final statement is suggested by the opening of the *Epistle to Burlington*, which appears not only to begin *in medias res*, but also to pick up precisely from where the preceding epistle leaves off. We shall look more closely at the interconnections between these two poems in the next chapter.

As is apparent from the notes to the edition of 1735, Pope wanted the *Epistle to Bathurst*, like the other three moral essays, to be considered part of a unit springing from and directly related to Epistle II of *An Essay on Man*. To enforce this relation all the more clearly, he appended a note to lines 161 ff. of the *Epistle to Bathurst*, specifically sending the reader back to the earlier epistle. The note reads:

> *that the Conduct of Men with respect to Riches, can only be accounted for by the Order of* Providence, *which works* the General Good *out of* Extremes, *and brings all to its* Great End *by Perpetual Revolutions*. See Book I Epistle 2 V. 165 &c. 207.

The passages of Epistle II of *An Essay on Man* to which Pope directs us have already been quoted as having direct relevance to the first two moral essays. Once again these passages have direct relevance to the *Epistle to Bathurst*. The passages explicitly noted by Pope are those on the Ruling Passion as a heaven-sent force. The first reads:

> A mightier Pow'r the strong direction sends,
> And sev'ral Men impels to sev'ral ends.

Like varying winds, by other passions tost,
This drives them constant to a certain coast.
Let pow'r or knowledge, gold or glory please,
Or (oft more strong than all) the love of ease;
Thro' life 'tis followed, ev'n at life's expence;
The merchant's toil, the sage's indolence,
The monk's humility, the hero's pride,
All, all alike, find Reason on their side.
(*Essay*, II, 165–74)

This passage contains references to the obsessive drives, the fantasies, the focus upon ends, and the grotesquerie that pervade the *Epistle to Bathurst*. The concluding line of the *Essay* passage has direct ironic application to all these, and to all the subjects of the poem's portraits. The *Essay* passage also directly relates to the verse-paragraph of *Bathurst* that comments upon Blunt's self-serving revelation of Britain's corruption:

'All this is madness,' cries a sober sage:
But who, my friend, has reason in his rage?
'The ruling Passion, be it what it will,
'The Ruling Passion conquers Reason still.'
Less mad the wildest whimsey we can frame,
Than ev'n that Passion, if it has no Aim;
For tho' such motives Folly you may call,
The Folly's greater to have none at all. (153–60)

This statement in turn echoes through the epistle's succeeding portraits which show the consequences of accumulating or hoarding wealth for its own sake, rather than for the purpose of righteous use. It is an effective transition because it turns the poem from the 'wild whimseys' that bulk so large in the first section towards the focus upon individual uses of wealth and their individual 'rewards' in the succeeding part of the poem.

The second of the direct line references to Epistle II of *An Essay on Man* is to the following passage:

Extremes in Nature equal ends produce,
In Man they join to some mysterious use;[23]
Tho' each by turns the other's bound invade,
As, in some well-wrought picture, light and shade,

[23] This is the form in which the couplet first appears, as a marginal addition in the first of the complete *Epistle to Bathurst* MSS.

And oft so mix, the diff'rence is too nice,
Where ends the Virtue, or begins the Vice.
(*Essay*, II, 205–10)

The *Epistle to Bathurst* explicitly echoes the opening couplet in the paragraph directly following on that describing the Ruling Passion:

Hear then the truth: ' 'Tis Heav'n each Passion sends,
'And diff'rent men directs to diff'rent ends.
'Extremes in Nature equal good produce,
'Extremes in Man concur to gen'ral use.'
Ask we what makes one keep, and one bestow?
That POW'R who bids the Ocean ebb and flow,
Bids seed-time, harvest, equal course maintain,
Thro' reconcil'd extremes of drought and rain,
Builds Life on Death, on Change Duration founds,
And gives th' eternal wheels to know their rounds. (161–70)

This passage is so directly an offshoot of the *Essay on Man* couplet that it both expands and clarifies the earlier statement. Where the use of 'Extremes in Man' was originally left as 'mysterious', in the *Epistle to Bathurst* we learn that 'Extremes in Man concur to gen'ral use'. This expansion offers us the assurance that Providence exercises ultimate control and directing power over all Nature, including Man, and seems to make this distinction in order to release our attention from the public effects of the misuse of riches so that we may concentrate for the remainder of the poem upon private concerns.

If the whole thrust of the poem is towards illuminating the centrality of virtue as the essential basis for individual happiness and eternal salvation, rather than being an exploration of extreme behaviour, the *Epistle to Bathurst* ought to show a connection with Epistle IV of *An Essay on Man* just as close as, if not closer than, its connection with specific parts of Epistle II. In Chapter I we showed that external data suggested this tie, particularly the evidence of the composition process and the Index of 1734. Internal evidence appears to bear out this observation. In addition to the very important thematic emphasis upon individual virtue as the source of happiness in the use of riches, which is also a central theme of Epistle IV of *An Essay on Man*, the *Epistle to Bathurst* shares with

Epistle IV of the *Essay* a number of marked verbal and metaphoric patterns.

One such pattern is that associating madness and extremes. This association appears early in Epistle IV:

> Take Nature's path, and mad Opinion's leave,
> All states can reach it, and all heads conceive;
> Obvious her goods, in no extreme they dwell,
> There needs but thinking right, and meaning well;
> (*Essay*, IV, 29–32)

'Thinking right' and 'meaning well' are the 'ends of being' which ensure the Man of Ross his future bliss; they are the 'ends' which become buried and lost in the obsessiveness that characterizes those who accumulate riches. Epistle IV also states the theme of present content and future salvation in connection with externals in another set of lines applicable to the *Epistle to Bathurst*:

> If then to all Men Happiness was meant,
> God in Externals could not place Content.
> Fortune her gifts may variously dispose,
> And these be happy call'd, unhappy those;
> But Heav'n's just balance equal will appear,
> While those are plac'd in Hope, and these in Fear:
> Not present good or ill, the joy or curse,
> But future views of better, or of worse.
> (*Essay*, IV, 65–72)

The contrasts in this passage recur in the section of Epistle IV that specifically treats riches:

> To whom can Riches give Repute, or Trust,
> Content, or Pleasure, but the Good and Just?
> Judges and Senates have been bought for gold,
> Esteem and Love were never to be sold.
> Oh fool! to think God hates the worthy mind,
> The lover and the love of human-kind,
> Whose life is healthful, and whose conscience clear;
> Because he wants a thousand pounds a year.
> (*Essay*, IV, 185–92)

The Man of Ross fits this description of 'the worthy mind' who loves human kind perfectly; it cannot be mere coincidence that he is described in a couplet so closely comparable to the final couplet quoted above:

> Of Debts, and Taxes, Wife and Children clear,
> This man possest—five hundred pounds a year.
> (*Bathurst*, 279–80)

The last phrase here not only belongs to one of the portions of the *Epistle to Bathurst* that was settled before 30 May 1731; it also occurs amongst the snatches of conversation about the ethic scheme recorded by Spence in May 1730. In contrast, the final four lines of the *Essay* passage last quoted above do not appear in any form in the Morgan manuscript draft, although most of the lines preceding them, and over a dozen that follow them, are present as at least recognizable variants of the final printed version.[24] This finding helps to corroborate the suggestion that the direction of influence was from the *Epistle to Bathurst* toward *An Essay on Man*, Epistle IV.

The same relationship seems true of another pair of closely corresponding passages. Early in the *Epistle to Bathurst* occurs an ironic passage that has been analysed earlier:

> What Nature wants, commodious Gold bestows,
> 'Tis thus we eat the bread another sows:
> But how unequal it bestows, observe,
> 'Tis thus we riot, while who sow it, starve.
> What Nature wants (a phrase I much distrust)
> Extends to Luxury, extends to Lust:
> And if we count among the Needs of life
> Another's Toil, why not another's Wife? (21–8)

Consider this passage on the impropriety of expecting external rewards from Nature with its counterpart in the *Essay*, Epistle IV:

> 'But sometimes Virtue starves, while Vice is fed.'
> What then? Is the reward of Virtue bread?
> That, Vice may merit; 'tis the price of toil;
> The knave deserves it, when he tills the soil,

[24] The Morgan draft of Epistle IV of the *Essay* contains about 150 lines of poetry identifiable as lines of the finished version of the epistle. This portion of the draft appears to have been written during late July and early August of 1731. See Chapter I, pp. 12, 24, and references there, and see also Leonard, 'Wit and Judgment: Pope and the Art of Revision', pp. 194–237.

The knave deserves it when he tempts the main,
Where Folly fights for kings, or dives for gain.

. . . .

But grant him Riches, your demand is o'er?
'No—shall the good want Health, the good want Pow'r?'
Add Health and Pow'r, and ev'ry earthly thing;
'Why bounded Pow'r? why private? why no king?'
Nay, why external for internal giv'n?
Why is not Man a God, and Earth a Heav'n?
Who ask and reason thus, will scarce conceive
God gives enough, while he has more to give:
Immense that pow'r, immense were the demand;
Say, at what part of nature will they stand?
(*Essay*, IV, 149–54; 157–66)

What is striking about these two passages is, once again, the probability that the lines of the *Epistle to Bathurst* inspired the creation of at least the last lines of the *Essay* passage.[25] These last six lines are virtually the only lines of section IV of the epistle not present in some recognizable form in the Morgan manuscript draft, whereas the *Bathurst* lines are present in the first full draft of the poem.

The concatenation of Fortune, Charity, temperance, and health that marks the eulogy to Bathurst also informs many passages in Epistle IV of *An Essay on Man*. One such passage is that specially devoted to riches, quoted above (lines 185 ff.). Another central one occurs much earlier in Epistle IV. Only the first four lines quoted here appear in the Morgan manuscript:

Know, all the good that individuals find,
Or God and Nature meant to mere Mankind;
Reason's whole pleasure, all the joys of Sense,
Lie in three words, Health, Peace, and Competence.
But Health consists with Temperance alone,
And Peace, oh Virtue! Peace is all thy own.
The good or bad the gifts of Fortune gain,
But these less taste them, as they worse obtain.
Say, in pursuit of profit or delight,
Who risk the most, that take wrong means, or right?
Of Vice or Virtue, whether blest or curst,
Which meets contempt, or which compassion first?

[25] See Leonard, op. cit., pp. 213–15, for a transcription and analysis of this portion of the manuscript draft. She also notices the similarity between the passages in *Bathurst* and Epistle IV of the *Essay*.

Count all th' advantage prosp'rous Vice attains,
'Tis but what Virtue flies from and disdains:
And grant the bad what happiness they wou'd,
One they must want, which is, to pass for good.
(*Essay*, IV, 77–92)

The connection between this poem and Epistle IV of *An Essay on Man* is, finally, more profound than the resemblances between any sets of passages. It lies in the whole direction of the poem, which is markedly unlike that of the *Epistle to Cobham* and the *Epistle to a Lady*. These poems do genuinely show their close affinity with Epistle II of the *Essay*, concentrating on the analysis of character as an end in itself. The *Epistle to Bathurst*, however, is primarily concerned with the achievement of happiness and the mad opinions preventing such achievement—the delusion that riches *per se* (like other externals) lead to happiness, the fantasy that schemes for reforming society ought to absorb man's attention, the error in supposing any necessary correlation between wealth and virtue. In focusing upon these themes, the *Epistle to Bathurst* shares with Epistle IV a concern for the relation of virtue and reward, and might be called a study 'Of Vice or Virtue, whether blest or curst'. It thus provides a set of concrete contemporary applications for the abstractions outlined in Epistle IV of the *Essay*, fulfilling Pope's hope, expressed in the prefatory 'Design' of the 1734 edition, that later epistles would particularize and chart more fully the effects the *Essay on Man* had outlined.

The *Epistle to Bathurst* nevertheless remains somewhat unsatisfying both in relation to Epistle IV and as an independent poem. Its bleak tone belies the promise and optimism the *Essay* achieves, and its structural pattern cannot be considered entirely satisfactory. It in turn needs completion and resolution. It seems to me that these resolutions of tone and structure do occur when one reads this epistle in conjunction with the *Epistle to Burlington*, whose own structural revisions may be a response to just this sort of awareness on Pope's part of the dependency of *Bathurst* upon other epistles in the larger ethic scheme.

CHAPTER V

THE *EPISTLE TO BURLINGTON*

THE *Epistle to Burlington* was published in December 1731. Of the eight completed epistles in the ethic scheme, it was the first to be published, preceding the next, the *Epistle to Bathurst*, by thirteen months. Its early publication points to its initial independence of the ethic system, and indeed the occasion for its original publication is made explicit on the title-page of the first edition, which reads, 'An Epistle to the Right Honourable Richard Earl of Burlington. Occasion'd by his Publishing Palladio's Designs of the Baths, Arches, Theatres, etc. of Ancient Rome'. This connection has led to the suggestion that it is not an ethical poem at all, let alone one that is integral to Pope's *opus magnum* plans.[1] Yet an examination of the poem indicates that it is indeed an ethic epistle and one that, especially in revised form, makes a genuine contribution to the *opus magnum*, acting as a complement to the *Epistle to Bathurst* and developing major themes of *An Essay on Man*.

There is a surviving autograph draft of the poem dating from some time before its first publication, which, unfortunately, is not nearly so helpful in tracing the poem's evolution as are the manuscript drafts of *An Essay on Man* or the *Epistle to Bathurst*. Mr. Bateson refers to this *Burlington* autograph manuscript in two footnotes. The first refers to it as 'an early autograph draft which shows the poem as it was before the architectural compliments to Burlington had been added';[2] the second calls it 'a fragment of some 70 lines'.[3] These

[1] 'In the end, then, instead of being an "ethic epistle" on the vice of prodigality, *To Burlington* turned out to be something of a hotch-potch, one-third philosophy, one-third gardening, and one-third architectural compliment', Twickenham III: ii, p. xxvi. A number of critics have challenged Bateson's famous remark; see, for instance, Martin Price, *To the Palace of Wisdom*, pp. 155–9; G. R. Hibbard, 'The Country House Poem of the Seventeenth Century' in *Essential Articles for the Study of Alexander Pope* (2nd edition, 1968), pp. 439–75; William A. Gibson, 'Three Principles of Renaissance Architectural Theory in Pope's Epistle to Burlington', *SEL 1500–1900*, xi (1971), 487–505.

[2] Twickenham III: ii, pp. xxvi–xxvii, n. 3.

[3] Ibid., p. xxxi, n. 1.

remarks may be somewhat misleading. The Pierpont Morgan manuscript is a single foolscap leaf, which contains sixty-four lines of the poem filling both sides and concluding with a catchword which suggests that there was a second leaf, now missing, that carried on the poem from line 88. (The catchword is 'Thro'—the first word of line 89.) The extant leaf contains, in order, the following lines: 1–21, 39–50, 57–76, 169–76, 79–88. This seems at first to be a jumble of sections, with many omissions and changes from the order we are familiar with. In fact, there is a close correspondence between the ordering of the manuscript draft and that of the first (1731) edition of the poem. The missing lines 22–38, presumably those implied by Mr. Bateson's reference to 'architectural compliments', follow line 180 in the edition of 1731. One may therefore assume with some confidence that they appeared in the missing later part of the manuscript of which the Morgan leaf constitutes only the opening page. Similarly, the omission of lines 51–6 is common to both the manuscript and the first editions of the poem; these lines enter the poem only in 1735. Lines 169–76 are also not out of place, as they might appear to be, since in the editions of 1731 these lines precede the description of Timon's villa. The manuscript draft is certainly rough in many respects: some sections, notably lines 57–76, show much erasure and rewriting; and the paragraph beginning 'Behold Villarios's ten-years toil compleat' (ll. 79–88) follows the 'philosophical' section, lines 169–76, beginning 'Yet hence the Poor are cloath'd, the Hungry fed'. However, these paragraphs are clearly marked for transposition to the order they follow in the published version of 1731. (The latter is marked '(3)', the former '(1)'; the paragraph presumably to follow on the missing next page (ll. 89–98) must have similarly been marked '(2)'.) The manuscript lines of the poem have, in general, reached a state very close to that of its form at first publication, and are therefore unlikely to constitute 'an *early* manuscript draft'. One wishes Mr. Bateson's term were correct, for the manuscript would then be likely to furnish more clues to the composition of the poem.[4]

Although we are without the help of a sequence of autograph

[4] See Sylvia Leonard, 'Wit and Judgment: Pope and the Art of Revision', pp. 253–7, for detailed attention to the revisions in this draft.

drafts, we do have a finished poem in two different states. As first published in 1731, the poem bore the half-title 'Of Taste', changing in the two editions of the next month (January 1731/2) to 'Of False Taste'. As may be gathered from the remarks about the manuscript, the major difference between the first editions and the edition of 1735 is that in the earlier versions all the compliments to Burlington are gathered together in the final portion of the poem. In the early editions the lines 'You show us, Rome was glorious, not profuse, / And pompous buildings once were things of Use' begin a climactic contrast to the earlier portions of the poem which stressed the misuse of riches. The twelve lines of more general praise (lines 177–90, with the exception of the couplet ll. 179–80) had not yet entered the poem, so that originally the entire conclusion of thirty lines following the section on Timon's villa was exclusively devoted to praising Burlington for his good taste and for his potential role as public benefactor. This emphasis is in accordance with the poem's original occasion, which was to preface a second volume of Palladio's drawings. When Pope included the epistle in his ethic scheme, he made, as we shall see, a number of transpositions and additions, yet the state of the poem as first published was from the beginning so apposite to the scheme that substantial recasting proved to be unnecessary. An examination of the poem's final casting will show its relation to the ethic scheme and especially to its 'companion-piece', the *Epistle to Bathurst*. Close connections with the latter poem in particular are evident in many individual passages, in the over-all structure, and particularly in the revised conclusion of the *Epistle to Burlington*.

The 'Epistle to Burlington' as an Ethic Epistle

The opening half of the poem uses the fashionable 'hobbies' of collecting, gardening, and building as examples of valueless, immoral expenditure. These examples are part of an underlying pattern that includes careful transitions and a developing movement from the personal and private world to the world of public morality and responsibility. The *Epistle to Burlington* thus reverses the movement of the *Epistle to Bathurst*, which begins with the public and social effects of riches and moves to focus almost exclusively on the private ends (in the double sense) of those who accumulate wealth.

The opening lines of the *Epistle to Burlington* introduce the theme of vanity, presenting the attack in terms far more general than the specific ostentations associated with collecting:

> 'Tis strange, the Miser should his Cares employ,
> To gain those Riches he can ne'er enjoy:
> Is it less strange, the Prodigal should waste
> His wealth, to purchase what he ne'er can taste?
> Not for himself he sees, or hears, or eats; (1–5)

This opening immediately links this epistle intimately with the *Epistle to Bathurst*; the speaker might easily be Bathurst himself, refreshed after his fatigue (see *Bathurst*, 338) and continuing the conversation by commenting upon Sir Balaam, then switching the topic from Sir Balaam and his acquisitive colleagues to a focus upon the corresponding vanity of prodigality. Pope's note underlines the close association and transition: 'The Extremes of *Avarice* and *Profusion* being treated of in the foregoing Epistle, this takes up one particular Branch of the latter; the *Vanity*.' The theme of vanity calls forth the plays on the phrase 'Not for himself' (ll. 5, 11–12) which, together with the stress on the absence of taste, suggests the unworthiness of collecting objects and patronizing the arts not on their merits, but simply to follow fashion and impress others. Pope uses the word 'taste' four times in the early lines (4, 14, 16, 17), once as a rhyme-word, where the mockery gains additional emphasis by being paired with 'waste'. The clustering of 'taste' with varying meanings carries the theme forward until 'taste' is explicitly put aside as secondary to 'something previous ev'n to Taste—'tis Sense' (42). Another emphasis in the passage is the movement from the vanity of spending money upon collections of various kinds to the vanity of spending money upon planting and building, two of the poem's major subjects. And finally, we should notice here that underlying the reiteration of the tastelessness that must result in spending money only for the sake of impressing others is the presence of a moral law suggested by the words 'punish' and 'sermon':

See! sportive fate, to punish aukward pride,
Bids Bubo build, and sends him such a Guide:
A standing sermon, at each year's expense,
That never Coxcomb reach'd Magnificence! (19–22)

'Magnificence', a virtue Pope associates with Bathurst as well as Burlington, is a word inevitably associated with Aristotelian ethics, and its use here is an important key to understanding the unity of the poem and its relation to the *Epistle to Bathurst*. Mr. Wasserman has discussed this relationship convincingly.[5] He writes in part:

Now, just as for Pope, who would speak not only against a vice but also against its contrary, so for Aristotle virtue is the mean between two contrary vices, one of excess and the other of defect. And, like Pope, Aristotle devoted considerable attention to the vices and virtues relating to riches, insisting, as Pope does in his prologue [to *Bathurst*] that only the use of riches, not the mere possession of them, is an ethical problem: 'wealth is not the Good we are in search of, for it is only good as being useful' (I. v. 8; see also IV. i. 6).

But Aristotle distinguished between two virtues in the use of riches: liberality, which is the mean between prodigality and niggardliness; and magnificence, which is called into play when large sums are involved and which lies between vulgar display and shabbiness (II. vii. 4–6). Hence Pope has supplied us with two epistles on the 'Use of Riches', one to Bathurst on liberality, and another to Burlington on magnificence . . .

Of the two extremes of magnificence—shabbiness, or deficiency of expenditure, and vulgarity, or tasteless extravagance—Pope's poem concerns itself with the latter. Since magnificence has its proper decorum which requires that the donor be an 'artist' in taste, vulgarity consists, says Aristotle, not in 'spending too great an amount on proper objects, but [in] making a great display on the wrong occasions and in the wrong way' (IV. ii. 4).

This explication of the poem's connection with Aristotle's ethics is enlightening. It makes clear, for instance, that the change of title from 'Of Taste' and 'Of False Taste' in the first editions to 'Of the Use of Riches' in 1735 implies a broader perspective (since the former is a part of the latter category) and makes more obvious the pairing of *Burlington* with *Bathurst*, but does not constitute a change of major significance. From the Aristotelian point of view, the one is

[5] Wasserman, *Pope's 'Epistle to Bathurst'*, p. 37. I follow Mr. Wasserman in using the Loeb translation.

inextricably intertwined with the other. As Mr. Wasserman suggests, Aristotle is explicit about the identification of virtue with taste: 'The magnificent man is an artist in expenditure; he can discern what is suitable, and spend great sums with good taste' (*Nicomachean Ethics*, IV, ii, 5).

Another passage from Aristotle shows that although he distinguishes between the virtues of liberality and magnificence, they are united in the very rich:

> The magnificent man will therefore necessarily be also a liberal man. For the liberal man too will spend the right amount in the right manner; and it is in the amount and manner of his expenditure that the element 'great' in the magnificent or 'greatly splendid' man, that is to say his greatness, is shown, these being the things in which Liberality is displayed. (*Nicomachean Ethics*, IV, ii, 10.)

Pope, like Aristotle, connects the two virtues, while limiting the virtue of magnificence and its allied vice of excess—vulgarity—to the very rich. Its potential for good or evil is in the hands of a very few, but the effect of its use or abuse may affect a great number. The subject of the epistle, which may at first seem to be of restricted significance, is of great importance.

The wedding of taste and expenditure operates throughout the poem and develops an ever deeper and more embracing ethical significance from section to section. From the opening, emphasizing the private and personal—from the choice of a whore or a wife to the collection of birds or butterflies—the poem moves gradually to the theme of architecture:

> You show us, Rome was glorious, not profuse,
> And pompous buildings once were things of Use.
> Yet shall (my Lord) your just, your noble rules
> Fill half the land with Imitating Fools;
> Who random drawings from your sheets shall take,
> And of one beauty many blunders make;
> Load some vain Church with old Theatric state,
> Turn Arcs of triumph to a Garden-gate;
> Reverse your Ornaments, and hang them all
> On some patch'd dog-hole ek'd with ends of wall,
> Then clap four slices of Pilaster on't,
> That, lac'd with bits of rustic, makes a Front.

> Or call the winds thro' long Arcades to roar,
> Proud to catch cold at a Venetian door;
> Conscious they act a true Palladian part.
> And if they starve, they starve by rules of art. (23–38)

Like the opening paragraphs of the poem, this section stresses the debasement that inevitably follows upon vain, empty imitation. Timon's villa is a particularly vivid example of the 'many blunders' made by mean-souled and improperly motivated imitators; and the concluding section of the poem shows the truly magnificent man in his most appropriate sphere, as an initiator of public works. Pope has shifted the passage quoted here from the conclusion as it existed in 1731, freeing the later form of the conclusion from its negative details, and in its new place allowing the stupidity of 'Imitating Fools' to link the vain behaviour of collectors more closely with the folly of Timon's villa.

From building, the subject turns now to planting, and the relevance of gardening instructions to 'Good Sense' becomes clear through a system of correspondences. As Good Sense, the 'gift of Heav'n', is the Light of the soul of Man, so the goddess Nature, the 'Genius of the Place', is the divine centre of the natural world. By attending to one's inner light one inevitably finds oneself co-operating with Nature's light, which 'paints as you plant, and, as you work, designs' (64). This is the abstract and aesthetic counterpart to the sympathetic and philanthropic use of natural resources described in the portrait of the Man of Ross (especially lines 253–60 of the *Epistle to Bathurst*). Within the *Epistle to Burlington* it is of course the positive counterpart to the abuses of the principle described in the passage about 'Imitating Fools', who inevitably 'of one beauty many blunders make', because they cannot perceive that the buildings in Burlington's drawings have an organic unity. Rules of gardening, of building, of collecting—all ways of spending money and all ways of living well—evolve from seeing the underlying unity of man and nature. Where there is such an understanding, the creation of beauty and magnificence, the proper ends of riches, must follow:

> Still follow Sense, of ev'ry Art the Soul,
> Parts answ'ring parts shall slide into a whole,

Spontaneous beauties all around advance,
Start ev'n from Difficulty, strike from Chance;
Nature shall join you, Time shall make it grow
A work to wonder at—perhaps a STOW. (65–70)

Embedded in the discussion of gardening, these lines also speak of '*ev'ry Art*', and the reader is surely being urged to extend the application to all uses of money and acts of creation. The *Epistle to Burlington* is itself an 'application' of the tenets the poem applies to gardening:

He gains all points, who pleasingly confounds,
Surprises, varies, and conceals the Bounds. (55–6)

The note to this couplet in the Twickenham text quotes a remark of Pope's to Spence:

All the rules of gardening are reducible to three heads: the contrasts, the management of surprises, and the concealment of bounds. . . . I have expressed them all in two verses (after my manner, in a very little compass), which are in imitation of Horace's *Omne tulit punctum*.

POPE *1742*[6]

The allusion to Horace is to his advice to the young writer: 'omne tulit punctum qui miscuit utile dulci, / lectorem delectando pariterque monendo' (*De Arte Poetica*, 343–4), suggesting the equal applicability of this principle to gardening and writing. Gardening is but one expression, though a highly significant one, of an all-encompassing view of man's creative activities.

The extended section on Timon's villa develops smoothly from the passage focusing on gardening by opening with a description of the grounds of the villa. The introductory lines of this section contain revealing similarities to a passage (pointed out by Maynard Mack) in Sir William Temple's essay 'Upon the Gardens of Epicurus; or, Of Gardening, in the Year 1685'. Temple writes:

The perfectest figure of a garden I ever saw, either at home or abroad, was that . . . made by the Countess of Bedford, esteemed among the

[6] *Anecdotes*, i. 254, no. 612; Twickenham, III: ii, p. 142. In 'The Garden and Pope's Vision of Order in the "Epistle to Burlington"' (*Durham University Journal*, N.S. xxxiv [1973], 248–59), Peter E. Martin cites this note and couplet at the beginning of an essay that relates the garden metaphor to the central aesthetic and moral concerns of the poem.

greatest wits of her time, and celebrated by Doctor Donne; and with very great care, excellent contrivance, and much cost; *but greater sums may be thrown away without effect or honour, if there want sense in proportion to money, or if nature be not followed; which I take to be the great rule in this, and perhaps in every thing else, as far as the conduct not only of our lives, but governments.*[7]

Pope's introductory lines read:

> At Timon's Villa let us pass a day,
> Where all cry out, 'What sums are thrown away!'
> So proud, so grand, of that stupendous air,
> Soft and Agreeable come never there. (99–102)

The echo of Temple's 'but greater sums may be thrown away without effect or honour' in Pope's 'What sums are thrown away!' is, like the Horatian echo in the gardening couplet, an example of Pope's 'manner, in a very little compass' of suggesting vast moral implications in a phrase. Timon's estate is the opposite of the Countess of Bedford's; it is an object of expenditure 'without effect or honour' and without taste, and is a symbol of the same defects in the English aristocracy at large.

The guided tour through Timon's estate corresponds to the climactic 'portraits' of the other moral essays. Indeed, Mr. Bateson refers to the 'character of Lord Timon'. Although it differs from the portraits in other epistles by describing less the person who uses riches than the uses to which the riches are put, the figure of Timon has aroused considerable interest. Most scholars have confined themselves to arguing for or against its specific application to James Bridges, Duke of Chandos, and his country-house, Cannons.[8] More recent investigations indicate some striking connections between Pope's portrait and Robert Walpole and his Norfolk estate, Houghton.[9] Yet one should not forget that Pope's Timon has a directly

[7] 'Upon the Gardens of Epicurus' in *Five Miscellaneous Essays by Sir William Temple*, ed. Samuel Holt Monk (Ann Arbor: University of Michigan Press, 1963), pp. 27–8 (italics mine). This reference comes from Mack, *The Garden and the City*, pp. 85–6.

[8] See, for instance, Twickenham, III: ii, pp. xxvi–xxxiii, 170–4, *et passim*, and George Sherburn, ' "Timon's Villa" and Cannons', *Huntington Library Quarterly* viii (1935), 131–52.

[9] Kathleen Mahaffey, 'Timon's Villa: Walpole's Houghton', *Texas Studies in Literature and Language* ix (1967), 193–222; Mack, *The Garden and the City*, especially Appendix F, pp. 272–8. A weakness in this identification is that although Mack

relevant literary lineage descending from Plutarch through Lucian and Shakespeare, and Pope's contemporaries would immediately have associated the figure with this tradition because of the continuous popularity of Shakespeare's play in Shadwell's adaptation throughout the first half of the eighteenth century.[10] The emphasis on misanthropy as the central characteristic of the traditional Timon goes hand in hand with emphasis upon the theme of indiscriminate spending. Dr. Johnson's remarks on the moral import of *Timon of Athens* make no explicit reference to misanthropy at all, saying only,

> The play of *Timon* is a domestick tragedy, and therefore strongly fastens on the attention of the reader. In the plan there is not much art, but the incidents are natural, and the characters various and exact. The catastrophe affords a very powerful warning against that ostentatious liberality, which scatters bounty, but confers no benefits, and buys flattery, but not friendship.[11]

Modern commentators have acknowledged the association of vanity and prodigality as Pope's rationale for choosing the name Timon. Mr. Bateson writes, 'Pope seems to have intended the name Timon to connote ostentatious magnificence rather than misanthropy. Both qualities were equally prominent in Shakespeare's Timon.'[12] And Kathleen Mahaffey, showing the applicability of Pope's Timon to Walpole, writes:

> The Timon of Pope's poem is not Timon the misanthrope, but Timon the prodigal tyrant, before his fall, hosting lavish entertainments attended by crowds of sycophants. He lacks the humanity and amiability of Shakespeare's prodigal, whose extravagance springs from a native gener-

considers some inconclusive evidence, neither he nor Mahaffey has discovered any association of the name 'Timon' with Walpole independent of the Pope portrait or any contemporary observer who identifies Houghton with Timon's villa.

[10] Shadwell's *Timon of Athens, the Man-Hater* was missing from the boards in only nine seasons between 1701 and 1745. See J. C. Maxwell, ed., *The Life of Timon of Athens* (Cambridge: Cambridge University Press, 1957), pp. xliii–xlvii.

[11] *Johnson on Shakespeare*, ed. Arthur Sherbo (New Haven & London: Yale University Press, 1968), p. 745. Modern commentators also interpret Shakespeare's Timon in terms that apply equally well to Pope's Timon. See, for instance, Robert C. Elliott, *The Power of Satire* (Princeton: Princeton University Press, 1960), pp. 141–67; Geoffrey Bullough, *Narrative and Dramatic Sources of Shakespeare* (London: Routledge and Kegan Paul, 1966), vi. 248 (where Bullough connects Timon with Aristotle's 'liberal' man); J. C. Maxwell, op. cit., pp. xxx–xxxiv.

[12] Twickenham III:ii, p. 173.

osity. Pride motivates the prodigality of Pope's Timon, magnifying the folly into a vice.[13]

The description of Timon's villa includes and elaborates upon all the categories of wealthy expenditure described in the first section of the poem, and in so doing, develops the moral implications of the misuse of riches even more deeply. One device whereby the moral implications are enforced is one we have noticed in connection with the *Epistle to Bathurst*: the grotesque inversion of man and nature. The section on Timon's villa provides a striking contrast to the preceding lines emphasizing the proportion, harmony, unity, and beauty that result from man and nature functioning in true co-operation. The estate is a vivid demonstration of the ludicrous and grotesque results of man's misguided wrenching of nature: nature becomes ridiculous; man becomes dehumanized.

The essence of Timon's villa is its utter lack of care for the humans who occupy and use it. This effect is a direct consequence of its owner's ignoble motives. It shows no regard to function and blatantly reveals Timon's ostentatious expenditure of wealth. Aristotle's description of the vulgar man corresponds closely to the introductory lines on Timon's villa:

> Such then is the character of the magnificent man. His counterpart on the side of excess, the vulgar man, exceeds, as has been said, by spending beyond what is right. He spends a great deal and makes a tasteless display on unimportant occasions: for instance, he gives a dinner to his club on the scale of a wedding banquet, and when equipping a chorus at the comedies he brings it on in purple at its first entrance, as is done at Megara. Moreover, he does all this not from a noble motive but to show off his wealth, and with the idea that this sort of thing makes people admire him; and he spends little where he ought to spend much and much where he ought to spend little. (*Nicomachean Ethics*, IV, ii, 20.)

Pope follows Aristotle in making the point here, as well as earlier in the poem, that the man who seeks only to impress others will not achieve his end. The disproportionate expenditure of money for

[13] Mahaffey, 'Timon's Villa: Walpole's Houghton', p. 196. Concentrating on the references to pride in the description of Timon's villa, Robert Folkenflik in 'Pope's Timon: A Possible Allusion to his Literary Identity' (*Études Anglaises*, xxxviii [1975], 72–4) suggests that Timon is also allusively Milton's Mulciber, the architect of Hell.

such ends and the ignobility that underlies such expenditure are so obvious and vulgar that no one can possibly be deceived into thinking them other than waste.

Timon's Folly re-echoes, particularizes, and adds metaphorical dimensions to many of the allusions in the preceding passage contrasting Burlington's accomplishments with those of 'Imitating Fools'. Just as these 'call the winds thro' long Arcades to roar, / Proud to catch cold at a Venetian door' (35–6), so 'Greatness, with Timon, dwells in such a draught / As brings all Brobdignag before your thought' (103–4). He becomes 'a puny insect, shiv'ring at a breeze!' (108), laughable in having ignored common sense to follow 'rules' in creating 'a Lake behind' which only 'Improves the keenness of the Northern wind' (111–12). Timon's efforts to achieve the grandiose and magnificent serve only to demean and diminish him. He becomes merely part of the 'huge heaps of littleness' he has created. Even before we reach the feast in the dining-room, the climax of the tour of the Villa, we have been bombarded by numerous details and numerous devices of irony and description, which together make a powerful indictment of Timon as one who has used his riches not to follow Nature or 'consult the Genius of the Place' or consider others, but who, indoors and out, has expended his wealth on artifice and on the exteriors of things, and who, moreover, takes special pride in displaying these superficialities, unaware of their hollowness and sham. Furthermore Timon embodies in one giant symbol the tasteless and extravagant expenditure that was typical of the many characters alluded to in the first hundred lines of the poem.

The accumulation of concrete detail and moral implications makes the caricature of eighteenth-century country house life one of immense power. In addition to its intrinsic power and its impact as the culminating example of false taste in the poem, the portrait gains effectiveness from its place in architectural and poetic tradition. William A. Gibson has recently shown the way in which the poem's positive tenets follow Palladian architectural theory in wedding beauty and use. And in his classic study of country-house poetry, G. R. Hibbard shows how Timon's villa is the obverse of the moral virtues lauded in *To Penshurst*. Timon's villa demonstrably ignores such fundamental virtues as the human scale of the building, the 'reciprocal interplay of man and nature in the creation of the good life', and 'the deep concern with the social function of the great house in the life of the community'.[14] As a negative example of all these features, Timon's villa really belongs to the 'decay-of-hospitality' tradition, hints of which appear in the shorter reference to the country estate of the Cottas in the *Epistle to Bathurst*. In the conclusion to the *Epistle to Burlington*, Pope has introduced a more complicated and comprehensive view:

> Yet hence the Poor are cloath'd, the Hungry fed;
> Health to himself, and to his Infants bread
> The Lab'rer bears: What his hard Heart denies,
> His charitable Vanity supplies.
> Another age shall see the golden Ear
> Imbrown the Slope, and nod on the Parterre,
> Deep Harvests bury all his pride has plann'd,
> And laughing Ceres re-assume the land. (169–76)

Pope calls this 'The *Moral* of the whole, where PROVIDENCE is justified in giving Wealth to those who squander it in this manner. A bad Taste employs more hands and diffuses Expence more than a good one' (note to 169 ff.), referring the reader back to the *Epistle to Bathurst*, verse 161, and its origin in the *Essay on Man*, Epistle II.

In the 1731 version of the poem, these lines had immediately preceded the Timon section, where, aided by the consistent change in possessive pronouns ('*thy* hard Heart', '*Thy* charitable Vanity', etc.), they apply to all those, like Villario and the son of Sabinus, who do not follow 'Good Sense' or the 'Genius of the Place' in devising their landscape projects. In the 1735 placement, the lines apply particularly to Timon and his vanity, making sharper the contrast between a single egregious example of the abdication of social responsibilities and the proper use of riches by the virtuous Bathurst and Burlington.

As originally conceived, the poem had only two verse-paragraphs following the Timon passage, that on the Imitating Fools and the

[14] 'The Country House Poem of the Seventeenth Century', p. 440; see also Mack, *The Garden and the City*, pp. 91–100.

paragraph which remains the concluding one in 1735. These appear to have been composed as a unit, as the original opening lines of each suggest:

> In you, my *Lord*, Taste sanctifies Expence,
> For Splendor borrows all her rays from Sense,
> You show us, Rome was glorious, not profuse,
> And pompous buildings once were things of Use.
> Just as they are, yet shall your noble rules
> Fill half the land with Imitating Fools; . . .
> Yet thou proceed; be fallen Arts thy care,
> Erect new wonders, and the old repair . . .

This 1731 conclusion creates an impression quite different from the 1735 version. In the earlier version, the emphasis is more emphatically upon the contrast between the wrong and right use of the architectural tradition, focusing upon the follies of others as a foil by which to enhance the compliment to Burlington.

When Pope revised the poem for the 1735 edition of the Moral Essays as a group, the conclusion of the poem developed a different character. Instead of narrowing in focus to a quite exclusive concern with architectural follies and virtuous possibilities, it expands so as to end on a much more inclusive, positive, optimistic note. The difference is achieved by changes in structure and the addition of a number of new lines. As we have noted, in the 1735 version the original penultimate paragraph (minus its opening couplet, which, slightly but significantly revised, remains as lines 179–80) appears in a position much earlier in the poem, where it anticipates and helps prepare for the Timon section. In a reverse direction, the eight-line passage which in 1731 had immediately preceded Timon's villa shifts in the 1735 version to follow it. This transposition alone causes it to apply not simply to the art of landscape, as it had done in the earlier position, but also to building, entertaining, and providing employment, characteristics that are illustrated in the Timon passage. In doing so it more fully expresses the moral emphasized by Pope's accompanying note, and also provides an important transition to the conclusion of the poem. At this stage, the poem has moved from the realm of the private and personal through a consideration of the individual in relation to nature, and now considers the individual and his public responsibilities. The final section of the poem reinforces the self-evident grotesqueness of Timon's misuse of riches by contrasting with it the right use of riches belonging to the virtue of magnificence.

The very rich have a special responsibility. Aristotle makes clear the idea that whereas the virtue of magnificence can be a characteristic of private expenditure, its real sphere is the public realm. He writes:

Now there are some forms of expenditure definitely entitled honourable, for instance expenditure on the service of the gods—votive offerings, public buildings, sacrifices—and the offices of religion generally; and those public benefactions which are favourite objects of ambition, for instance the duty, as it is esteemed in certain states, of equipping a chorus splendidly or fitting out a ship of war, or even of giving a banquet to the public. . . . But great public benefactions are suitable for those who have adequate resources derived from their own exertions or from their ancestors or connexions, and for the high-born and famous and the like, since birth, fame, and so on all have an element of greatness and distinction. The magnificent man therefore is especially of this sort, and *Magnificence mostly finds an outlet in these public benefactions, as we have said, since these are the greatest forms of expenditure and the ones most honoured.* But Magnificence is also shown on those private occasions for expenditure which only happen once, for instance, a wedding or the like, and which arouse the interest of the general public, or of the people of position; and also in welcoming foreign guests and in celebrating their departure, and in the complimentary interchange of presents; *for the magnificent man does not spend money on himself but on public objects*, and his gifts have some resemblance to votive offerings. It is also characteristic of the magnificent man to furnish his house in a manner suitable to his wealth, since a fine house is a sort of distinction; and to prefer spending on permanent objects, because these are the most noble. (*Nicomachean Ethics*, IV, ii, 11–16o; my italics.)[15]

Although Providence will operate despite the vanity and ill-use of riches, the man who sees and shares this responsibility is properly making 'votive offerings'. The Aristotelian equation of public benefactions and religious performance has a parallel in Pope's use of diction with clear religious associations. The use of 'grace' and

[15] Wasserman considers the categories of Magnificence (see *Pope's 'Epistle to Bathurst'*, p. 38), but does not make special reference to the public sphere as more important than the private.

'sanctifies' intensifies the passage naming and praising Bathurst and Burlington:

> Who then shall grace, or who improve the Soil?
> Who plants like BATHURST, or who builds like BOYLE.
> 'Tis Use alone that sanctifies Expence,
> And Splendor borrows all her rays from Sense. (177–80)

This passage is a compound of a new couplet and a revised one. Like the new ten-line passage following it, it embeds the practice of virtue, with all its traditional classical and religious associations, in the life of the wealthy landed nobility:

> His Father's Acres who enjoys in peace,
> Or makes his Neighbours glad, if he encrease;
> Whose chearful Tenants bless their yearly toil,
> Yet to the Lord owe more than to the soil;
> Whose ample Lawns are not asham'd to feed
> The milky heifer and deserving steed;
> Whose rising Forests, not for pride or show,
> But future Buildings, future Navies grow;
> Let his plantations stretch from down to down,
> First shade a Country, and then raise a Town. (181–90)

This important passage, added to the poem in 1735, envisages a new generation creating widespread peace and prosperity through the proper use of riches. The vision embodied in this verse-paragraph follows the order of ever-widening circles of responsibility and benefaction that the poem as a whole has followed. Its parallel phrases describe the personal use of inherited wealth, then the responsibility to tenants, next the fruitful use of nature, and finally the use of the products of a well-tended estate in the service of the country at large.

The same sense of promise informs the concluding tribute to Burlington:

> You too proceed! make falling Arts your care,
> Erect new wonders, and the old repair,
> Jones and Palladio to themselves restore,
> And be whate'er Vitruvius was before:
> Till Kings call forth th' Idea's of your mind,
> Proud to accomplish what such hands design'd,
> Bid Harbours open, public Ways extend,
> Bid Temples, worthier of the God, ascend;

Bid the broad Arch the dang'rous Flood contain,
The Mole projected break the roaring Main;
Back to his bounds their subject Sea command,
And roll obedient Rivers thro' the Land;
These Honours, Peace to happy Britain brings,
These are Imperial Works, and worthy Kings.

Thomas R. Edwards, Jr. writes that 'This vision of useful art is perhaps the most "Augustan" passage Pope ever wrote. Our full appreciation of what it positively asserts depends on our recollection of the alternatives, the kinds of fruitless activity described in the other *Moral Essays*.'[16] Such alternatives are, of course, to be found witihin the *Epistle to Burlington* itself, as well as the other Moral Essays.

The power of the vision, furthermore, comes not only from 'our recollection of the alternatives', but also from the suggestiveness of the diction in the passage. As Mr. Wasserman and Mr. Bateson note,[17] there are suggestions of the return of the Golden Age. Mr. Bateson notes that the whole passage is full of echoes of Dryden's version of the sixth book of the *Aeneid*, and particularly singles out 'Bid Temples, worthier of the God, ascend' (198), and the final line 'These are Imperial Works, and worthy Kings', the last a reminiscence of Dryden's 'These are Imperial Arts, and worthy thee', referring to Rome's special mission in the world as distinct from the special gifts of Greece. We may also notice the emphasis on 'restoration' in the earlier portion of the paragraph, and the focus upon the extension of peace and prosperity on a profound scale, characteristics of the Golden Age in general and of Dryden's translation of the Augustan vision in particular.[18]

[16] *This Dark Estate*, p. 71.

[17] Wasserman, op. cit., p. 38; Twickenham III: ii, p. 156.

[18] See, e.g., Dryden's *Aeneid* vi. 1055, 1079–81, 1105–8, 1118. During the time Pope was composing the *Epistle to Burlington*, he playfully used the same elevated language in a letter of 11 September 1730 chastising Lord Bathurst for neglecting him: 'I know the succeeding Reign, as it was a Time of greater Actions & Designs, and a Busier Scene, both at home and abroad, did much engross your Lordships Thoughts & hours, & hurryd you (like all other true Patriots) to the public paths of Glory from the private one of Friendship, Amusement & Social Life. I also am sensible, that many Great & Noble Works, worthy a large Mind & Fortune, have employd your cares & time; such as Enclosing a Province with Walls of Stone, planting a whole Country with Clumps of Firs, digging Wells . . . , erecting Palaces, raising Mounts, undermining High ways, & making Communications by Bridges.' (*Correspondence*, iii. 130.)

The conclusion of the *Epistle to Burlington* has brought us far from the opening, whose jibes at vain collectors emphasized the wholly private and personal, through the countryside where gardens and estates are conspicuous expenditures and imply public responsibilities, to the national and imperial spheres in which art, taste, good sense, and virtue have their most far-reaching import. Far from being a jumble, the poem, as we have seen from investigating its structural pattern, its diction and selection of detail, and its traditional associations, is a unified whole with an important moral theme.

The final vision is expressed as a hope, rather than a statement. Burlington is bidden to proceed with his plans 'Till Kings call forth th' Idea's of your mind'. Nevertheless it is, as Mr. Edwards calls it, 'an intellectual possibility'. In this respect, it differs from the dark pessimism of the *Epistle to Bathurst* where Cotta's son is considered a fool for loving the House of Hanover and his country, and where the King is associated with the Devil in unfeelingly dividing Sir Balaam's wealth.

'*Bathurst*', '*Burlington*', *and the* '*Opus Magnum*'

The closing portion of the *Epistle to Burlington* has distinct and powerful reminders of the *Epistle to Bathurst.* The visionary quality of the final two verse-paragraphs relates to the *Epistle to Bathurst* in several ways. First, the optimistic visions at the end of *Burlington* balance the pessimistic visions with which *Bathurst* begins. The 'gen'ral Flood' of corruption is recalled in the 'dang'rous Flood' that projects like Burlington's will contain. The kings of the future will be worthier and more responsive than the current insensitive avaricious king. In this immediate corrupt age Cotta's son may be a zealous fool for giving lands, timber, and wool to his country, but future generations are enjoined to do the same for 'future Buildings, future Navies'. If the Man of Ross can with modest means divert waters, create walks, and teach the 'heav'n-directed spire to rise', surely Burlington may 'Bid Harbors open, public Ways extend, / Bid Temples, worthier of the God, ascend'. The conclusion of *Burlington* expresses a profound hope that the wealthy landowners will co-operate with Providence in assuring a blissful resolution of the violent oscillations portrayed in *Bathurst*. The two poems together forcefully describe a *concordia discors*. In doing so, the two may be seen as completing the theme Pope had apparently originally planned to create in three poems. Spence's note on Pope's plans, quoted in Chapter I, may be repeated here:

Mr. Pope's poem grows on his hands. The first four or five epistles will be on the general principles, or of 'The Nature of Man', and the rest will be on moderation, or 'The Use of Things'. In the latter part, each class may take up three epistles: one, for instance, against avarice, another against prodigality, and the third on the moderate use of riches; and so of the rest.[19]

In November 1730, the date of this entry, Pope was engaged in writing the *Essay on Man*, the *Epistle to Bathurst*, and the *Epistle to Burlington*. Even earlier in the year (May 1730), Spence reports Pope's remarks to much the same effect:

We should not speak against one large vice without speaking against its contrary. As to the general design of Providence, the two extremes of a vice serve like two opposite biases to keep up the balance of things. Avarice lays up (what would be hurtful); Prodigality scatters abroad (what may be useful in other hands). The middle [is] the point for virtue.[20]

Other evidence also contributes to the reading of the poems as a closely linked pair of companion pieces, despite their different origins. The *Epistle to Bathurst*, although about both avarice and prodigality, concentrates upon the greedy and miserly accumulation of wealth, whereas the *Epistle to Burlington* offsets that emphasis by its own stress upon the prodigal expenditure of wealth. This set of complementary characteristics finds a highly significant basis in the *Nicomachean Ethics*. Aristotle writes,

This [i.e. profligacy] then is what the prodigal comes to if he is not brought under discipline; but if he is taken in hand, he may attain the due mean and the right scale of liberality. Meanness on the contrary is incurable; for we see that it can be caused by old age or any form of weakness. Also it is more ingrained in man's nature than Prodigality; the mass of mankind are avaricious rather than openhanded. Moreover Meanness is a far-reaching vice, and one of varied aspect: it appears to

[19] *Anecdotes*, i. 131, no. 299.

[20] Ibid. i. 130–1, no. 297.

take several shapes. . . . Meanness is naturally spoken of as the opposite of Liberality; for not only is it a greater evil than prodigality, but also men more often err on the side of Meanness than on that of Prodigality as we defined it. (IV, i, 36–8, 44)

The *Epistle to Bathurst* and the *Epistle to Burlington* together constitute a powerful development of these observations, which in turn provide a capsule commentary upon the appropriateness of the optimism and narrower range of texture and *exempla* in the *Epistle to Burlington* in relation to the deep pessimism, complexity, and numerous *exempla* in the *Epistle to Bathurst.*

An awareness of the close connection between the two epistles also helps us to see a possible reason for the seeming abruptness with which the *Epistle to Bathurst* closes. Mr. Alpers, who was quoted in the last chapter, calls the Sir Balaam tale a 'pseudo-conclusion' and for this reason finds the poem faulty. But if we see that the poem was planned to appear ultimately as part of a larger whole, then a totally final resolution to the *Epistle to Bathurst* is not only unnecessary, but perhaps even undesirable. The *Epistle to Burlington*, as we noticed, opens as if a conversation upon the subject of the *Epistle to Bathurst* were in process. The two poems thus constitute one continuous conversation which opens and closes with a focus on the social and national implications of the use of riches and in the middle—in the last portion of the *Epistle to Bathurst* and the first part of the *Epistle to Burlington*—casts a scathing eye on the effects of the use of riches upon the individual. If so close a connection is valid, then the ending of the *Epistle to Bathurst* is deliberately, not erroneously, a 'pseudo-conclusion' and in this sense corresponds to the conclusions of each of the first two epistles of *An Essay on Man*, whose overt and scathing pessimism was illusory, and which were not independent statements, but signs of stages arrived at on the way to the optimistic conclusion of Epistle IV. In like manner, the uncompromising pessimism of the end of the *Epistle to Bathurst* may be seen as an incomplete and partial statement awaiting a larger perspective. Lord Bathurst, praised not at the conclusion of the earlier poem but in an earlier, ambiguous passage, receives clear and emphatic praise in the new couplet added to the 1735 version of the *Epistle to Burlington*. This new couplet had not of course yet appeared in print when Pope told Swift that he would 'see pretty soon, that the letter to Lord Bathurst is a part of [the whole scheme of my present Work]' and that Swift would 'find a plain connexion between them, if you read them in the order just contrary to that they were publish'd in'.[21] The only poems published at that time were the epistles to Burlington and to Bathurst, although the first three epistles of the *Essay on Man* were to follow the same spring. Clearly the *Epistle to Burlington* was very early envisaged as belonging to the scheme, and the revisions of 1735 become only a more explicit rendering of a union which Pope appears to have borne in mind during the composition of the *Epistle to Bathurst*.

The relation of the *Epistle to Burlington* (like that of the *Epistle to Bathurst*) with Epistle II of *An Essay on Man* appears to be subordinate to its relation with Epistle IV of the *Essay*, despite Pope's efforts to suggest the contrary in the notes and format of the 1735 edition. There are of course significant connections with Epistle II, particularly in the ways in which both the *Epistle to Bathurst* and the *Epistle to Burlington* show that money exacerbates the workings of the passions and fosters the illusions that provide individuals with 'strange comforts'. A major focus of the *Epistle to Burlington* is upon the principle enunciated at the end of Epistle II of the *Essay*:

> Each individual seeks a sev'ral goal;
> But HEAV'N's great view is One, and that the Whole:
> That counter-works each folly and caprice;
> That disappoints th' effect of ev'ry vice;
>
> . . . . . .
>
> That Virtue's ends from Vanity can raise,
> Which seeks no int'rest, no reward but praise;
> And build on wants, and on defects of mind,
> The joy, the peace, the glory of Mankind.
>
> (*Essay*, II, 237–40, 245–8)

However, Epistle II of the *Essay* is at this point moving from a concentration upon Man '*as an Individual*' to a consideration of man as a social being, and the anecdotes of 1730 suggest that the poems 'Of

[21] *Correspondence*, iii. 348. See also Chapter I, p. 7 and n. 2. The couplet (lines 177–8) apparently derives from a tentative marginal jotting in the first complete *Epistle to Bathurst* MS. See Wasserman, pp. 90–1.

the Use of Riches' (the final entry in the Index of 1734 for the work 'Of the Use of Things') were conceived from the beginning as relating to the *Essay*'s final conclusions. In May 1730 Pope significantly connects the 'gardening poem' in particular with 'prodigality', 'wrong tastes', and his 'prose collections on the happiness of contentment'.[22] It is possible that in 1730 Pope did not yet see the 'prose collections on the happiness of contentment' as one of the 'four or five epistles . . . on the general principles, or of "The Nature of Man" ', yet there is every reason to see both the *Epistle to Bathurst* and the *Epistle to Burlington* as a pair expressing the rewards and happiness associated with the right use of riches and the virtues of benevolence, the themes of the *Essay*, Epistle IV. The richly optimistic promise of the future that concludes the *Epistle to Burlington* is also the tone of Epistle IV's promise of bliss in virtuous living. The order of composition suggests that the *Epistle to Burlington*, like the *Epistle to Bathurst*, was itself partly responsible for the themes, shape, and tone of the *Essay on Man*, another sign of the early and close interrelation of parts of the moral scheme before 1735.

In his 'Introductory Notice to the Moral Essays and Satires', W. J. Courthope writes as follows:

The Moral Essays themselves present no indications of being integral parts of a single design. They are indeed superficially connected by the appearance in each of the theory of the Ruling Passion, but, even as they stand in the text, they proceed by no such gradations of reasoning as we find (for instance) in a didactic poem like the 'De Rerum Natura'. Besides the order in which they were originally published precludes the notion that they were produced by a sustained effort of philosophic thought.[23]

Courthope is misled by Warburton's later outline of the scheme into attributing to Pope a claim for 'a sustained effort of philosophic thought' and a clear conception and straightforward execution of the *opus magnum* that Pope did not claim for himself. On the contrary, Pope makes Courthope's own distinction between the 'didactic poem like the "De Rerum Natura" ' and the more casual and 'less

[22] See Chapter I, pp. 11–12, and references there.

[23] *Works of Alexander Pope*, ed. Whitwell Elwin and William John Courthope (London, 1881), iii. 46.

dry' charts that followed upon it. Nor does 'follow' imply that they were composed in logical order after the completion of the *Essay*, only that they are printed as a group following the *Essay*. 'The order in which they were originally published' and even more significantly the order in which they were conceived and composed, suggests the complexity of the interaction between all the epistles in the scheme. The notes and arrangement of the 1735 edition have unfortunately perpetuated the notion that the only connection is the after-the-fact and arbitrary one of being 'superficially connected by the appearance in each of the Ruling Passion'.

The eight epistles so far examined constitute the only completed portions of Pope's *opus magnum*. As we shall see, Pope continued to speak of the plan, although it waned for a time after 1735 and revived again only after Pope and Warburton met in 1740. Many suggestions about the interrelation of the eight epistles have been presented in the foregoing chapters, and the reader may not find all of them equally convincing. Certainly persuasive, however, is the sheer amount of evidence, however fragmentary, amorphous, and confusing, attesting to Pope's wholehearted concern with the scheme, beginning in 1729 and continuing through the planning and composition of the epistles he collected and published together in 1735 as Books I and II of the Ethic Epistles.

In the process of composing these, Pope had begun another, related project, the 'Imitations of Horace'. Although he speaks of these rarely in his letters, when he does so he consistently distinguishes them from those epistles that are within his 'system'.[24] In accordance with Pope's own division of these poems into two distinct categories, there are a number of observable differences between the two. Most conspicuously, the poems that were eventually collected and published as the 'Imitations of Horace' almost all have specific Horatian antecedents, adversaries who play an active role in the lively dialogue form, a more obvious focus upon the contemporary political or literary scene, and a much more central concern with the role of the poet and a clear sense of the poet in *propria persona*. One may with ease make exceptions of individual poems or parts of poems in either category for which this group of distinctions does not

[24] See Chapter I, pp. 13–15, and references there.

hold true, and one can certainly find many of the serious philosophical and moral concerns, themes, and allusions we have studied in the preceding chapters also present in the 'Imitations', but the general distinction is, I hope, both useful and valid. It derives in part from the fact that many of Pope's 'Imitations' are of Horace's satires rather than his epistles, and modern students of Horace distinguish Horace's own epistles from his satires in a way that parallels this distinction between Pope's epistles within the system and the Horatian poems he was writing concurrently. E. P. Morris, for instance, referring to Epistles II, VI, and XVI of Horace's Book I, writes, 'What is new here is the tone. The Satire treats these desires as follies, to be ridiculed; the Epistle treats them almost as sins—if this is not too modern a word—to be preached against.'[25] And Niall Rudd remarks that in the epistles of Horace, 'the moralist absorbs the satirist'.[26] There is, to be sure, no absolute distinction to be made between the two groups of Horatian adaptations—at least not in this place. What for Pope appears to have begun as a kind of *jeu d'esprit* to provide relaxation from the greater moral seriousness demanded by the *opus magnum* project came in turn to possess its own moral earnestness and intensity.

Although the poems we have studied at length are nowadays often read with great pleasure as wholly independent units—as if they were, in fact, separate Horatian adaptations—nevertheless it has, I hope, proved rewarding to take Pope at his own word and consider the ways in which a reading of the poems within the system profits from an understanding of their interdependence and their accordance with the demands of the plans for the larger ethical project of which they were intended to form only a part.

[25] 'The Form of the Epistle in Horace', Yale Classical Studies ii (1931), 88.

[26] *The Satires of Horace* (Cambridge, 1966), pp. 157–8. See also p. 172. Comparable comments may also be found in Edmond Courbaud, *Horace, sa vie et sa pensée à l'époque des Épîtres* (Paris, 1914), pp. 11, 169; A. Y. Campbell, *Horace: A New Interpretation* (London, 1924), pp. 257–8; Edouard Fraenkel, *Horace* (Oxford, 1957), p. 309. This is a distinction Bateson obscures when he speaks of the moral essays as 'essentially four Horatian satires' (Twickenham, III:ii, p. xx).

CHAPTER VI

POPE'S ETHIC SCHEME AFTER 1735

IN March 1743 Pope told Spence,

> What was first designed for an Epistle on Education as part of my Essay scheme is now inserted in my fourth *Dunciad*, as the subject for two other epistles there—those on civil and ecclesiastical government—will be treated more at large in my *Brutus*.[1]

This anecdote identifies the two projects that Pope clearly associated with his *opus magnum* scheme other than *An Essay on Man* and the four *Moral Essays*. Pope's plans for an epic on Brutus form the basis for Chapter VII; this chapter explores the implications of the first part of the anecdote: the plans for an epistle or epistles on Education, the origins of the fourth or 'new' *Dunciad*, and the relation of the *New Dunciad* to *An Essay on Man*. Pope's remark, however, is a retrospective one, and a proper exploration of it requires, at least initially, a resumption of the chronological arrangement employed in Chapter I. Accordingly, the first section below picks up where Chapter I left off, and then chronicles and analyses in sequence all Pope's allusions to the *opus magnum* from 1736 to 1739 in correspondence and in the revised notes and format of printed editions of the 'ethic epistles' between these dates. The second section examines William Warburton's role in rekindling Pope's interest in the ethic scheme and in completing his last new poem, the *New Dunciad*. This section begins with Warburton's meeting with Pope in 1740 but then turns to evidence suggesting that some of the material for the *New Dunciad* originates as far back as 1728. The final section of this chapter considers some of the thematic links and image patterns connecting the *New Dunciad* and *An Essay on Man*.

[1] *Anecdotes*, i. 151, no. 337.

Pope's Ethic Scheme in Decline, 1736–9

Griffith calls 1735 Pope's '*annus mirabilis*'.[2] In that year, Pope published sixty-eight books, either new works or reprints; prominent among these were the various editions of his collected *Works*, Volume II, containing Books I and II of the ethic epistles. No further portions of the ethic work were to be completed, and even before 1735 there are signs that the 'system' is on the wane. In 1734 Pope withdrew from the folio edition of *An Essay on Man* the index that outlined the project in more ample terms than he apparently wished to commit himself to filling; his correspondence also contains a number of references suggesting disenchantment with continuing the project. They suggest further that the disenchantment resulted not from a simple unwillingness to write more epistles but from having tried to do so without achieving satisfactory results. In April 1734, in a letter to Swift quoted in Chapter I, Bolingbroke had said that the *Essay on Man* was finished and that 'the others will soon follow for many of them are writ or crayoned out'. This must be a pointer to parts of the system beyond the *Moral Essays* because, of the four, only the *Epistle to a Lady* had not been printed. In September 1734 Pope asked a significant favour of Swift: 'I have only one piece of mercy to beg of you; do not laugh at my gravity, but permit me to wear the beard of a philosopher, till I pull it off, and make a jest of it myself.'[3] This remark, too, implies that Pope was still planning more epistles for the 'system'. Yet by December 1734, in another letter to Swift, Pope's tone had changed:

> I am almost at the end of my Morals, as I've been, long ago, of my Wit; my system is a short one, and my circle narrow. Imagination has no limits, and that is a sphere in which you may move on to eternity; but where one is confined to Truth (or to speak more like a human creature, to the appearances of Truth) we soon find the shortness of our Tether. Indeed by the help of a metaphysical chain of ideas, one may extend the circulation, go round and round for ever, without making any progress beyond the point to which Providence has pinn'd us: But this does not satisfy me, who would rather say a little to no purpose, than a great deal.[4]

[2] R. H. Griffith, *Alexander Pope: A Bibliography in Two Parts* (Austin: University of Texas Press, 1922–7), I, 329. (The phrase is in the Headnote for 1736.)

[3] *Correspondence*, iii. 433.

[4] Ibid. iii. 445.

The weary tone of this passage seems to imply that Pope attempted further epistles and was frustrated by his lack of success with them. If this conjecture is right, the difficulty would appear to be that Pope found that he was being repetitive, unable to state his basic themes in a fresh way even though in different contexts. In May 1735 (a month after the quarto and folio *Works*, Volume II, had been published) Pope wrote to Caryll:

I want to make you a present of all I'm worth, the 2d (and perhaps the last) volume of my *Works*, which are now become so voluminous, as to outweigh their author. It is high time after the fumbling age of forty is past, to abandon those ladies [i.e. the Muses], who else will quickly abandon us.[5]

Although this is probably one of Pope's disingenuous statements, nevertheless, regarded in connection with the letter last quoted, it should not be altogether dismissed. Nor can we altogether dismiss Spence's observation that in expressing doubt as to whether he would go on with his epistles on government and education, Pope 'spoke a little warmer as to the use of [his moral scheme], but more coldly as to the execution'.[6]

These remarks of 1734 and 1735 gain even more significance in the light of the following extract from Pope's letter to Swift in March 1736:

If ever I write more Epistles in Verse, one of them shall be address'd to you. I have long concerted it, and begun it, but I would make what bears your name as finished as my last work ought to be, that is to say, more finished than any of the rest. The subject is large, and will divide into four Epistles, which naturally follow the Essay on Man, *viz.* 1. Of the Extent and Limits of Human Reason, and Science, 2. A view of the useful and therefore attainable, and of the un-useful and therefore un-attainable, Arts. 3. Of the nature, ends, application, and the use of different Capacities. 4. Of the use of *Learning*, of the *Science* of the *World*, and of *Wit*. It will conclude with a Satire against the misapplication of all these, exemplify'd by pictures, characters, and examples.

But alas! the task is great, and *non sum qualis eram*! My understanding indeed, such as it is, is extended rather than diminish'd: I see things more

[5] Ibid. iii. 455 (bracketed addition from Sherburn's footnote).

[6] See Chapter I, p. 29, and *Anecdotes*, i. 133, no. 301. Sadly, Spence's entries about Pope for the year 1734 are the only ones Mr. Osborn cannot pin to a specific date or month.

in the whole, more consistent, and more clearly deduced from, and related to, each other. But what I gain on the side of philosophy, I lose on the side of poetry: the flowers are gone, when the fruits begin to ripen, and the fruits perhaps will never ripen perfectly.[7]

The letter to Swift can really be said to be a rather striking example of speaking 'a little warmer as to the use of it than before; but more coldly as to the execution'. The phrase 'what I gain on the side of philosophy, I lose on the side of poetry' once more suggests that Pope has tried and failed to compose more epistles 'in order of the system'.

This outline of 1736 in Pope's letter to Swift is very different from the Index of 1734, with which it should nevertheless be compared. The Index (transcribed above, p. 28) is a list of titles of all the units of the ethic scheme at its most comprehensive; the paragraph in the letter to Swift is an expanded version of one portion of the projected continuation of the *Essay*, that stemming from the subject-matter of Epistle I. It does not refer to completed epistles nor to epistles that might develop from other parts of the *Essay*. What is not clear from the 1736 letter is whether the outline there conforms to what Pope had in mind when he made the comment, recorded by Spence and discussed in Chapter I, that he had drawn in his plan 'much narrower than it was at first',[8] or whether other developments of the *opus magnum* scheme were still being contemplated in 1736. In the Index of 1734, 'Of the Use of Education' was classed with the work 'Of the Principles and Use of Civil and Ecclesiastical Polity'. The unifying principle at that time was presumably the institutional character of these subjects, as offshoots of Epistle III of *An Essay of Man* 'with respect to society'. Although Pope does not use the word 'education' in the outline to Swift, we may consider it a part of his plan, since the topic can as easily list under an intellectual heading as under a study of social institutions. As we shall see, Pope certainly claimed afterwards to have been thinking of his epistle on education in this connection.

Another epistle specifically mentioned in the Index that does not appear in the outline to Swift is 'A View of the Equality of Happiness

[7] *Correspondence*, iv. 5.

[8] *Anecdotes*, i. 132, no. 300, and Chapter I, above, pp. 30–1.

in the several Conditions of Men'. The wording of item three of the outline to Swift, 'Of the nature, ends, application, and the use of different capacities' may possibly suggest a connection, but the outline is surely restricted to intellectual capacities, whereas the Index topic seems to have much wider application and to be firmly anchored to Epistle IV of *An Essay on Man*, 'with respect to happiness'. Perhaps another reason that Pope does not mention it is that it too is not a project of the future, but has already been at least partially absorbed in the epistles to Bathurst and Burlington, as our earlier discussions suggested. The same rationale would obviously apply to the epistles on 'the Knowledge and Characters of Men' and 'the particular Characters of Women'.

The remaining topics of the Index can definitely be assigned a place in the 'drawn-in' plan presented to Swift in 1736. They are those comprising the single first unit of the Index's Book II: 'Of the Limits of Human Reason', 'Of the Use of Learning', and 'Of the Use of Wit'. The outline of 1736 appears to resolve the issue which confronted us in Chapter I, as to whether the printing format implied a subordinate relationship of subjects and mezzo-subjects. What in Chapter I we neutrally labelled a unit or a group here clearly emerges as a distinct book. That it is a book of four epistles seems entirely natural since the four ethic epistles had also been printed together as a book and both these units appear to have been so constituted in order to conform to the four-epistle form of Book I of the Ethic Epistles, *An Essay on Man*.

The coalescence of the pattern of this unit on intellectual capacities, pursuits, and ends from 1734 and 1736 thus follows the pattern of composition of the *Essay on Man* itself, and the format of the Index may be considered a parallel to the period in the evolution of the *Essay* when Pope was uncertain as to how many epistles it would contain. The phrase in the conversation of 1730 about 'settling and ranging the part of it aright' seems in retrospect to refer not only to the ordering of topics within the epistle or epistles, but also to the formal structure of the work itself. As the *Essay* was to be what a scale is to a book of maps (a metaphor Pope introduced in 1730 and was continuing to use in 1734), it seems that in 1736 at least, Pope saw the ratio as four to one. As Book I contained four epistles, so each epistle of Book I would yield another four-part book. Such a ratio, while too systematic to apply to all the planning stages of the scheme, does seem to provide a credible and suggestive basis for placing the stage marked by the outline to Swift in the line from the conception of the scheme in 1729 through its vacillating course up to Pope's death in 1744. At the earliest stage, the *Essay* itself slowly evolved into four-epistle form; the final stage of the scheme, the epic, also only gradually assumed a four-book outline; the unit on intellectual capacities, pursuits, and ends marks the same process occurring at a midway point in the project's history.

Pope's letter to Swift implies at least a partial reason for the subsequent abandonment of the plan. The first epistle listed, 'Of the Extent and Limits of Human Reason, and Science', is that for which the final eight lines of verse in the Harvard manuscript (transcribed in Chapter I) were intended. Those lines are headed 'Incipit Liber Secundus. Epist. I. of Y^e^ Limits of Reason'. In Chapter III we suggested the possibility that some of the material originally intended for this epistle might have been absorbed into the first section of the *Epistle to Cobham.* The change of title in the letter to Swift may carry the related possibility that by 1736 Pope had altered an earlier conception, and was now planning to include attention to the state of knowledge in general rather than focusing on the limits of reason. But we have no way of knowing the proposed contents of the epistle or how far Pope had proceeded with it. Conjectures about the form and substance of the next two epistles also seem fruitless, except to suggest that the two seem to complement each other in that the second suggests treatment of the Arts, rather than Man, and the third suggests a possible particularization of various types of men in accord with various 'Arts'. The fourth seems less abstract and more social and concretely contemporary than the others, particularly as it is to 'conclude with a Satire . . . exemplify'd by pictures, characters, and examples'. This last sentence may seem to imply a fifth epistle, but this seems unlikely; it is not numbered, and is covered by Pope's introductory remark that 'the subject is large and will divide into four Epistles'.

The subject is indeed large. The outline evokes the paradoxical observation that if, in comparison with the number of topics listed in the Index of 1734, the plan is being 'drawn in narrower than it was at first', in another way it is actually being considerably expanded in relation to the size of its component parts. It seems, in fact, to have become inflated beyond realizable dimensions, and the paragraph following the outline in the letter to Swift suggests that Pope diagnosed his difficulty with some precision. He appears to have felt that he could not compose more and fresh epistles on a subject he had worked on so long, and consequently temporarily abandoned the whole project.[9]

The project remained dormant until the meeting with Warburton in the spring of 1740 reawakened Pope's interest in it.[10] The octavo edition of *Works*, Volume II, in April 1736 is essentially a reprint of the octavo editions of 1735. Signalling the lowest ebb of all in the plans for the 'Ethic Work' are the changes in the notes and format of the edition of January 1739. The format dissociates the ethic epistles from *An Essay on Man*. The half-title to *An Essay on Man* still reads, as before, 'An Essay on Man, Being the First Book of Ethic Epistles, to Henry St. John L. Bolingbroke', the heading of the first page of poetry reads 'Ethic Epistles, the First Book. To

[9] The letter to Swift immediately continues as follows: 'The climate (under our Heaven of a Court) is but cold and uncertain: the winds rise, and the winter comes on. I find myself but little disposed to build a new house; I have nothing left but to gather up the reliques of a wreck and look about me to see what friends I have! Pray whose esteem or admiration should I desire now to procure by my writings? whose friendship or conversation to obtain by 'em? I am a man of desperate fortunes, that is a man whose friends are dead: for I never aimed at any other fortune than in friends' (*Correspondence*, iv. 5–6). The possible hyperbole of this outcry should not be allowed to disguise the fact that it records a very real and staggering loss of close friends within a short period. Gay had died in December 1732; Pope's mother in June 1733; Arbuthnot in February 1735; Peterborow in October 1735; and Caryll in April 1736. Furthermore, Bolingbroke, Pope's 'guide, philosopher, and friend', had left England in May 1735 to settle permanently in France. If, in consequence, Pope felt temporarily unequal to his 'great task', we ought not be to surprised.

[10] In the period 1736–9, Pope's publishing interests were the Imitations of Horace (of which he makes little mention in his letters) and collections of his earlier correspondence (of which his letters are full). He wrote relatively few letters in this four-year period, and they are not especially pleasant to read. Those to and from Swift and to and from the Earl of Orrery concerning Swift make melancholy reading, because Orrery was convinced, and succeeded in convincing Pope, that Swift's death was imminent; and Swift's letters to Pope are positively lugubrious, lamenting on his own decay and the loss of all mutual friends. Bolingbroke lived with Pope at Twickenham from July 1738 to April 1739, and there is no extant correspondence from the period of his residence in France. Nor are there any letters to or from the Earl of Oxford, nor to or from Spence, who was abroad from May 1737 until February 1738.

H. St. John, L. Bolingbroke', and the concluding page reads 'End of the First Book of Ethic Epistles'. But so far as this edition is concerned there is no second book. The next half-title reads only 'Epistles to Several Persons' and covers eleven epistles, the first four of which are the epistles to Cobham, to a Lady, to Bathurst, and to Burlington which had formerly been grouped separately as 'Ethic Epistles, the Second Book'. Unlike all previous collected editions, however, these are not designated 'Ethic Epistles' or 'the Second Book', nor are they prefaced by an outline of 'Contents'.

The change in format is supported by changes in the notes. Three new notes are totally different from any notes in the 1735 editions. They are all to the *Essay on Man*. The note to the passage beginning 'Far as Creation's ample range extends, / The scale of sensual, mental pow'rs ascends' (I, 207–8) reads, 'The Extent, Limits, and Use of *Human Reason* and *Science*, the Author design'd as the subject of his next Book of Ethic Epistles'. Again in 1739 Pope added a final sentence to the 'argument' to the line ' 'Twas then, the studious head or gen'rous mind' (III, 283), which reads, 'The Deduction and Application of the foregoing Principles, with the *Use* or *Abuse* of *Civil* and *Ecclesiastical Policy*, was intended for the subject of the third book'. The same process occurred in the fourth Epistle. To the line 'Fortune her gifts may variously dispose' (IV, 67) the 'argument' of 1735 is followed by a new note reading, 'The Exemplifications of this Truth, by a view of the *Equality* of *Happiness* in the several particular *Stations* of Life, were design'd for the subject of a future Epistle'.

The most striking feature of these notes is the one they have in common. All of them employ the past tense and thus signal Pope's apparently total abandonment of the project. These notes also confirm the evidence of the format, in 'erasing' the identification of the ethic epistles as Book II. In their place is 'The Extent, Limits and Use of *Human Reason* and *Science*'. This substitution confirms the views advanced above in discussing the Index of 1734 and the outline to Swift of 1736, first that this group had a direct correlation to Epistle I of *An Essay on Man*, and second, that it was meant to form a complete book. The next note correlating the epistles on Civil and Ecclesiastical Policy as Book III, and stemming directly from Epistle III of the *Essay*, is further confirmation of this pattern. The epistles on the Use of Riches appear to be acknowledged by the reference to the 'view of the Equality of Happiness in the several Particular Stations of Life' as a future *epistle* rather than an entire book. If, as earlier chapters have argued, the completed epistles to Bathurst and Burlington have their primary connections with Epistle IV of the *Essay*, then only a portion of the final book was to have been a project of the future.

Variant phrasing in a number of other notes conforms to the wording of these new notes. Two earlier notes, given on p. 35 above, change their readings 'See Book I . . .' to read in the 1739 edition 'See the Essay on Man . . .'. Similarly, the entire sentence constituting the cross reference, 'The Use of this doctrine, as apply'd to the knowledge of Mankind, is one of the subjects of the second book', is omitted from the note to *An Essay on Man*, Epistle II, 133 ff. (cited above, p. 33).

The major perplexity of the 1739 edition is the total absence of references to what was in 1735 called 'Ethic Epistles, the Second Book'. Even if we may conjecture that the 1735 arrangement was a makeshift one and that thereafter Pope may have quietly chosen to dissociate the final pair of epistles from the first pair and from the 'Second Book', this conjecture does not explain the apparent consignment to oblivion of the *Epistle to Cobham* and the *Epistle to a Lady*. Pope's notes leave no room for them. The scale-maps pattern ought to provide for five books altogether, including *An Essay on Man*, but the 1739 notes, even upon the most generous interpretation, suggest only four. There is no hint of epistles or of a book, past, present, or future, stemming from Epistle II of the *Essay*. One can only assume that in 1739 neither the *opus magnum* scheme nor any of its permutations or combinations interested Pope very much, and that he was therefore either not aware of or not bothered by inconsistencies of this kind.

Faint hints of the 1735 two-book 'Ethic Epistles' scheme still remain in the edition of 1739, in the references to *An Essay on Man* as the 'First Book of Ethic Epistles' and also in the unaltered note to the *Epistle to Bathurst*, line 86, about Wharton: 'See his character in the first epistle of the Second Book'. Despite these vestiges of the

1735 format, it is clear that in preparing the 1739 edition Pope was intent upon laying the ghost of the plan in all its forms.[11]

Warburton and the 'New Dunciad'

Records of the specific time and place of Pope's first meeting with Warburton differ, as do interpretations of the nature of the relationship between Pope and Warburton thereafter. Despite the scantiness and conflicting quality of the evidence, what is certain is that with the advent of Warburton, the moral scheme came to life once more. The most detailed account of Pope's determination to revive the scheme comes from the son of Lord Chancellor Hardwicke, Charles Yorke, then a Cambridge undergraduate, who wrote to his brother Philip in June 1740:

> Mr. Warburton has lately been near a fortnight with Mr. Pope at Twickenham. He speaks of him in strains of rapturous commendation. He says that he is not a better poet than a man, and that his vivacity and wit is not more conspicuous than his humanity and affability. He tells me that Mr. Pope is tired with imitating *Damasippus*, and intends to do it, but that the great scheme which he has in view is the continuation of the Essay. The first, you know, was only a general map of man, wherein the extent and limits of his faculties were marked out. The second is to treat of false science at large, and the third is to inquire into the use and abuse of civil society.[12]

That the continuation of the *Essay* should be one of the major topics of conversation at this early meeting is not surprising, since the occasion for meeting was Pope's gratitude for Warburton's *Vindication of Mr. Pope's Essay on Man*, published in issues of *The History of the Works of the Learned*, beginning in December 1738 and continuing to 1739. This is a series of polemical open letters defending the orthodoxy and regularity of *An Essay on Man* against

[11] Maynard Mack cites the concluding couplet of the *Epilogue to the Satires: Dialogue II* ('Alas! alas! pray end what you began, / And write next winter more *Essays on Man*') as evidence that 'In 1740 Pope seems to have been seriously meditating a continuation of the *Essay*' (Twickenham III:i, p. xii, n. 4). But in addition to being a poetic plea delivered by a fictitious friend, Dialogue II's publication in July 1738 predates the January 1739 edition of *Works*, vol. ii, that we have been discussing, by over six months.

[12] George Harris, *The Life of Lord Chancellor Hardwicke* (London, 1847), i. 475–6. Also quoted entire in A. W. Evans, *Warburton and the Warburtonians* (London: Humphrey Milford, 1932), pp. 83–5.

attacks by the aged Professor Jean-Pierre de Crousaz. Pope had been hoping to meet Warburton for some time, but they did not meet until late April 1740 when, according to Joseph Warton, 'Their very first interview was in Lord Radnor's garden, just by Mr. Pope's at Twickenham. Dodsley was present; and was, he told me, astonished at the high compliments paid him by Pope as he approached him.'[13] Pope's letters from this meeting until his death reciprocate the 'strains of rapturous commendation' Charles Yorke noted Warburton using of Pope. The most frequently quoted instance is in Pope's letter to Warburton of 27 October 1740: 'You Understand my Work better than I do myself',[14] about which Joseph Warton notes: 'This is one of the most singular concessions made by any author; and a fulsome strain of flattery indeed.'[15] Although one would like to agree with George Sherburn that 'this obvious flattery is not too serious',[16] the remark cannot be altogether dismissed; Pope was certainly mightily impressed by Warburton, who became his literary mentor for the final period of his life, as Swift and Bolingbroke had been for earlier periods.

Warburton's definite activities on behalf of Pope consisted of participating in the writing of notes for the *New Dunciad*, co-editing the new issues of Pope's earlier works, and, by Pope's will, profiting from 'such editions as he shall publish without future alterations'.[17] His indefinite influence upon Pope's career is difficult to assess. Joseph Spence was abroad from September 1739 to November 1741, so his usually reliable notes are missing from this crucial early period of collaboration, and almost all the information available other than that in Pope's own letters comes from Warburton himself. This information, however, is suspect for several reasons. First, Warburton's personality was such as to encourage him always to attribute to himself a greater role than was perhaps warranted. Second, many of his remarks postdate by many years the events they describe. And third, manifold evidence exists of Warburton's lack of editorial judgement, his insensitivity to Pope's poetry, and his

[13] Joseph Warton, ed., *Works of Alexander Pope* (1797), iv. 342 n.
[14] *Correspondence*, iv. 288.
[15] Warton, op. cit., ix. 346 n.
[16] *Correspondence*, iv. 288, n. 3.
[17] *Gentleman's Magazine* xiv (1744), 313; cited in Frank Brady, 'The History and Structure of Pope's *To a Lady*', *SEL 1500–1900*, ix (1969), 447.

willingness to tamper with Pope's works without the authorization of the poet.[18] We must nevertheless do what we can with the evidence at hand.

According to Owen Ruffhead, whose biography of Pope was written at Warburton's urging and under his close supervision, the fourth book of the *Dunciad*, the single new work Pope wrote and published in the period 1740–4, owed its composition to Warburton, who urged 'that it was a pity so fine a poem as the *Dunciad*, should remain disgraced by the meanness of its subject; and that he ought to raise and ennoble it by pointing his satire against minute philosophers and free-thinkers'.[19] Pope's letters of the period corroborate Warburton's role as catalyst. The first such reference is vague both in content and in year date. The date is 12 August and Professor Sherburn suggests 1741 as the year in which Pope wrote to Warburton: 'I thank you heartily for your Hints; & am afraid if I had more of them, not on this only but on other Subjects, I should break my resolution, & become an author anew.'[20] This 'resolution' is also referred to again in October 1741, when Pope wrote to the Earl of Marchmont 'that I am determined to publish no more in my life time, for many reasons; but principally thro' the Zeal I have to speak the *Whole Truth*, & neither to praise or dispraise by halves, or with worldly managements'.[21] But at Pope's urging Warburton arrived at Twickenham in late November for a lengthy visit, and on 1 January 1742 Pope wrote to Hugh Bethel:

> One of my amusements has been writing a Poem, part of which is to abuse *Travelling*. . . . I little thought 3 months ago to have drawn the whole polite world upon me, (as I formerly did the Dunces of a lower Species) as I certainly shall whenever I publish this poem.[22]

[18] See, for instance, the findings of Brady, op. cit., Griffith, 'Early Warburton? or Late Warburton?', *Studies in English* (Austin: University of Texas Press, 1940), pp. 123–31; Mack, 'Pope's Horatian Poems: Problems of Bibliography and Text', *Modern Philology* 41 (1943), 33–44; Twickenham, III:ii, pp. xiv–xv, l–li, *et passim*.

[19] Owen Ruffhead, *Life of Alexander Pope, Esq.* (London, 1769), p. 391. For an analysis of the extent of Ruffhead's dependence upon Warburton, see Robert M. Ryley, 'Warburton, Warton, and Ruffhead's *Life of Pope*', *Papers on Language and Literature* 4 (1968), 51–62. Note also that Ruffhead's *Life* appeared the year after the death of Joseph Spence, the man most able to challenge the Warburton–Ruffhead version of Pope's literary projects.

[20] *Correspondence*, iv. 357.

[21] Ibid. iv. 364.

[22] Ibid. iv. 377.

The *New Dunciad* was published less than three months later, on 20 March 1742. After another year and a half, in which Pope worked on revisions of the original three-book *Dunciad*, the *Dunciad* in four books was published in October 1743. During the autumn of 1742 Pope wrote many letters to and about Warburton, acknowledging his encouragement and active participation. He wrote to Warburton on 4 December: 'If any thing more can be done for the Dunciad, it must be to acquaint the public that You have thought it worth your Care by bestowing some Notes upon it to make it more Important and Serious.'[23] Later in the same month, Pope wrote to Ralph Allen: 'The true Edition is at last completed, & pray when you write tell Mr. W. how much it is owing to him that it is complete, & how much I think it advantaged by his Notes & Discourse before it.'[24] And the very next day (28 December 1742), Pope wrote again to Warburton:

I have always so many Things to take kindly of you, that I don't know which to begin to thank you for. I was willing to include Our whole account of the Dunciad, at least, & therefore stayd till it was finished. The Encouragement you gave me to add the fourth book, first determind me to do so: & the Approbation you seemd to give it, was what singly determind me to print it. Since that, your Notes, & your Discourse in the Name of Aristarchus, have given its Last Finishings & Ornaments.[25]

Against this gathering of evidence of Warburton as inciting force and active participant in the *New Dunciad*, there is some counter-evidence, although none is conclusive or substantial. The first such indication raises some doubt as to whether Warburton wrote all the notes to the *Dunciad* that carry his initials. In at least one instance, he did not. In a letter of November 1742, predating the acknowledgements quoted above, Pope wrote to Warburton:

A Project has arisen in my head to make you in some measure the Editor of this new Edit. of the Dunc. if you have no scruple of owning some of the *Graver Notes* which are now added to those of Mr Cleland and Dr Arb. I mean it as a kind of Prelude or Advertisement to the publick of your Commentarys on the Essays on Man, and on Criticisme, which I propose to print next in another Volume, proportiond to This. I have scratched out a sort of *Avis au Lecteur*, which I'l send you to this effect, which if you disapprove not, you'l make your own. I have a

[23] Ibid. iv. 429. [24] Ibid. iv. 433. [25] Ibid. iv. 434.

particular reason to make you Interest your self in Me & My Writings. It will cause both them & me to make the better figure to Posterity. a very mediocre Poet, one Drayton, is yet taken some notice of, because Selden writ a very few Notes on one of his Poems.[26]

Amid the flattery are some clear facts, one of which is happily supported by other evidence. The 'sort of *Avis au Lecteur*' to which Pope refers exists in manuscript as part of Egerton 1950 (which also contains the *Brutus* plan). It is in Pope's hand, yet upon its publication in 1743, as 'Advertisement to the Reader', is initialled by 'W.W.'.[27]

Presented with this evidence, one may with justice wonder how many other notes are Warburton's only nominally. Pope, after all, speaks of Warburton 'owning some of the *Graver Notes* which are now added', making the notes sound like a *fait accompli*, and only the attribution new. No definite answer is available on this whole issue which may, in any case, be thought highly peripheral, especially as it deals not with Pope's poetic composition, which is our real concern, but with the notes, which at all stages were a collaborative venture.[28] The point is that the circumstance here casts doubt on the authority of other statements made in Warburton's name, to which we shall have occasion to refer later.

A second kind of evidence concerns the possible inception of the Fourth *Dunciad* before the advent of Warburton.[29] The most

[26] *Correspondence*, iv. 427–8.

[27] For final text, see Twickenham, V, 251; cf. William Cleland's function in the earlier *Dunciad*, described in Twickenham, V, xxv. Another instance like the 'Avis au Lecteur' may be implied in Pope's letter to Warburton a week later (see *Correspondence*, iv. 429–30); on the other hand, it may be, as Mr. Sherburn thinks, a repetition of the request of the previous week, which had had no response from Warburton.

[28] Although, as Professor Sutherland writes (Twickenham, V, xxxi), 'It would be idle to speculate on Warburton's contribution to the *New Dunciad*', nevertheless, according to Warton, Pope's contemporaries indulged in just such speculation. See Warton's note to lines 243–4 of Book IV, quoted in Twickenham, V, 367.

[29] In May 1739, a year before Pope first met Warburton, he wrote to Swift: 'Since my *Protest* (for so I call the Dialogue of 1738) I have written but ten lines, which I will send you. They are an Insertion for the next New Edition of the Dunciad, which generally is reprinted once in 2 years. In the second Canto, among the Authors who dive in Fleet ditch, immediately after *Arnall.* Vers. 300, add these' (*Correspondence*, iv. 178). These ten lines (ii. 305 ff.) constitute by far the most extended addition to the poem since 1729, and may possibly signify that some sort of major revision of the poem was being contemplated around this time. Mr. Sherburn also comments, 'Significantly, perhaps, Pope first wrote *for the new Edition* and then crossed out and wrote *for the next new Edition*. One doubts whether the general revision of *The Dunciad* was at this time decided upon, but possibly it was' (*Correspondence*, iv. 178, n. 4).

ambitious hypothesis for early dating is offered by Robert W. Rogers in an appendix, 'The Missing *Dunciad* MSS.', to his *Major Satires of Alexander Pope*. He summarizes the substance of a two-page annotation in Jonathan Richardson's hand that appears on a blank leaf preceding the title page of a 1736 edition of the *Dunciad* in the Berg Collection of the New York Public Library. As described by Mr. Rogers, the sketch is of material ultimately to occupy a large portion of the 'Fourth *Dunciad*' yet is headed 'Canto 2d'. It has Theobald as hero, and includes amongst the satiric materials universities, virtuosi, Bentley, and the French refugee Governor with his pupils, all of whom are portrayed as 'telling Dullnes[s] & their King Tibbald, what they will perform with [L]ives & Fortunes for her, & what they have done in [br]inging up ye Youth to such Ends for y next Age . . .'.[30] Mr. Rogers then concludes:

> This sketch presents material for the most exciting kind of speculation; but unfortunately there are no grounds for positive claims. The difficulty lies in the impossibility of dating the sketch. It could conceivably represent a proposed revision of the second book, drawn up sometime between 1736 and 1740. If the time is correct, then it would seem that Pope may have planned to eliminate the games from his poem and to substitute an attack on education. The trouble with this explanation is that the notes should be in Pope's autograph rather than in Richardson's, if it were true. Furthermore, one passage appearing on the flyleaf (*Dunciad*, [1729], II, ll. 1–12) is an obviously inferior version of the passage as it was first printed in 1729. These difficulties suggest that this summary may represent an early plan for the second book, . . . aimed at abuses in learning rather than at the vices of publishers, authors, patrons, and journalists. Lacking more evidence one hesitates to press this extravagant hypothesis too far; one can only regret Richardson's failure to provide more information about the significance of this passage, as well as about that of many others he records. What might have been the principal source of knowledge about the development of the poem is now a source of frustration and debate.[31]

Using Mr. Roger's account of the annotation, one may indulge in even further speculation, of particular relevance to Pope's *opus magnum*. Several pieces of evidence contribute to this line of thought.

[30] R. W. Rogers, *Major Satires of Alexander Pope* (Illinois Studies in Language and Literature, vol. 40; Urbana: University of Illinois Press, 1955), p. 123.

[31] Ibid.

The first is that the sketch is headed 'Canto 2^{d}'. This title could, as Mr. Rogers points out, conceivably apply to a proposed revision of Book II of *The Dunciad* after 1736; it could also apply to Book II of the *Essay* scheme as outlined in Pope's letter to Swift of 1736, particularly its final epistle, 'Of the Use of *Learning*, of the *Science* of the *World*, and of *Wit*. It will conclude with a Satire against the Misapplication of all these, exemplify'd by pictures, characters, and examples.' Charles Yorke's report of Warburton's first visit to Pope spoke of the plan as still alive: 'The second is to treat of false science.' Finally, as Spence records, Pope himself twice made the connection explicit. In March 1743, in the anecdote quoted at the beginning of this chapter, Pope said:

What was first designed for an Epistle on Education as part of my Essay scheme is now inserted in my fourth *Dunciad*, as the subject for two other epistles there—those on civil and ecclesiastical government—will be treated more at large in my *Brutus*.[32]

A year later, in April 1744, Pope again asserted this relationship with a slight expansion: 'I had once thought of completing my ethic work in four books. The first, you know, is on the nature of man. The second would have been on knowledge and its limits. Here would have come in an Essay on Education, part of which I have inserted in the *Dunciad*.'[33]

Unfortunately, this exciting conjecture about the relation of the two projects is seriously undercut by a first-hand examination of the annotation itself, and I am forced to the conclusion that Mr. Rogers's second 'extravagant hypothesis' (as he himself calls it in the extract quoted above) is more likely to be the correct one: the annotation is probably a copy of a working draft of *The Dunciad* prior to its first publication in 1728. Two features of the annotation of the 1736 *Dunciad* in the Berg collection lend force to this conclusion. The sketch of 'Canto 2^{d}' is only one, although by far the most extensive, of a great number of annotations in the Berg copy, all of which fall under the statement, handwritten at the top of its title page, reading, 'This Book is altered from the Second MS; as ye 1st ed. 1728 is from the First MS. A. Pope.' The 1728 annotated edition, also in the Berg collection, bears the companion inscription, 'This Book

[32] *Anecdotes*, i. 151, no. 337. [33] Ibid. i. 134, no. 302.

corrected from the First Broglio MS. as the Ed. 1736 is from the Second.'[34] One concludes, therefore, that as in other cases, Jonathan Richardson annotated these two printed texts from the original working manuscripts for Pope to use as reference copies in preparing revised editions of *The Dunciad*. Although the second MS. may date from after 1728, it nevertheless seems more likely that the two manuscripts bore a time-relation analogous to the pairs of surviving draft manuscripts for *An Essay on Man* and the *Epistle to Bathurst*. In both these cases, the manuscripts appear to have been written in close conjunction with one another, and preceded the first published edition of the poem.[35]

Close inspection of the 'Canto 2^{d}' outline itself also tends to support the conjecture that the annotation is a copy of a pre-publication manuscript. The first entry under the heading is a series of cue words, beginning 'The Sons of Dullness meet' and continuing with seven words in a vertical column at the left margin of the page, which turn out to be the words beginning lines 15–22 of Book II (originally (1728) the opening passage of Book II). This series of cue words indicates that Pope must have jotted down these openings quickly in the process of copying this part of the draft from an earlier manuscript. The next section is the one referred to by Mr. Rogers in the paragraph quoted above, an early state of the first twelve lines of Book II as revised in 1729. Its opening lines, 'High on a Bed of state, that far outshone / Fleckno's proud Seat, or Querno's nobler Throne / —— exalted sate. Around him bows', are a recognizable version of the printed lines, but in a highly tentative and unfinished state. The third section is the following prose outline that closely corresponds to the eventual fourth book:

Addresses & Homages p^{d} to ye New King; Tibbalds Satire on ye Universities,[2] Inns of Court,[1] Governors to Travelling Noblemen Academy of Musick, Virtuosos. (& Corruptions of each)

1. B——y with ye Cantabrigians 2. wth ye Oxonians.
3. A French Refugee Governor with his Pupils
   (Addresses spoke by these 3)

[34] Rogers mentions both these annotations, op. cit., p. 120, text and n. 3.

[35] Compare also the description of Richardson's transcript of the Morgan MS. of the *Essay on Man*, given by Mack, 'Introduction' to *An Essay on Man. Reproductions*, section IV, pp. xxiv–xxviii.

4. Inns of Court Students. 5. Travell^{g} Physicians, to mak fine Gentlemen at Paris, not collect Simples at Alexandria
6. Virtuosos Useless. Editions, Statues, Painting; Silly affectation of Taste. Then introduce ye Directors of Musick with a[ll] their Set of fine Gentlemen of Taste. All telling Dullnes & Their King Tibbald what they will perform with Lives & Fortunes for her, & What they have done in bringing up ye Youth to such Ends for ye Next Age. Virt

Here the first page ends. In fact it seems to break off. Yet overleaf the annotation begins with a verse section corresponding to the first numbered item listed above, 'B——y with ye Cantabrigians', for it begins with a version of IV, 199–208, and continues with a trial version of Bentley's address totally unrelated to the final version. One line reads, 'Behold ye youth educated by my Precepts are presented to Thee.' Although part of a verse sequence, the line has not yet reached anywhere near final form, since it has neither metrical pattern nor a rhymed companion line. Finally, this second page concludes with a few prose annotations. These read in full:

Satire on Neglect of Politeness in B——ly's address & Timeserving.
Oxf^{d} Description of a Head of a House.
Tutors Leading up their Pupils
His Address, A Satyr on ye Bad Education, Mad Principles.

When seen in its entirety and at first hand, this sketch bears a close resemblance to the kind of early draft represented by the Morgan version of Epistle IV of *An Essay on Man* and, as we shall see, to the *Brutus* manuscript, representing a state so early in the composing process that many of the ideas for the poem have not yet evolved from prose jottings to poetic statement. Yet the sketch, however rudimentary, does have shape. The first prose section attempts to create an outline of the entire unit. In this over-all outline the first three points refer only to the central speaking character of each group. The second prose section fills in this basic outline with details of two kinds. Of the four notes in the second prose section, two (the first and last) contain suggestions for the thrust of the direct addresses of the main speakers, and the middle two contain ideas for the lines surrounding the direct address. This two-part pattern of basic outline plus a separate collection of suggestions of greater detail is typical of Pope's usual procedure and ought to do much to assure us that although the annotation is undatable and not in Pope's hand, it is nevertheless a reliable transcription of Pope's manuscript planning in its early stages.

It is quite possible that the ideas outlined in the sketch remained dormant in the form conveyed here, until many years later, when Pope, having abandoned them as a possible portion of the original *Dunciad*, revived them as a possible portion of the *opus magnum*. Perhaps it is significant that Pope dedicated the *Dunciad* of 1729 to Swift and also introduced his outline for Book II of the *opus magnum* in his letter to Swift of 1736 with the words, 'If ever I write more Epistles in Verse, one of them shall be address'd to you.' It was not until at least 1736 that Jonathan Richardson copied the materials from the 'Second MS.' into the *Dunciad* edition of that year; perhaps his work refreshed Pope's memory and occasioned the plans outlined to Swift. Whatever the case, in after years, as we saw from the Spence anecdotes of 1743 and 1744, Pope associated the origin of the section on 'education' with the *opus magnum* rather than with the *Dunciad*. Such a reconstruction may result at least partly from Bishop Warburton's influence.

Of Warburton's influence, Mr. Rogers concludes:

> William Warburton undoubtedly made some contributions to the fourth book; but what these were it is difficult to determine. Certainly he gave moral support; and he supplied a number of notes. A few details may have been introduced into the poem at his suggestion. . . . Except for such details, however, there is little that can reasonably be attributed to him. . . . We must, therefore, come to the conclusion that Pope's friend did not really exert an important influence upon the fourth book of the *Dunciad*.[36]

Mr. Rogers may be correct in assuming that Warburton is unlikely to have made any substantial contribution in regard to basic subject-matter, particularly if it is true that much of the material of Book IV, in outline at least, antedates not only his friendship with Pope, but also the original 1728 edition of the poem itself.[37] Nevertheless,

[36] Rogers, pp. 112–13.

[37] Warburton may, however, have had a good deal of influence upon the religious import of the final version of the *Dunciad*. In 'The Mystery of the Cibberian *Dunciad*', *SEL 1500–1900*, viii (1968), 463–74, William J. Howard discusses this point and also notes that in the winter of 1741–2, Pope and Warburton were together visiting Ralph Allen at Bath for a month to six weeks, during which time the poem was largely being finished.

despite my personal desire to join Mr. Rogers and many of Pope's friends and later editors in minimizing Warburton's beneficent influence on Pope, it seems impossible to do so in this case. Specifically, it is not unreasonable to assume, from the combination of evidence presented so far, that in 1740 Warburton encouraged Pope both to 'write more *Essays on Man*' and to elevate the *Dunciad* and enlarge its references. These suggestions appear to have coalesced in Pope's mind and inspired him to turn the abandoned essay materials (which in turn may have developed partly from abandoned *Dunciad* materials) into a new *Dunciad* book. If this hypothesis is acceptable, we must be grateful to Warburton, for however intangible his influence in some cases, and heavy-handed in others, he must be considered the catalyst productive of Pope's only complete new work in the last five years of his life, and a major achievement of his career.

'The Essay on Man' and the 'Fourth Dunciad'

To determine just which insertions in the *Fourth Dunciad* are possible fugitives from the ethic scheme is impossible with the scanty evidence we have. A few general relationships may however be noted. Aubrey Williams's remarks on the whole new *Dunciad* are particularly appropriate to the fourth book:

> And the more one explores the increasing inclusiveness of the *Dunciad* (through the addition of the notes and the Fourth Book), the more one is aware of its implicit kinship with *An Essay on Man*, of the latter's status as a more sober counterpart to the ironic examination conducted in the *Dunciad*. As one of the finest statements in English of the principles of Christian Socratism, *An Essay on Man* provides the best background against which one may view the lack of self-knowledge which is so inseparable a part of Pope's characterization of Scriblerus and of duncery in general.[38]

In Epistle I of *An Essay on Man*, man's pride was most tellingly expressed in images that describe him as exceeding his proper bounds. Man wants to 'act or think beyond Mankind', wants to 'be the GOD of GOD', and tries to do *more* than befits his proper role and sphere:

[38] Aubrey Williams, *Pope's 'Dunciad': A Study of Its Meaning* (London: Methuen, 1955), p. 84.

In Pride, in reas'ning Pride, our error lies;
All quit their sphere, and rush into the skies.
Pride still is aiming at the blest abodes,
Men would be Angels, Angels would be Gods.
Aspiring to be Gods, if Angels fell,
Aspiring to be Angels, Men rebel;
And who but wishes to invert the laws
Of ORDER, sins against th' Eternal Cause.
(*Essay*, I, 123–30)

In contrast, the inversion of the laws of order in the *Fourth Dunciad* takes the form of emphasizing the reduction of man's reasoning capacities to *less* than their proper function. The schoolmaster proudly states his role: 'When Reason doubtful, like the Samian letter, / Points him two ways, the narrower is the better' (151–2). As described in the *Fourth Dunciad*, man's folly is not that of self-aggrandizement, but of repressing his full potential and focusing only on fragments and minutiae. Instead of aspiring upward, men 'reason downward, till [they] doubt of God'.[39] The unit on education proper, in its progressive movement from words to fragments of words to sounds and finally to '*Air*, the Echo of a Sound' (322), forms but one of the many illustrations in the *Fourth Dunciad* of the 'misapplications of *Learning*, of *Science* of the *World*, and of *Wit*', all of which are examples of the abuse of man's capacities by using *less* than his full reasoning powers. The unit on education recalls, too, the *Essay's* questions, 'Why has not Man a microscopic eye?' . . . 'Say what the use, were finer optics giv'n' (*Essay*, I, 193, 195) in Bentley's proud proclamation that 'We only furnish what he cannot use' (261), and the university curriculum achieves this end by treating man precisely as if he were a fly with microscopic eye:

The critic Eye, that microscope of Wit,
Sees hairs and pores, examines bit by bit:
How parts relate to parts, or they to whole,
The body's harmony, the beaming soul,
Are things which Kuster, Burman, Wasse shall see,
When Man's whole frame is obvious to a *Flea*. (233–8)

[39] The complicated religious controversies alluded to in these passages are, of course, not being addressed here.

Modern commentators agree that the section on education is the one with the closest links to the essay scheme,[40] but other portions of Book IV may also have earlier been connected with the *opus magnum*. Certainly many other related passages exhibit the same downward, reductionist movement. The Goddess's opening speech praises the 'Wits', the textual critics, for mincing standard authors to bits. The most zealous of the collectors of minutiae who press round the throne of Dulness with gifts are a florist and a butterfly-collector. In praising them, Dulness urges all men to follow their example:

> 'O! would the Sons of Men once think their Eyes
> And reason giv'n them but to study *Flies!*
> See Nature in some partial narrow shape,
> And let the Author of the Whole escape:
> Learn but to trifle; or, who most observe,
> To wonder at their Maker, not to serve.' (453–8)

Trifling, typical of the education process, is similarly the mark of the two philosophers, the gloomy Clerk and Silenus. They too 'let the Author of the Whole escape' by taking one of several 'partial narrow' downward paths. And Silenus recapitulates the training of Dulness's band:

> 'From Priest-craft happily set free,
> Lo! ev'ry finish'd Son returns to thee:
> First slave to Words, then vassal to a Name,
> Then dupe to Party; child and man the same;
> Bounded by Nature, narrow'd still by Art,
> A trifling head, and a contracted heart.' (499–504)

Not all passages in the *Fourth Dunciad* illustrate this complementary yet opposing relationship to the movement in the *Essay on Man*. Some passages in fact reveal emphases very similar to passages in the *Essay*. An exception to the emphasis on the downward movement occurs, for instance, within the speech of the gloomy Clerk. The final alternative he offers closely echoes the phrasing of the passage from the *Essay*, Epistle I, just quoted, in which man's egotism drives him to 'be the GOD of GOD'. The Clerk says:

> Or, at one bound o'er-leaping all his laws,
> Make God Man's Image, Man the final Cause,

[40] See, for instance, *Anecdotes*, i. 133, 151; Twickenham, V, xxxi; Williams, p. 111.

> Find Virtue local, all Relation scorn,
> See all in *Self*, and but for self be born:
> Of nought so certain as our *Reason* still,
> Of nought so doubtful as of *Soul* or *Will*. (477–82)

Ultimately each of the extremes leads man to the same disastrous end: away from God and towards folly, dullness, and pride. The gifts of the Goddess Dulness, 'Firm Impudence, or Stupefaction mild' (530), 'Kind Self-conceit' (533), and 'Int'rest' (537, 538), afford the same 'strange comforts' bestowed by Pride and described at the end of the *Essay*, Epistle II. As the Goddess says,

> All my commands are easy, short, and full:
> My Sons! be proud, be selfish, and be dull. (581–2)

Only in Epistle IV of *An Essay on Man* does a proper and desirable rising movement replace that of excessive and improper aspiration:

> See! the sole bliss Heav'n could on all bestow;
> Which who but feels can taste, but thinks can know:
> Yet poor with fortune, and with learning blind,
> The bad must miss; the good, untaught, will find;
> Slave to no sect, who takes no private road,
> But looks thro' Nature, up to Nature's God;
> Pursues that Chain which links th' immense design,
> Joins heav'n and earth, and mortal and divine;
> Sees, that no being any bliss can know,
> But touches some above, and some below;
> Learns, from this *union of the rising Whole*,
> The first, last purpose of the human soul;
> And knows where Faith, Law, Morals, all began,
> All end, in LOVE of GOD, and LOVE of MAN.
> (*Essay*, IV, 327–40; italics mine.)

Here, significantly, the vision and bliss of the 'rising whole' are contrasted to sectarianism, solipsism, and partial, fragmentary knowledge.

The downward, reductionist, fragmentary pattern appears to be the dominating movement of the *Fourth Dunciad* just as the excessive, aspiring pattern marks so many passages of *An Essay on Man*, Epistle I. Yet in each poem these movements are part of a greater, complex whole, and since Pope makes no explicit connection between the two it is hard to say whether he planned the movement of the later poem as a deliberate contrast to the movement of the *Essay*.

Ian Jack comments on the epistolary style of parts of the *Fourth Dunciad*, and notes that 'One reason for the mixture of styles in *The Dunciad* is manifestly the fact that passages now incorporated in it were written at various times and with various purposes'.[41] But there are many missing links in the chain binding the *Essay on Man* and the *Dunciad*, and the most crucial one is the absence of the epistles or detailed outline of the epistles that were to precede the concluding satire. There is in fact no firm evidence that Pope developed the episodes 'inserted in my fourth *Dunciad*' significantly beyond the 'brouillion' stage marked by the transcription in the 1736 edition of the *Dunciad* until after 1740. On the contrary, we know that he seems to have had the habit of suggesting that his work was much nearer completion than it actually was, and it is possible to assume that the Richardson annotations in the 1736 edition constitute the insertions Pope spoke of to Spence in 1743 and 1744.

It is, however, more likely that Pope did spend concentrated time and effort developing the sketch for the four-epistle work, and particularly its concluding satire, that was supposed to follow the *Essay on Man*. Even if we conclude that the Richardson transcription represents a portion of a manuscript that pre-dates and was written as a tentative version of the 1728 *Dunciad*, the assumption that Pope (whom Maynard Mack describes as 'never a man to forget a good thing, either his own or another's'[42]) worked on it to a significant extent *circa* 1736 would help to account for why he subsequently associated it with the 'Epistle on Education' intended for the *Essay* scheme. In Aubrey Williams's words, 'For practical purposes, in fact, we may perhaps view Book IV as having accomplished, in however altered a form, most of Pope's plan [as described to Swift]. It *is* a satire against the "misapplication of" human capacities, "exemplified by pictures, characters, and examples." '[43]

[41] Ian Jack, *Augustan Satire* (Oxford: Clarendon Press, 1952), p. 128.

[42] *Reproductions*, p. xxxiii, quoted, with reference to the *Epistle to a Lady*'s substantial dependence upon fragments of poetry composed by Pope before 1730, by R. M. Schmitz, 'Peterborough's and Pope's Nymphs: Pope at Work', *Philological Quarterly*, xlviii (1969), 200.

[43] Williams, p. 111.

CHAPTER VII

'BRUTUS'

POPE's other, but incomplete, new project of his final years was the plan to write an epic called 'Brutus'. The coupling of *Brutus* with parts of the fourth *Dunciad* as transformed portions of Pope's *opus magnum* in Spence's entry for March 1743 (quoted in the last chapter) comes as a rather surprising announcement. There is no earlier reference to a projected epic. It is nowhere mentioned in Pope's extant correspondence; and in Spence's *Anecdotes* up to and including the very month of the entry quoted, Pope never mentions *Brutus* in referring to epics he did write or would have written had he not translated Homer. The most perplexing of these references to *not* writing an epic is the following entry:

> If I had not undertaken that work [the Homer translation] I should certainly have writ an epic, and I should have sat down to it with this advantage—that I had been nursed up in Homer and Virgil.
>
> POPE *March 1743.*[1]

The peculiarity here is the date, for it was also in March 1743 that Pope told Spence, as we have seen, that 'the subject for two other epistles there [i.e. in his *Essay* scheme]—those on civil and ecclesiastical government—will be treated more at large in my *Brutus*'. That Pope should at the same time be speaking of writing an epic as part of a 'conditional sentence contrary to fact' and of writing an epic upon the subject of which he is prepared to expand at some length seems most unlikely. In his textual note to the first entry quoted above, Mr. Osborn reports a variant of the anecdote, dated 1742, which reads, 'I should certainly have written an Epic Poem if I had not engaged in the translation of Homer.'[2] Unless some sort

[1] *Anecdotes*, i. 83, no. 195.

[2] Ibid. ii. 702 (textual note to no. 195). Osborn continues, 'Because it is a duplication it is omitted in the text', and prints the later entry in accordance with his decision always to follow the latest text in Spence's own hand.

of phrase is missing, common sense would seem to demand that we consider 1742 rather than 1743 as the period during which Pope represents himself as *not* planning an epic.

Among the series of conversations of March 1743 is one in which Pope details the epic he *is* planning:

> The idea that I have had for an epic poem of late turns wholly on civil and ecclesiastical government. The hero is a prince who establishes an empire. That prince is our Brutus from Troy, and the scene of the establishment, England.
>
> The plan of government is much like our old original plan, supposed so much earlier, and the religion introduced by him is the belief in one God and the doctrines of morality.
>
> Brutus is supposed to have travelled into Egypt, and there to have learned the unity of the Deity, and the other purer doctrines, afterwards kept up in the mysteries.
>
> Though there is none of it writ as yet, what I look upon as more than half of the work is already done, for 'tis all exactly planned.
>
> 'It would take you up ten years?' [asked Spence.]
>
> Oh, much less, I should think, as the matter is already quite digested and prepared. POPE *March 1743*[3]

This entry once more raises the question of dating. The implication of Pope's remarks of either April or August 1742 (the two occasions when, according to Mr. Osborn, Pope was in Spence's company in that year) leads us to assume that Pope had not begun to plan *Brutus* before some time in 1742. But since Pope so firmly says that 'the matter is already quite digested and prepared' there has been an attempt to place the date of the inception of the epic plans earlier. Warburton's note to the final stanza of a poem titled, 'On receiving from the Right Hon. the Lady Frances Shirley a Standish and two Pens', published for the first time in Volume IV of Pope's *Works* of 1751, suggests the period 1739–40. The editors of the Twickenham edition of Pope's *Minor Poems* date it *c.* 1739, noting that Warburton 'is the sole authority for the text and genuineness of this poem'.[4] Published as an appendix to the *Epilogue to the Satires*, the poem's tentative date comes from its allusion to the February 1739 threat of prosecution by the House of Lords on account of Pope's two dialogues of 1738. The final stanza reads:

[3] *Anecdotes*, i. 153, no. 343. [4] Twickenham, VI, 378–9.

'Come, if you'll be a quiet soul,
That dares tell neither Truth nor Lies,
I'll list you in the harmless roll
Of those that sing of these poor eyes.'

Warburton's annotation of the opening two lines of this last stanza reads: 'i.e. If you have neither the courage to write satire, nor the application to attempt an Epic poem.—He was then meditating on such a work'. Although Ruffhead's biography of Pope (naturally) and the Elwin–Courthope edition of Pope's *Works* repeat this interpretation, it is hard to agree that the lines are intended to have so exact an application, and harder still to feel that Warburton's statement, made over a decade later, should receive credence when there exists no other suggestion to counter the series of remarks by Pope to Spence at least up to April 1742 suggesting that he was *not* 'meditating on such a work'.[5] Moreover, Pope presents the idea as one he had had 'of late', a term which could include ten months or so, but is less likely to refer to a period of years.

Two documents exist to lend substance to Pope's claim that 'though there is none of it writ as yet' the epic is 'all exactly planned'. An outline of the *Brutus* plan has long been available in Ruffhead's *Life of Alexander Pope*.[6] An autograph manuscript version of the outline survives as part of the contents of Egerton MS. 1950 in the British Museum. The Egerton version received its most extensive and minute examination by Friedrich Brie.[7] Finding that Ruffhead's plan was far more extensive than the Egerton manuscript outline, Brie gives a transcription of the Egerton version so that the two may be compared. However Brie, like Ruffhead, rearranges the manuscript outline so as to give a much more orderly and connected appearance to Pope's sketch than the manuscript itself does.

The *Brutus* outline occupies three leaves of the Egerton 1950 collection. The first two leaves are large, $12\frac{1}{2}'' \times 7\frac{1}{2}''$. The opening page, numbered '4', carries the heading, 'BRUTUS Great Grandson of

[5] See Owen Ruffhead, *Life of Alexander Pope, Esq.* (London, 1769), pp. 348–50; *Works of Alexander Pope*, edd. W. Elwin ahd W. J. Courthope (London, 1889), v. 337.

[6] Ruffhead, pp. 409–22.

[7] Friedrich Brie, 'Popes *Brutus*', *Anglia*, lxiii (1939), 144–85. The only other major article on the epic plan is the excellent one by Donald J. Torchiana, 'Brutus: Pope's Last Hero', in *Essential Articles for the Study of Alexander Pope*, ed. Maynard Mack (Hamden, Conn.: Archon Books, 2nd ed., 1968), pp. 705–23.

Aeneas. 66 Years after ye destr. of Troy.', and describes 'Lib. 1'. Page 4 verso is blank, page 5 describes 'Lib. 2' on one side, 'Lib. 3', the concluding book, on the other.[8] The third leaf (page 6) is a fragment. It contains the beginning of the epic, eight full lines and three partial lines of blank verse, the rest torn away. This fragmentary page is the back of a discarded letter, and 'paper-sparing' Pope, we discover, has used even the reverse for his epic jottings, interweaving them with the lines of the original letter.

The sketch of the epic as it appears on the first three pages is as follows: Book I is a council scene. Brutus and his band are at the Straits of Calpé and are debating whether to enter the Atlantic. Brutus' resolution is described, and Hercules appears in a vision to confirm his sentiments. Book II describes the voyage northward, with stops at the Canary Islands and Lisbon. Book III describes Brutus and his band settling in Britain. They land in the South-West, having had adventures in Ireland, Mona, the Hebrides, and possibly other neighbouring islands. The final battle is with the giants of Cornwall, and 'These being finally reduced, ye whole Iland submits to good Government wch ends ye Poem'.

This fairly straightforward outline, however, occupies only a part of each page. The pages are divided vertically in half, and in each case, the bare outline of the book's action occupies only one block of script on the left hand side of the page. Surrounding it and usually filling the right side of the page are annotations of source material, greater expansion of detail, additional adventures, digressions, and background explanations. For instance, page 4, devoted to Book I, starts the outline of the action *in medias res*, while the right side of the page sketches the antecedent action and its rationale:

Benevolence ye First Principle and Predominant in Brutus. Thence a strong Desire to redeem ye Remains of his countrymen (ye descend^{ts} frō Troy) now captive in Greece: & To establish their freedom & felicity in a Just Form of Governmt. . . . The Love of his Country induces his Voyage. He travels to gather together ye descend^{ts} of ye Trojans, who were dispers^{d} ab^{t} Greece (& consequently had learn^{d} ye Policies & Customs of different States) after he has collected these, he consults ye Oracle to incourage

[8] In what clearly seems to be a binding error, the leaf is attached to the folder so that Lib. 3' precedes 'Lib 2'.

them—wch promises a land in ye mid Ocean, mark'd out by some circumstances to be Britain . . .

This use of right and left halves of each page is consistent throughout. Another instance appears on the page devoted to Book III. The concluding paragraph of the basic outline reads:

> The People of ye Giants dominion overrun with Superstition, tell him there are Islands near y^{m} possest by Titans, or Hero's Ghosts frō wch Thunders & Tempests guard all access. He undertakes these adventures to disperse Tyranny & error & Spread Truth & good Governm^{t}.

The extensive annotation opposite on the right side of the page does something to dispel the vagueness of the basic outlines. There, three points follow upon the heading 'False Policies', providing a kind of gloss on 'these adventures' in the basic outline:

1. The Island Mona und^{r} *Superstition* govern^{d} by *Priests.* Tacit. Ann. 14:30
2. Others und^{r} dismal *Anarchy* fire Buildings Laws like ye Peruvians at first, & Cyclops of old, infesting their Neighbours & eating Captives, carrying away Virgins. An Episode of a Lover carrying Brutus to reconquer one.
3. The third und^{r} *Tyranny*, stronger y^{n} others, taken for Giants. . . .

Below this gloss is another and later marginal addition, also in point form, headed by the instruction, 'Add Difficulties with his own people during this time, a Character of a kinsman of Brutus young fierce, ambitious & brave, to excess. an Achilles.'

Perhaps the best way to describe the disordered state of the manuscript with its core outlines and additions, explanations, and annotations growing round about is to liken it to the Morgan manuscript draft of *An Essay on Man*, Epistle IV, or the *Dunciad* sketch from the 'Second Broglio MS.'. There is a distinct family resemblance, although the *Brutus* outline represents an even earlier stage. It has as yet no poetry. Whereas the draft of Epistle IV of the *Essay* shows Pope hammering out clusters of verse couplets from his 'prose collections', the *Brutus* plan shows Pope developing detailed 'prose collections' from the bare bones of the basic outlines. The two share such features as numbered propositions, editorial annotations which cite both classical and contemporary sources, and the general appearance of the page on which clusters of reasonably legible script are surrounded by later additions often in cramped, hurried, and much less legible handwriting.

Owen Ruffhead's outline is much more orderly, and richer in detail. He introduces it with these words:

A sketch of this intended piece, now lies before the writer of these sheets; and as the plan seems to be noble, extensive, and edifying, he trusts that an account of it will not only be entertaining, but instructive; as the design may serve as a model to employ some genius, if any there be, or shall hereafter arise, equal to the execution of such an arduous task.[9]

This introductory paragraph is a fair sample of Ruffhead's style throughout. As E. D. Snyder noted in 1919, Ruffhead elaborates and 'emotionalizes' Pope's sketch. Snyder compares a passage from the Egerton manuscript with Ruffhead's version. The original (from Brutus' speech in the council scene of Book I) reads:

He answers he was but a Mortal like them, & if their Virtue were superior to his, they wd be as much Gods as He. Y^e^ Way is open to Heaven by Virtue. Lastly he resolves to go in a single ship, & reject all Cowards.

Ruffhead transmutes this as follows:

To which Brutus, rising with emotion, answers, that Hercules was but a mortal like them; and that if their virtue was superior to his, they would have the same claim to divinity: for that the path of virtue was the only way that lay open to Heaven.

At length he resolves to go in a single ship, and to reject all dastards as dared not accompany him.[10]

Although Ruffhead's pompous rephrasing is an irritant, the outline, as George Sherburn says, is certainly the most valuable part of his biography. The outline is even more valuable than might first appear, for missed by Snyder but noticed by Brie is the fact that the sketch that Ruffhead says he has in front of him is not Egerton 1950, but a later, fuller version of the plan.[11] Along with some insignificant detail, Ruffhead introduces additions of a very specific kind, such as the names of characters, geographical place-names, and additional episodes, as well as further particularization of episodes already sketched out in the Egerton draft. Brie considers and rejects two

[9] Ruffhead, p. 410.
[10] Edward D. Snyder, 'Pope's Blank Verse Epic', *JEGP*, 18 (1919), 580.
[11] Brie, pp. 147–8.

possible alternatives to the hypothesis that Ruffhead is working from another sketch, and his findings seem irrefutable. The first alternative is that Ruffhead has concocted the details himself, but Brie rejects this suggestion on the ground that Ruffhead by all accounts is a stolid, unimaginative, and reliable figure. The second alternative is that Ruffhead has more pages of the Egerton manuscript in front of him than are now extant. Brie rejects this alternative too, because of the nature of the additions, which are interspersed throughout and dovetail into the familiar parts of the outline unobtrusively. Examples of such details are that whereas Egerton's description of the council scene in Book I gives only Brutus' speeches at length, Ruffhead's version includes the counter-proposals of other speakers, all of whom he names. And to the beginning of Book II, Ruffhead adds an opening showing God on high, and gives further details for the Canary Island section, adding, for instance, the precise number of persons Brutus left behind as a colony to Egerton's more general 'yet they leave ye old Men & Women & ye fearful, & those unfit for Service, to find their Quiet; & build them a City, etc.'. In Ruffhead's version the journey northwards includes a landing in Norway where the Trojan descendants fight the natives, and where they first observe the *aurora borealis*.

The *aurora borealis*, which does not figure in the book-by-book outline in the Egerton transcript, does appear as a part of the jottings that can be deciphered from the palimpsest-like manuscript fragment (page 6) on which ideas for the epic are written over Pope's crossed-out letter. Also part of this fragment are phrases such as 'other Isles, Orcades, Hebrides, etc.', 'overthrow by Jupiter', 'Thunders, Tempests, etc.', which are incorporated into what is perhaps the most significant new feature of Ruffhead's outline: the addition of a complete book. In Ruffhead's version, the outline of Egerton's Book III becomes Book IV, and Book III now expands on the trials that beset the Trojans before they land at Torbay in south-west England, describing the voyage from Norway to the Orcades, where Brutus resolves to land in order to dispel fears stemming from a legend that makes these northern islands the place where 'some of the Titans were confined after their overthrow by Jupiter' (thus incorporating the phrasing of the discarded letter).

Here they are subject to the violence first of a hurricane and then of a volcano. Brutus' companion, Orontes, flies in fear, but Brutus prays to God, who answers by sending a guardian angel who explains the phenomena, and directs him to the south-west parts of England.

The jottings on the letter must point to a draft subsequent to the Egerton outline, since in the latter the outlines of Books II and III occupy both sides of a single leaf. There cannot have been an intervening Book-outline at that stage. The letter fragment is thus an independent confirmation of Brie's conclusion that Ruffhead had a subsequent draft in front of him that is now lost. According to Ruffhead's version, then, which can safely be assumed reliable, the epic was finally to have a four-book form. This fact is important, for it brings *Brutus* in line with all the other four-part components of the *opus magnum*. And like the other units, it seems to have only gradually assumed its four-part structure.

Ruffhead's version, although a marked expansion of the Egerton outline, seems nevertheless still rather far removed from the stage Pope reports to Spence in March 1743—the stage at which 'the matter is already quite digested and prepared'. In April 1744, a year later, and just a few weeks before his death, Pope, outlining his ethic work for the final time, tells Spence again that his *Brutus* 'is all planned already' and adds 'and even some of the most material speeches writ in prose'.[12] These two reports a year apart may possibly correspond, respectively, to the two stages marked by the autograph version and the Ruffhead version. However, the advance marked by the Ruffhead version certainly does not appear to involve a year's work, even if much interrupted. Two alternatives present themselves. The first is that there were later, more developed versions that have not come down to us. This is certainly possible, but it seems unlikely that Warburton would not have known of them, and preserved and lent them to Ruffhead instead of an earlier draft. The other alternative, although highly conjectural, accords with Pope's attitude at earlier stages in his career. This hypothesis assumes that Ruffhead's version is the one lying behind Pope's conversations with Spence, and that Pope, as in the case of the *Essay on Man*, is being over-optimistic about the work yet to be done upon the epic.

[12] *Anecdotes*, i. 134, no. 302.

Although Pope seems never to have reached the stage of transforming his manuscript notes into verse (with the exception of the few lines of the exordium), the marginal annotations suggest that he had spent considerable time reading or re-reading background material. In the section of his edition of Spence's *Anecdotes* called 'Pope on Ancient Writers', Osborn gives the following entry:

Mr. Pope has still a most excellent memory, and that both of the sensible and local kind. When I consulted him about the Hades of the ancients, he referred immediately to Pindar's second Olympic Ode, Plutarch's treatise *De Iside et Osiride*, the four places that relate to it in the *Odyssey* (though this was so many years after he had done that translation), Plato, Lucretius, and some others, and turned to the very passages in most of them with a surprising readiness. SPENCE *March 1743*.[13]

As an independent feat of memory, this listing by Pope does indeed deserve Spence's tribute, as Mr. Osborn notes in his comment. But the date of the entry coincides with the date on which Pope outlined his epic to Spence, including the passage, 'Brutus is supposed to have travelled into Egypt, and there to have learned the unity of the Deity, and the other purer doctrines . . .' and we may therefore be justified in concluding that Pope was not recalling material he had not seen for many years but instead had recently been dipping into classical sources to select material relevant to portions of his projected new epic.

The major source of Pope's epic is, of course, Geoffrey of Monmouth's *Historia Regum Britanniae*, a work with which Pope had long been familiar. Two references to his knowledge of, and attitude towards, the legend come from the period during which Pope was translating Homer. One of these appears in Pope's comic 'Receit to make an Epick Poem', published in *The Guardian* of 10 June 1713 and later republished as a chapter of 'The Art of Sinking in Poetry', where Pope mentions Geoffrey of Monmouth as a useful source for a suitable epic fable, presumably casting an ironic glance at Blackmore's *Prince Arthur*.[14] Four years later (1717), he found himself

[13] *Anecdotes*, i. 224, no. 532.

[14] Some other details in the 'receit' correspond rather alarmingly to the Egerton jottings. In 1713, Pope wrote ironically: 'For the Machines . . . If you have need of Devils, draw them out of Milton's Paradise, and extract your spirits from Tasso'; 'For the Under-Characters, gather them from Homer and Virgil, and Change the Names as occasion serves'; 'For a Tempest. Take Eurus, Zephyr, Auster and Boreas, and cast

actively involved with the Brutus legend, although in a minor capacity. His neighbour, Aaron Thompson, was engaged in making the first English translation of Geoffrey's *History of the Kings of Britain*, and prevailed upon Pope to versify the prayer of Brutus to Diana that results in Diana's prophecy specifying Britain as the hero's destined goal.[15] Once again, as in the more general 'receit', Pope's attitude is one of disrespectful irony. Corresponding with Edward Blount about Thompson's project, Pope writes:

> If I durst mix prophane with sacred history, I would chear you with the old Tale of *Brutus* the wandering *Trojan*, who found on that very Coast the happy End of his Peregrinations and Adventures.
>
> I have very lately read *Jeffery of Monmouth* (to whom your *Cornwall* is not a little beholden) in the Translation of a Clergyman in my neighbourhood. The poor man is highly concerned to vindicate *Jeffery's* veracity as an Historian; and told me he was perfectly astonished, we of the *Roman* Communion could doubt of the Legends of his Giants, while we believ'd those of our Saints? I am forced to make a fair Composition with him; and, by crediting some of the wonders of *Corinaeus* and *Gogmagog*, have brought him so far already, that he speaks respectfully of St. *Christopher*'s carrying Christ, and the Resuscitation of St. *Nicholas Tolentine*'s Chickens. Thus we proceed apace in converting each other from all manner of Infidelity.
>
> *Ajax* and *Hector* are no more, compared to *Corinaeus* and *Arthur*, than the *Guelphs* and *Ghibellines* were to the *Mohocks* of ever-dreadful memory. This amazing Writer has made me lay aside *Homer* for a Week, and when I take him up again, I shall be very well prepared to translate with belief and reverence the Speech of *Achilles*'s Horse.[16]

them together in one Verse. Add to these of Rain, Lightning and of Thunder (the loudest you can) *quantum sufficit*'; 'For the Language . . . Here it will do well to be an Imitator of Milton.' Comparable extracts from the Egerton draft read: 'The machinery. names of good spirits, names of evil frō Milton'; 'add . . . a character of a kinsman of Brutus young, fierce, ambitious, & brave to excess. an Achilles'; 'Thunder Tempests, etc.'

[15] The prayer of Brutus Pope wrote for Thompson's translation appears in Twickenham, VI, 193. A quite separate project, Pope's 'Two Choruses to the Tragedy of Brutus', appeared for the first time in Pope's Works, 1717 (see Twickenham, VI, 151–5). These poems were written for the Duke of Buckingham's tragedy adapted from Shakespeare's *Julius Caesar*. Apparently confusing the legendary Brutus with the historical one, Nicolson and Rousseau (*'This Long Disease, My Life'*, p. 87 n.) suggest that these choruses might also have found a place in Pope's epic. The second, addressed to 'tyrant Love' and speaking of Brutus' love for Portia, Cassius' for Junia, is decidedly inappropriate, but the first has several references to the 'bleak Atlantic' and to 'Britain's utmost shore'.

[16] *Correspondence*, i. 425 (Pope to Blount, 8 Sept. 1717).

Although in 1717 Pope apologized to Blount 'for all this Trifling', by 1743 the Brutus epic was no longer a trifling matter but a serious if short-lived commitment. The story of Brutus freeing the Trojans from slavery and leading them on their northward journey to settle in Britain occupies Part I of Geoffrey of Monmouth's *History of the Kings of Britain*. This legend must have seemed to Pope eminently appropriate as a framework for developing the themes of Epistle III of *An Essay on Man*. It provided excellent material by which Epistle III's concerns with freedom, benevolence, the nature of good governments and bad, the contrasts between primitive and civilized peoples, and the virtues of self-love transformed into social love could be given concrete development. In keeping with the thrust of the *Essay*, Pope's outline shows that he eschews Geoffrey's picture of Brutus winning bloody and brutal battles 'in transports of Joy' (Thompson's wording), and supplants it with a characterization of Brutus as a lawgiver whose ruling passion was benevolence. One of the most appealing parts of Geoffrey's *History* must have been the sentence introducing the last paragraph of Part I: 'After *Brutus* had finished the Building of the City, he made Choice of Citizens that were to inhabit it, and prescribed them Laws for their peaceable Government.'[17]

Others besides Pope were moved by all the ferment of the period —archeological, patriotic, euhemeristic—to compose national epics upon classical models, and unfortunately all the precedents are ominous. In 1572 Ronsard had published four books of *La Franciade*, whose hero Francis, the son of Hector, similarly gathered together the Trojan survivors from the Mediterranean area and journeyed northward to found the French nation and the dynasty of French kings. This never-completed epic is considered Ronsard's most disastrous literary venture. More immediately relevant to Pope's plans is another abortive epic, this one using the Brutus legend. In 1735 Hildebrand Jacob published the first five books of his epic, *Brutus the Trojan: Founder of the British Empire*. This rightly obscure work is not mentioned by Pope or by other writers in connection with Pope's epic plans, but in an anecdote appearing for the first time in Osborn's edition of Spence, Pope indicates familiarity with

[17] Aaron Thompson, *The British History, Translated into English from the Latin of Jeffrey of Monmouth* (London, 1718), p. 38.

Jacob's works: 'Hildebrand Jacob wrote a bawdy poem when young which had something of spirit in it, but everything else of his is low and flat—as dead as ditch-water!'[18] There is no evidence for associating this remark specifically with Jacob's epic, but one may certainly see the likelihood of the association, especially because the date, 1742, is appropriate to the connection. Jacob's epic certainly bears out Pope's general opinion of his works. The epic is written in totally undistinguished blank verse which possesses no poetic quality or imaginative power. It embodies no moral reflections, only action, and the action is basically Virgil's. It is perhaps best looked at as a perfect example of the product of following the 'Mechanick Rules' Pope advocated in 1713 for the poet wholly without genius. Its appearance may have aroused Pope's interest purely as a sort of negative catalyst.

Friedrich Brie's careful research into the sources of Pope's manuscript annotations allows us to see clear and potentially fruitful connections between the classical writers and texts Pope cites or alludes to and the interests, ideas, and pursuits of Pope and his contemporaries, turning on 'civil and ecclesiastical government'. Through these annotations citing ancient and modern sources, Brie traces Pope's interest in *topoi* such as the noble savage, the golden age, the destruction of superstition and its supersession by Reason; in natural phenomena such as earthquakes, volcanoes, eclipses; and in such current ideas as the influence of climate upon national groups. Brie's explorations are exhaustive and conclusive, and they provide clear and convincing evidence of Pope's eclectic interests and the range and depth of his 'research' into those areas of social and political thought adumbrated in *An Essay on Man*, Epistle III.

In most cases, however, it is difficult to see precisely how Pope would have resolved these idea clusters into satisfying poetic unity. There is one portion of the manuscript that seems tenuous and cryptic but affords us a more clearly defined picture of Pope's poetic strategy. This reference centres on Pope's interest in the baneful effects of superstition, a subject that recurs repeatedly in

[18] *Anecdotes*, i. 213, no. 499. The only other reference to Jacob's epic I have seen is in Ernest Jones, *Geoffrey of Monmouth, 1640–1800* (University of California Publications in English, V, 1944), pp. 409–10. The edition in the Bodleian library is, according to David Foxon, one of only three known extant copies.

various passages of the epic plan—in positing superstition as the cause of the downfall of Troy, in elaborating upon the priestly tyranny described in the *Essay*, Epistle III, and in depicting the grovelling subjection to uncontrollable natural phenomena by men, individually and in social groups.

On the Egerton manuscript page describing 'Lib. 3', the final book of his epic at that stage, Pope's outline reads:

> . . . Stories are told by Britains as Giants: whom he helps y^m^ to conquer. The People of ye Giants dominion overrun with Superstition, tell him there are Islands near y^m^ possest by Titans, or Hero's Ghosts frō wch Thunders and Tempests guard all access.

Opposite this part of his outline, Pope notes as source material, first, 'Plut', and then, immediately underneath, 'Fonten. of Oracles'. The first of these annotations refers to Plutarch's essay on 'The Obsolescence of Oracles', and more particularly to one passage within it. Plutarch's essay is in the form of a rather desultory and digressive conversation amongst participants who all agree that oracles are truly prophetic, that daemons (that is, demigods) are in charge of them, and that these oracles have lately ceased to function. Amongst the many anecdotes offered by the speakers to support their observations is one recounted by Demetrius:

> Demetrius said that among the islands lying near Britain were many isolated, having few or no inhabitants, some of which bore the names of divinities or heroes. He himself, by the emperor's order, had made a voyage for inquiry and observation to the nearest of these islands which had only a few inhabitants, holy men who were all held inviolate by the Britons. Shortly after his arrival there occurred a great tumult in the air and many portents; violent winds suddenly swept down and lightning flashes darted to earth. When these abated, the people of the island said that the passing of someone of the mightier souls had befallen. 'For,' said they, 'as a lamp when it is being lighted has no terrors, but when it goes out is distressing to many, so the great souls have a kindling into life that is gentle and inoffensive, but their passing and dissolution often as at the present moment, fosters tempests and storms, and often infects the air with pestilential properties.' Moreover, they said that in this part of the world there is one island where Cronus is confined, guarded while he sleeps by Briareus; for his sleep has been devised as a bondage for him, and round about him are many demigods as attendants and servants.[19]

[19] *Plutarch's Moralia*, trans. F. C. Babbitt (Loeb edition, 1936), v. 403–5.

That this is the particular passage Pope meant by his vague annotation 'Plut' is clear not only because of its specific references to 'islands lying near Britain', their tempests and storms, and the significance of these, but also because he couples 'Plut' with 'Fonten. of Oracles' in his marginal gloss. In his *History of Oracles and the Cheats of the Pagan Priests*, Fontenelle paraphrases the whole of this particular account by Demetrius, and then adds scoffingly:

Has not *Demetrius* made a very curious Relation of this Voyage? And is it not pleasant to see such a Philosopher as *Plutarch* coldly relate to us such wonderful things?[20]

This expansion of Pope's brief annotation allows us to speculate with some profit upon Pope's strategy in the epic. By juxtaposing the treatment of ancient and modern authorities on such issues as gods, religion, superstition, and the causes of violent and frightening natural events, Pope is apparently creating a multi-level narrative. In this instance, he can attribute to the inhabitants of the islands the 'ancient' explanations and points of view; within the same framework, he can have his hero rationalize the phenomena and bring modern enlightenment to bear on superstition and replace the fear and terror of the primitive peoples with the beneficent effects of a new reign. Support for this hypothesis comes from Pope's exhortation to himself in the next paragraph of the Egerton outline, to 'moralize ye old Fables concerning Brutus. Gogmagog etc. the Fables being made ye Peoples acct. of y^{m}. When Brutus goes, ye Enchantments vanish.' Similarly, the outline continues in a new paragraph immediately following, 'Priests, Conjurers, Magic, resist him. as Priests of Delphi had Secrets y^{t} past for Supernatural'. The creation of multiple points of view relieves Pope of the need to impose his 'moral' from without; instead he can weave it into the very fabric of the epic story.

The Plutarch–Fontenelle example is a useful and clear-cut clue to a procedure that may be implicit in Pope's outline at other points. In some of the clusters of ancient and modern sources Pope was apparently planning to exploit, there is considerable congruity of detail and meaning. One such collection of references ('Fortunate Islands',

[20] *The History of the Oracles and the Cheats of the Pagan Priests.* In Two Parts. Made English by A. B. (London, 1688), p. 28.

'Teneriff', 'inarata', 'Land of Laziness', 'Capua') pertains to the Canary Islands episode, in which all the motifs combine to suggest the desirability of an escape from a corrupt civilization to a new and primitive land whose characteristics evoke the picture of the golden age. Other traditional motifs are more controversial, yet their very discord may have been as fruitful to Pope as the opposition between Plutarch and Fontenelle. Another example is the exploitation of the idea that Egypt was the motherland of the best arts, best laws, and purest religious doctrines. Another set of contradictory views, handed down from classical times, were those about the nature of druidic society as, on the one hand, a peaceful, noble, and enlightened society, and on the other hand, containing elements of barbarism such as human sacrifice and the fearful awe of the people towards their priestly governors. These last two strands coalesce in the belief that Moses—like Orpheus, Hercules, Homer, Pythagoras, Solon, Plato, Plutarch, and (according to Pope) Brutus—had journeyed into Egypt and that 'the Druids of Britain . . . had . . . thier Religion from thence'.[21]

Another important clue to Pope's poetic procedure may lie in the outline's departures from the structure of Homeric and Virgilian epics. Friedrich Brie notes with approval that Pope appears to eschew entirely such epic conventions as the visit to the underworld, the funeral games, and the obstacles created by sexual entanglements.[22] That these features are absent from the epic outline does not, of course, preclude their presence in the finished poem; their omission from the outlines does, however, suggest that Pope here, as in his other works, is not automatically following his models in every respect. Other less obvious departures from classical epic pattern constitute shifts in emphasis rather than matters of omission or commission. Two broad structural shifts of focus, each affecting one half of the traditional pattern, seem worthy of special notice.

[21] William Warburton, *Divine Legation of Moses* (1738), i. 136. For a lucid and comprehensive study of many of these controversies, see Don Cameron Allen, *Mysteriously Meant: The Rediscovery of Pagan Symbolism and Allegorical Interpretation in the Renaissance* (Baltimore & London: The Johns Hopkins Press, 1970), esp. pp. 35–40, 107–33 on the significance of Egypt in the transmission of religious ideas; 53 ff. on Euhemerus and Christian euhemerists; pp. 78–9 on the development of the 'discussion of predictive utterances' from Plutarch to Fontenelle.

[22] Brie, p. 153.

In both the *Odyssey* and the *Aeneid*, the action of the poem begins with the hero nearly at his destination, recounting his journey as part of the poem's antecedent action. According to the outline drafts of *Brutus*, the scene also opens as the hero is in the midst of his journey, but in this case the portion of the voyage yet to come would appear to occupy a much more significant place in proportion to the antecedent action than is true of the classical epics. Brutus has yet to enter the ocean, journey northward, and visit and adventure among many island and mainland peoples. Pope seems to have wished to make the journey portion of the epic more prominent for two reasons: to concentrate upon the variety of political organizations encountered by Brutus and his band, and to focus upon the need for an accomplishment of Brutus' educative role. The first of these purposes is very much in accord with Pope's vision of the epic as a substitute for the original third book of the *opus magnum* as projected in 1734, a group of essays on civil and ecclesiastical government; the second is closely linked with the first, and is made clear early in the outline itself, when Brutus rejects his people's proposal to settle in the Canary Islands: 'He refuses, because it does not answer his purpose of Extending Benevolence, & polishing & teaching Nations, despises ye mean thought of making only themselves happy. . . .' The plan suggests Pope's intention to describe other communities not merely as potential allies or enemies, but as integral objects of Brutus' altruistic concern, and as subjects central to the poem's concern.

Pope's plans for the second half of the epic also suggest an emphasis somewhat different from the classic pattern and in greater accord with the themes of Epistle III of the *Essay*. Whereas Odysseus must restore order to his own fatherland and Aeneas must initially carve out a new home in one particular locale of Italy, Brutus' mission is to spread good government and benevolence through the whole of the British Isles as well as to establish a new homeland. The accomplishment of Brutus' mission in broadest terms is part of the explicit central action of the poem, whereas the comparable mission of Aeneas is forecast throughout the *Aeneid* as an achievement of the future. In Pope's epic models, the hero himself becomes increasingly aware of his role and becomes increasingly worthy of it.

Pope's plan suggests no such focus upon the hero: Brutus' moral worth, intellectual stature, and powers of leadership appear to be accomplished facts before the epic opens; the outline action of the epic concentrates on portraying the dissemination of similar enlightenment to his own followers and to the communities he encounters. Brutus, as Mr. Torchiana writes,

> is the perfect human being, who is clear-minded in the best eighteenth-century way: there is one God, a few simple rules for government, and the primary virtues. As an instrument of providence, possessed of a guardian angel, Brutus is also an agent of plenitude. Benevolence can take no other course than to extend itself. Brutus does not falter and recover himself as does Aeneas; he must instead persuade others to virtue; he only kills monsters of superstition, fanaticism, and error.[23]

Pope's sketch appears to show that he is departing from his classical models in being much less interested in the hero's adventures, moral development, and conquests than in political and social structures, concepts, and ideals. We must therefore take Pope seriously when he says to Spence, 'The idea I have had for an epic poem of late turns *wholly* on civil and ecclesiastical government' (my italics). The epic outlines thus show Pope still very much committed to the project that had begun to absorb him in 1729, one that he had long felt demanded further treatment of '*the Nature and State of* Man, *with respect to* Society', the subject of *An Essay on Man*, Epistle III.

Many sections of the epic plan, even in its skeleton form, suggest that Pope had Epistle III of the *Essay* in mind as he formulated concrete episodes corresponding to the earlier more generalized descriptions of the development of society. In Epistle III (147–60), the description of the 'State of Nature' as 'the reign of God' is curiously vague and unlocalized:

> Pride then was not; nor Arts, that Pride to aid;
> Man walk'd with beast, joint tenant of the shade;
> The same his table, and the same his bed;
> No murder cloath'd him, and no murder fed.
> In the same temple, the resounding wood,
> All vocal beings hymn'd their equal God:

[23] Torchiana, p. 717.

The shrine with gore unstain'd, with gold undrest,
Unbrib'd, unbloody, stood the blameless priest:
Heav'n's attribute was Universal Care,
And Man's prerogative to rule, but spare.
(*Essay*, III, 151–60)

In the Brutus outline, Pope plans a closely comparable but much more particularized picture of the druidic society in the west of Britain who perform 'no bloody sacrifices' and whom Brutus meets 'at an Altar of Turf in an open place offering fruits and flowers to heaven'. Similarly, the epic outline provides vivid and forceful examples of the violence and destruction bred by superstitious belief that accord closely with the general description of the nature and effects of superstition and tyranny in Epistle III (246–60). As a final example, the epic outline shows Pope's continuous preoccupation with the problem that lies uneasily unresolved in Epistle III's account of the decline and subsequent restoration of the ideal state. In a marginal comment occupying a prominent position in the upper left portion of the first page of the Egerton outline, Pope writes:

How came the Arts and Civility he introduced into Britain to be lost again? A Prophecy delivered to him by an old Druid that the Britons shou'd degenerate in an age or Two, and Relapse into a degree of Barbarism, but that they shou'd be Redeemd again by a Descendant of his Family out of Italy, Julius Caesar, under whose successors they shou'd be Repolishd and that the Love of Liberty he had introduced, the Martial Spirit, and other Moral Virtues should never be lost. With Observations upon the Impossibility of an Institution being Perpetual without some Changes.

Pope does not indicate the place in the epic where this prophecy will fit, nor does it appear in Ruffhead's more ample description. Its mere appearance, however, suggests that Pope was aware of the inadequacy of Epistle III's description of restoration following decline:

'Twas then, the studious head or gen'rous mind,
Follow'r of God or friend of human-kind,
Poet or Patriot, rose but to restore
The Faith and Moral, Nature gave before.
(*Essay*, III, 283–6)

These three sets of correspondences between epic plan and Epistle III of the *Essay* correspond to the three topics Friedrich Brie outlines in his thorough analysis of the epic outline: the origin of society from a state of nature, the corruption of society through superstition and tyranny, and the restoration of society upon true principles through self-love being transmuted to social love.

In April 1744 Pope told Spence that the third book of his ethic work 'was to have treated of government, both ecclesiastical and civil—and this was what chiefly stopped my going on. I could not have said what I *would* have said without provoking every church on the face of the earth, and I did not care for living always in boiling water. This part would come into my *Brutus*, which is all planned already . . .'[24] Had Pope completed the epic, one doubts that he would have avoided controversy, yet one can see that the epic form might seem to be a good way of developing the ideas he originally planned in epistle form. In contrast to the epistle form, the epic form could distance criticism, and could make it appear to apply to another time and to other, legendary nations. The epic form would eschew direct contemporary references, yet provide ample scope for descriptions of various forms of government, good and bad, of various leaders, good and bad, of theories and ideas of good and bad forms of civil and ecclesiastical polity.

In his comprehensive analysis of the epic plan, Donald Torchiana sees *Brutus* not only as a concrete working out of the general argument of the *Essay on Man*, Epistle III, but also as a potential contribution to the literature of the Patriot Opposition and, in its outline of Brutus' career, 'a corrective to the "*Abuse* of *Civil* and *Ecclesiastical Policy*" in the 1743 *Dunciad*, especially in Book IV where the Empire of Dulness is restored'.[25] Although all three points are related, the connection with the *Fourth Dunciad* is of particular interest from the point of view of the *opus magnum* scheme. If the *Dunciad* and *Brutus* are linked together as anti-epic and epic, as pictures of disorder and restoration, they are of course linked as the final forms of the planned epistles on education and on civil and

[24] *Anecdotes*, i. 134, no. 302.

[25] Torchiana, pp. 713–14. Torchiana is quoting part of the note to *Essay*, III. 283 (' 'Twas then, the studious head or gen'rous mind'), added in the 1739 edition of Pope's *Works*. See Chapter VI, p. 138.

ecclesiastical polity first listed in the Index of 1734. Subsequently Pope seems to have linked the Epistle on Education to the first unit of Book II in the Index, 'Of the Limits of Human Reason', 'Of the Use of Learning', and 'Of the Use of Wit', as developments from the *Essay*, Epistle I, but its original association with the epistles on Civil and Ecclesiastical Polity, as developments from Epistle III of the *Essay*, may have been the reason why Pope found whatever he had already written so easy to adapt to the *Fourth Dunciad*, which is, of course, also very much about 'Civil and Ecclesiastical Polity'. The two final expressions cannot be compared: the *Fourth Dunciad* has thoroughly absorbed its origins; the *Brutus* plan has not got beyond the stage of prose notes. Apparently, however, Pope began the latter as he completed the former, and this relationship makes for a felicitous rounding-off of the *opus magnum.* As Pope in 1729 turned from the *Dunciad* to the beginning of the moral scheme and plans for *An Essay on Man* as the positive and optimistic counterpart to his attacks on vice and folly, so once again in 1742–3 he turned from the *New Dunciad* to preparing plans for an epic, once again to be the positive and idealistic counterpart to his now much more politically oriented attacks on vice and folly.

The existence of the Egerton manuscript symbolizes not only the end of a project but the end of an era, for amongst the Egerton papers is the scrap bearing Pope's tentative opening lines for the epic in blank verse. The poet who had written all his major works in heroic couplets was now planning to write in a wholly different verse form.

CHAPTER VIII

THE FINAL *OPUS MAGNUM* PLANS, 1744

THE conversation of April 1744, parts of which have been quoted earlier, is Pope's final description of his *opus magnum*. The note in its entirety reads:

> I had once thought of completing my ethic work in four books. The first, you know, is on the nature of man. The second would have been on knowledge and its limits. Here would have come in an Essay on Education, part of which I have inserted in the *Dunciad*. The third was to have treated of government, both ecclesiastical and civil—and this was what chiefly stopped my going on. I could not have said what I *would* have said without provoking every church on the face of the earth, and I did not care for living always in boiling water. This part would come into my *Brutus*, which is all planned already, and even some of the most material speeches writ in prose. The fourth would have been on morality, in eight or nine of the most concerning branches of it, four of which would have been the two extremes to each of the cardinal virtues.
>
> POPE *14–21 April 1744*[1]

Mr. Osborn follows this entry with a note beginning, 'This conversation, which occurred just a few weeks before Pope's death, records still another modification of Pope's grand design.'[2] Although undoubtedly a variation upon earlier descriptions, if only because the epic itself is a major new addition, it nevertheless tallies remarkably closely with earlier descriptions of the project, particularly the most detailed previous outline, the Index of 1734. There are of course some obvious differences. According to the Index order, the epistle 'Of the Use of Education' was allied with that on 'Civil and Ecclesiastical Polity' rather than with the group 'On Human Reason', but the outline in the 1736 letter to Swift has already suggested that the epistle on education had coalesced with those stemming from Epistle I of the *Essay*. The epic is a substitute for

[1] *Anecdotes*, i. 134, no. 302. [2] Ibid., i. 134.

the earlier 'Epistle of the Principles and Use of Civil and Ecclesiastical Polity' partly, at least, for the reasons Spence conjectured a decade earlier. The fourth Book 'on morality' assuredly corresponds closely to the group consisting in the Index of 1734 of 'A View of the Equality of Happiness in the Conditions of Men' and 'Of the Use of Riches, etc.'. Of this part of the 1744 outline, Mr. Osborn writes,

> The fourth book seems to have progressed no further than the preliminary sketching. Of the four cardinal virtues—fortitude, justice, prudence, and temperance—no extended passages 'on the two extremes of each' are known, unless Pope's lines on avarice and prodigality . . . can be so considered.[3]

Mr. Osborn seems not to subscribe to the consideration he posits, yet he refers the reader to earlier 'Anecdotes', one of which seems particularly apposite. In November 1730 Spence reports, as we recall,

> Mr. Pope's poem grows on his hands. The first four or five epistles will be on the general principles, or of 'The Nature of Man' and the rest will be on moderation, or 'The Use of Things'. In the latter part, each class may take up three epistles: one, for instance, against avarice, another against prodigality, and the third on the moderate use of riches; and so of the rest.

It seems undeniable that there is a clear line stretching from this outline of 1730 through the Index of 1734 to the final, if too systematic, description of the fourth book in April 1744. We may suppose, moreover, that Pope considered at least the *Epistle to Bathurst* and the *Epistle to Burlington* to be contributions to this book 'on morality', not only on account of their content and accompanying notes, but also because the new note of 1739 makes reference to lapsed plans for a hypothetical future *epistle*, rather than a whole book, on the subject of virtue and happiness, unlike other notes in the 1739 volume that refer to the abandonment of entire *books* of ethic epistles. The phrasing and ambitious scope of this portion of the 1744 outline may reflect the influence of William Warburton.

There is, however, one significant omission in this final outline to Spence. It takes no account of the epistles *To Cobham* and *To a*

[3] *Anecdotes*, i. 134.

Lady, or of a book to correspond with Epistle II of the *Essay*. This pair of epistles was listed after the unit on Reason in the Index of 1734, and seemed there to be identified with Epistle II of Book I. A possible reason for their omission from Pope's description is that they are a 'sub-unit' that he found impossible to develop and that destroys the aesthetic symmetry of the pattern of four which the *opus magnum* seems always to evoke.

Another solution to the problem of the omission of explicit mention of any of the *Moral Essays* may be found in the last outline of all. This is the detailed outline titled 'Advertisement' and given in the opening pages of the rare 1744 edition of *Epistles to Several Persons* prepared by Pope and Warburton as a companion to the 'standard' editions of *An Essay on Man* and *An Essay on Criticism*. It is perhaps the best known and most cited of all descriptions of the plan, yet we do not know what authority it has. Although readily available in transcription in the Introduction to the Twickenham edition, it is included here for easy comparison with earlier outlines:

The ESSAY ON MAN was intended to have been comprised in four Books:

The *First* of which, the Author has given us under that title, in four epistles.

The *Second* was to have consisted of the same number:

1. Of the extent and limits of human Reason.
2. Of those Arts and Sciences, and of the parts of them, which are useful, and therefore attainable, together with those which are unuseful, and therefore unattainable.
3. Of the Nature, Ends, Use, and Application of the different Capacities of Men.
4. Of the Use of Learning, of the Science of the World, and of Wit: concluding with a Satyr against the Misapplication of them, illustrated by Pictures, Characters, and Examples.

The *Third* Book regarded Civil Regimen, or the Science of Politics, in which the several forms of a Republic were to have been examined and explained; together with the several Modes of Religious Worship, as far forth as they affect Society; between which, the Author always supposed there was the most interesting relation and closest connection; so that this part would have treated of Civil and Religious Society in their full extent.

The *Fourth* and last Book concerned private Ethics or practical Morality, considered in all the Circumstances, Orders, Professions, and Stations of human Life.

The Scheme of all this had been maturely digested, and communicated to the L. Bolingbroke, Dr Swift, and one or two more, and was intended for the only work of his riper Years: But was, partly thro' ill health, partly thro' discouragements from the depravity of the times, and partly on prudential and other considerations, interrupted, postponed, and, lastly, in a manner laid aside.

But as this was the Author's favourite Work, which more exactly reflected the Image of his strong capacious Mind, and as we can have but a very imperfect idea of it from the *disjecta membra Poetae* that now remain, it may not be amiss to be a little more particular concerning each of these projected works.

The FIRST, as it treats of Man in the abstract, and considers him in general under every of his relations, becomes the foundation, and furnishes out the subjects, of the *three* following; so that

The SECOND Book takes up again the *First* and *Second* Epistles of the *First* Book, and treats of man in his intellectual Capacity at large, as has been explained above. Of this, only a small part of the conclusion (which, as we said, was to have contained a Satyr against the misapplication of Wit and Learning) may be found in the *Fourth* Book of the *Dunciad*, and up and down, occasionally, in the other *three.*

The *Third* Book, in like manner, reassumes the subject of the *Third* Epistle of the *First*, which treats of Man in his Social, Political, and Religious Capacity. But this part the Poet afterwards conceived might be best executed in an EPIC POEM; as the Action would make it more animated, and the Fable less invidious; in which all the great Principles of true and false Governments and Religions would be chiefly delivered in feigned Examples.

In pursuance of this design, he plan'd out a Poem on the subject of the fabulous BRUTUS . . .[4]

The FOURTH and last Book pursues the subject of the *Fourth* Epistle of the *First*, and treats of *Ethics*, or practical Morality; and would have consisted of many members; of which the four following Epistles were detached Portions: the *two first*, on the *Characters of Men and Women* being the *introductory* part of this concluding Book.

The first thing to be said of this outline relates not to its contents, but to its authorship. The division of responsibility between Pope and Warburton for the 'suppressed edition' of the *Epistles to Several Persons* which this outline prefaces, is a vexing problem. The edition is presumably the one that figures in possibly the most famous of all Spence's *Anecdotes* that quote Pope: 'Here am I, like

[4] For the full summary of the epic, see Twickenham, III: ii, pp. xviii–xix.

Socrates, distributing my morality among my friends, just as I am dying. (On sending about some of his Ethic Epistles as presents, about three weeks before we lost him.)'[5] Yet this edition was withdrawn from circulation and not reissued until 1748.[6] Mr. Bateson and more recently Mr. Brady discuss the possibility that some of the features of the edition were added by Warburton after Pope's death.[7] Even if all parts of this edition were seen and sanctioned by Pope, Pope's attitude was, as Mr. Bateson puts it, 'not the spirit in which to undertake a final and meticulous revision of highly finished verse'.[8] Pope was very ill for some time before his death, yet was anxious that the standard edition of his works move forward as rapidly as possible. As he told Spence in January 1744, 'I *must* make a perfect edition of my works, and then I shall have nothing to do but to die.'[9] In these circumstances, he may have entrusted to Warburton a good deal more authority and responsibility than was his wont. Both Mr. Bateson and Mr. Brady make this point convincingly with respect to textual variants in the poetry, and other features of the edition.[10]

Neither Mr. Bateson nor Mr. Brady raises either question—of posthumous changes or of Pope's too great willingness to defer to Warburton in the months before he died—specifically in connection with the 'Advertisement'. In a note to the transcription of the above 'Advertisement', Mr. Bateson writes only, 'How much of it Pope himself is responsible for is not clear.'[11] Mr. Bateson's description of Warburton's habit of mind—'A certain officious "tidiness" was one of Warburton's most pronounced intellectual characteristics'[12] —is applicable to this outline, which is therefore open to the same questions about authorship as other new and variant features of the

[5] *Anecdotes*, i. 261, no. 631 (10 May 1744).

[6] See *Correspondence*, iv. 504 n.; Twickenham, III: ii, p. xiii; Brady, 'The History and Structure of *To a Lady*', *SEL 1500–1900*, ix (1969), 439–62, *et passim*.

[7] See, for instance, Twickenham, III: ii, pp. xiii–xiv, 41–4, *et passim*, and Brady, op. cit.

[8] Twickenham, III: ii, p. li, n. 1.

[9] *Anecdotes*, i. 258, no. 622 (10–14 January 1744; italics as in original).

[10] See the 'General Note on the Text' as well as the notes preceding each poem in Twickenham, III: ii, and Brady, op. cit. Brady's charges that Warburton behaved both highhandedly *and* underhandedly in his part in the deathbed edition are detailed especially on pp. 444–51 of his article.

[11] Twickenham, III: ii, p. xix, n.

[12] Ibid., p. xiv.

1744 edition. The use of the third person throughout, although appearing to support the conjecture that the outline is not Pope's, is unfortunately not a certain guide, since notes in earlier editions, assuredly written by Pope, also use the third-person reference to 'the author' in just the same way.

As is obvious, the 'Advertisement' divides into two parts, with the second particularizing the first and showing the way in which the *disjecta membra Poetae* fit into the four-book scheme. The opening outline is familiar and need not detain us long. The most surprising feature of it is that the description of the second book is more than merely familiar; it is identical with the description of it in the letter to Swift of 1736 which appears to have been used as a copy-text for this part of the outline.

The second part of the description takes into account the omissions we noticed above in Pope's description to Spence, by explaining that the second book, on intellectual capacities, was to draw not only on Epistle I of *An Essay on Man*, but also on Epistle II, and by further explaining that the epistles *To Cobham* and *To a Lady* are the introductory epistles of the unfinished fourth book. I do not find the latter explanation a satisfying one. In effect, it is a corollary of Pope's 1735 arrangement of the four ethic epistles as offshoots of Epistle II, and much the same suggestion of an artificial yoking together of the four that was put forth there is applicable here. The epistles *To Cobham* and *To a Lady* do indeed bear a family resemblance to the epistles *To Bathurst* and *To Burlington*, but whereas the latter pair appears primarily to 'pursue the subject of the fourth Epistle of the *First* and treat of *Ethics*', the former pair even more clearly seems to pursue the subject of the Second and treat psychology and the Ruling Passion. This outline strikes me as a belated effort to create a 'tidy' arrangement of all parts of the *opus magnum*, that ignores the evidence of the Index of 1734 and the edition of 1735. These earlier arrangements admittedly contradict one another with regard to the disposition of the epistles on the Use of Riches, but they are in accord with each other and with common sense in relating the epistles on the characters of men and women to Epistle II of the *Essay*. The authority of the Index is by no means sacrosanct; Pope withdrew it from circulation, and his own statements thereafter indicated departures from it. The 1735 edition seems itself to be a response to Pope's statement that he had considerably drawn in his plan from the dimensions implied in the Index. If, however, we wish to explore the relation between the epistles and the *opus magnum*, the earlier versions of the plan appear to be the ones we must reckon with. They date from the time that the ethic scheme was most fully occupying Pope's thoughts and influencing the composition of the epistles.

If we wish to know how Pope thought of his plan after he had begun to withdraw his attention from it as a unified and coherent scheme, the 1744 Advertisement may be an accurate pointer to his views—or again it may not. Although some parts of it are clearly attributable to Pope in that they transcribe his own earlier statements, it does not necessarily follow that other portions have comparable authority. Although the outline has a great deal of appeal because of its clarity and comprehensiveness, it is also suspect for the same reason. These virtues do not characterize Pope's independent outlines, even the retrospective ones.

The editorial notes in editions of *An Essay on Man* and the *Moral Essays* are of no significance following the important edition of 1739, discussed in Chapter VI. The 'non-Warburton' editions of 1740 and 1743 are close reprints of the edition of 1739. In the editions of 1743 and 1744 in which Warburton collaborated with Pope and in which Warburton's commentaries tend to occupy more space than Pope's poetry, most of the cross-reference notes, a feature of editions from 1735 through 1743, are excised. Pope presumably considered Warburton's lengthy notes a dignified, systematic, and elaborate substitution. Readers less sympathetic to Warburton's poetic sensibilities are more likely to consider them Warburton's tribute to the Goddess of Dullness:

> For thee explain a thing till all men doubt it,
> And write about it, Goddess, and about it;
> So spins the silk-worm small its slender store,
> And labours till it clouds itself all o'er.

Much of Warburton's annotation of *An Essay on Man* is an exact transcription of his earlier defence of the poem against the attacks of Professor Crousaz.

Some of the notes, however, have another source. An example is the opening of the commentary:

> THE Opening of this poem, in fifteen lines, is taken up in giving an account of the Subject; which, agreeably to the title, is an ESSAY on MAN, or a Philosophical Enquiry into his *Nature* and *End*, his *Passions* and *Pursuits*.
>
> The Exordium relates to the Whole work, of which this was only the first book. The 6th, 7th, and 8th lines allude to the subjects of this present book, *viz.* the general Order and Design of Providence; the Constitution of the Human Mind, whose Passions cultivated are Virtues, neglected, Vices; the Temptations of Misapplied Self-love; and the wrong pursuits of Power, Pleasure, and Happiness. The 10th, 11th, 12th etc. have relation to the subjects of the books intended to follow, *viz.* the Characters and Capacities of Men, and the limits of Learning and Ignorance. The 13th and 14th, to the Knowledge of Mankind, and the various Manners of the age.

With the recognition that Warburton has copied this note from the opening page of the Harvard manuscript of *An Essay on Man*, we have come full circle, back to the origins of the *opus magnum* project some fifteen years earlier.

Curiously, the reports of the over-all plan that date from the period 1729–35, when Pope was most deeply engaged in planning and executing his ethic scheme, are vague, fragmentary, and unsystematic, and do not give a clear and consistent picture of the project's pattern or scope. This phenomenon has led to the suggestion that the larger scope of the plan was an *ex-post facto* imposition upon the already completed epistles. However, our survey has clearly shown that the plan existed from the very beginning and that the conception shaped the composition of *An Essay on Man* as well as the moral epistles. The explanation of the lack of clear and systematic outline of the project during its most productive period seems to lie in the fact that Pope was so deeply engaged in the scheme that he saw its numerous possibilities and complexities rather than a neat and systematic delimitation of its scope.

The notes and format of the edition of 1735 suggest a belated attempt to give the impression of tight organization, most specifically to the four epistles that follow the *Essay* in that edition. This effort resulted in an attempt to link the two final moral epistles directly with the first two and with Epistle II of the *Essay* rather than with Epistle IV. By placing the evidence provided by this edition against the background of other external evidence up until 1735 and by an examination of the poems themselves, we suggested that such a close connection was a distortion of Pope's plans, and militated especially against seeing the relationship of the final pair of epistles to Epistle IV of the *Essay*.

After 1735 Pope published no more epistles having a direct connection with his system. He did, however, cherish the plan and was unwilling to abandon it altogether. Indeed, as soon as he drew away from intensive work upon it and began to see it in perspective, the outlines of its constituent parts and its entirety are described in much more systematic fashion, as a four-to-one pattern, in which successive books are each to have four epistles and each book is to grow out of and illuminate one epistle of the *Essay on Man*. This concern for symmetry and scale can be considered not only an effect of oversimplifying earlier complexities, but also a cause contributing to the temporary abandonment of the plan, since it called for an expenditure of effort and a kind of systematized thinking and patterning alien to Pope's genius. However, even in this period, there is much evidence to suggest that Pope considered the project unfinished and worthy of finishing. In particular, the notes to the 1739 edition and the 'Brutus' outline suggest Pope's awareness of the incomplete nature of the *Essay on Man*. The moral epistles already completed are not included in Pope's outlines of this later period, and this omission also contributes reinforcement to the suggestion that the yoking together of the four moral essays as one complete book was a temporary gesture towards rigour that Pope soon found unsatisfactory.

With the advent and stimulus of Warburton, Pope revived the plan once more, but issued no more completed poems in direct connection with the project. Instead, he wove some at least of his abandoned materials into the *New Dunciad*, used other portions of it to initiate plans for an epic, and finally turned to preparing a standard edition of his works, leaving this project, as he left the *opus magnum* project, incomplete at his death. The tailing-off of the project after 1735 should not, however, prevent us from seeing that the scheme held the same recognizable shape throughout its fifteen-year span, even though during that period it was sometimes uppermost in Pope's mind, sometimes peripheral to other publishing projects. No other single project, in fact, absorbed him so fully and over so long a period, and for the period 1729–35 at least, his commitment to it largely determined both the small details and the general direction and pattern of almost all his major works.

INDEX